A DIRECTOR'S

METHOD

FOR FILM

AND TELEVISION

RON RICHARDS

A DIRECTOR'S
METHOD
FOR FILM
AND TELEVISION

Focal Press
Boston London

Focal Press is an imprint of Butterworth–Heinemann.

Recognizing the importance of preserving what has been written, it is
the policy of Butterworth–Heinemann to have the books it publishes
printed on acid-free paper, and we exert our best efforts to that end.

Library of Congress Cataloging-in-Publication Data

Richards, Ron.
    A director's method for film and television / Ron Richards.
      p.   cm.
    Includes index.
    ISBN 0-240-80119-9 (pbk.)
    1. Motion pictures—Production and direction.
    2. Television—Production and direction. I. Title.
PN1995.9.P7R5 1991
791.43'0233—dc20   91-16861
                                                      CIP

British Library Cataloguing in Publication Data

Richards, Ron
    A director's method for film and television.
    I. Title
    791.450233

    ISBN 0-240-80119-9

Butterworth-Heinemann
80 Montvale Avenue
Stoneham, MA 02180

10 9 8 7 6 5 4 3 2 1

Printed in the United States of America

CONTENTS

PREFACE

When I started in this business I was certain I knew how to direct. I had practical and professional experience as an actor and stage director and had studied basic television techniques at RCA Institute trade school. I was then hired as a television director. After directing for a while, I found that my work seemed pedestrian; I wanted more than that.

So I returned to school. I received my BFA from Columbia University's School of Dramatic Arts college, and my MFA from New York University, where I was the first graduate of its new master's program. Upon graduation I was invited to teach other master's candidates. To me, this seemed to validate me as a director.

I went on from there to direct commercials, industrials, stage plays, and low-budget feature films. I even directed a sequence for the New York City ballet. I frequently joked, "If it moves and pays a fee, I am available to direct it."

The years raced by; but, eventually, I became dissatisfied. I felt my work had become repetitious and predictable. When I looked at the work of my fellow directors and discovered that they seemed to be able to exploit the medium and invent sequences that seemed new and exciting, I began to explore what made those directors innovative and unique.

It occurred to me directors like John Huston, Billy Wilder, Preston Sturges, Alfred Hitchcock, and Frederico Fellini were writers. The pattern of writers becoming directors is familiar. As recently as 1986 the Academy of Motion Pictures and Directors Guild of America chose Oliver Stone, a writer, as best director for his feature film *Platoon.* I theorized that screenplay writing was a way of learning how to be a director.

There is no doubt that screenplay writing is an art. Yet upon investigating further, I realized that translating those words from the screenplay into visual images is the unique skill of the director.

Nicholas Roeg, the eminent director of *Don't Look Now* and *Walkabout,* has stated that the screenplay is just a device to get the money people to back the making of it into a film; the screenplay has little to do with film-making or its process.

Elia Kazan, the famed director, noted for his classic *On the Waterfront,* stated, "The director is the true author of the film. The director tells the story on film, using a vocabulary, the lesser part of which is the arrangement of words."

This began my pursuit to understanding the process of selecting pictures and arranging them in a specific order to tell the story. This resulted in structuring and naming the 12 Cinema Languages discussed in Part 4 of this book.

In addition, knowledge of how to work with actors and how actors work with directors is critical. Together, the director and the actor can make a formidable creative force.

The power of a creative partnership can be seen in the number of film actors who have become stars: Martin Scorsese with Robert DeNiro in *Mean Streets* and *Raging Bull*; John Ford with John Wayne, starting with *Stagecoach*; Alfred Hitchcock with Robert Donat and Madeline Carroll in the classic *39 STEPS*—just to cite a few. For actors to know directors is as important as the directors knowing the actors.

The premise that film and television acting are different from stage acting is quite true. Some teach film acting as if it were stage acting, which is incorrect. Though some techniques apply, the practice of continuous rehearsal for the stage is different from that of little or almost no rehearsal in film acting tradition and practice. It is rare that the film actor can count on more than two to three rehearsals, and often those rehearsals are fragmented as well. Those directors and actors not understanding the difference have created theatrical or wooden films.

Another crucial partner is the producer. The director should include the producer in the creative process because, as Roeg and Kazan have implied, the director's creative choices have serious ramifications for the budget. Some producers, including some studio heads, do not understand this creative process. This book will aid film professionals in making the processes of filmmaking a joyful collaboration, which is necessary to protect the integrity of the film before and during its entrance into the marketplace.

I finally determined that there are four components to directing: the written word, the visual language, the actor's language, and the production itself. It seemed if I could create a form that would incorporate those four parts on a single sheet of paper that would guide me, shot by shot, through the entire production, then I would have a winning formula that would free me to deal with emergencies and remain creative at the same time. I called this sheet of paper the checklist form, and it can be found in Chapter 18.

After reading this book the reader will be able to fill out the checklist form. This book will take the mystery out of directing and bring a greater emphasis to artistic filmmaking.

ACKNOWLEDGMENTS

I have been talking about writing this book for years and have finally done it. There are a few who have hung in there with me whom I must single out.

First, John Rhone, a dear, good friend without whose support none of this would have happened. John is someone I will be grateful to forever, not only for encouraging me to do this book but for his unconditional love and support. He will always be in my heart.

To a special lady, Barbara Van Diest, who has been a friend for many years and has always encouraged and supported me. I will always be grateful because she inspired me to finish this book and to conclude the year of 1990 with a positive statement. She too will always be in my heart.

To my colleague and extraordinary friend Mark Warren, who supported and encouraged me over the years, I simply say, thank you for being there.

To my dear, mercurial friend Merritt Davis, who keeps spreading rumors that he beats me in tennis, I say, what is more important, a good backhand or a word processor? Thank you for your humor and encouragement.

To Alexander Singer, who spent a lot of time going over the material, whose wonderful, unique mind gave me clarity and insight, thank you.

To my two beautiful daughters, Juliet and Alicia, who knew I was working on the book but never bugged me. They simply accepted me for having to do it. I love them.

To Jerry Jampolosky, who never laid eyes on this manuscript but whose guidance helped me to get here. Thank you, Jerry.

To my editor Sharon Falter, thank you. To Karen Speerstra, your patience and help were wonderful.

Finally, to all my friends, colleagues, and students who put up with me for years as I promised to write this book, thank you for your patience. Yes, I *did write it after all!*

PART  1

A CREATIVE CONCEPTUALIZATION

Chapter **1**

....

INTRODUCTION

This book details my directing method and its terms. It grew like the proverbial Topsy and is based on my experience as a director, writer, and producer. I developed this system in order to survive the pitfalls of production.

When I first began my career, I directed or wrote anything I could get hired for, from television to stage plays to commercials, and even feature films, just to survive.

I spent hours preparing, developing systems, anticipating all kinds of problems. But no matter what I did, it never seemed to work out the way I envisioned it. My fervent wish was to survive the vagaries of production caused by incompetence, my own ignorance, and undirectable scripts. Then it hit me like a thunderbolt: *it was not supposed to work out!* Production was supposed to be a growth process. The best I could expect was the best we could do.

This realization spawned my method. The system has worked for me and I have shared it with fellow directors in my seminars at the Directors Guild and with some British directors in London. In addition, I have shared it with students at UCLA Extension, USC, and AFI, and many of the reports I have received are forthright endorsements.

• • • • • • • • • • • • • • • • • • •

THE METHOD

Creative conceptualizing is the basis of this method. Each film has a unifying idea, or central theme, that makes it intrinsically different. This concept or idea is the reason why the story is being told. This understanding of the central theme is the basis of all the creative work the director is going to do, and it makes the difference between art and chaos. Chapter 2 deals with this concept in detail.

This method organizes the process of directing the narrative film. It prevents errors of omission or breaches in the central theme and frees the director to explore other creative choices. But, no matter how lost the director may get, the method is there to guide her through the shoals of production and, if followed, it is a fail-safe procedure.

• • • • • • • • • • • • • • • • • • •

THE CHECKLIST

This fail-safe method is made operational by the checklist in Chapter 18. This list works the same way as that used by a pilot before launching his craft into the air, except that this one launches the director into making a film.

The checklist form is used for every shot in the film. It requires the director to prepare shot by shot and step by step, which results in clarity and unity. This book was designed so that after reading it, the reader will easily be able to use the checklist.

• • • • • • • • • • • • • • • • • • •

LANGUAGES OF THE FILM DIRECTOR

In addition to the central theme and the checklist, a good comprehension of the languages of the film director is vital to understanding the method. Just as there are other national languages, such as French or German, there are also different languages in making motion pictures. The director should be fluent in most of these languages, and there are four that he must know. These four languages constitute Parts 2 through 6 of this book. Following is a brief discussion of each.

The Literary Language

The literary language is the language of the screenplay. It addresses such things as empathy, characters, and structure, which are problems that have to be resolved early or they will plague the production and can eventually lead to the project's demise. Because these areas are so important, Part 2 begins with an examination of the rules and limitations of a screenplay.

The Visual Language

The visual language (Parts 3 and 4) is really the director's language because it deals exclusively with the arrangement of pictures. This has a dynamic and lasting effect on the film.

The selection and arrangement of the pictures of the film is dictated by the use of one or more of the 12 cinema languages. The screenplay writer by knowing these cinema languages may subtly suggest the use of a cinema language by writing it into the screenplay.

Supported by correct composition and picturization, selection of one of the 12 cinema languages answers the perennial nagging question, "Where do you place the camera?"

The Actor's Language

Actors are vulnerable. Directors must protect the actor and make him or her safe. This results in a creative partnership, or *rapport*. The bond that subsequently develops between the director and the actor can only make the film better. How the director and the actor choose to express this artistic bond depends on their personal preference. Part 5 includes discussion of 20 acting techniques, with the emphasis on film-acting disciplines, although there are some stage-acting techniques that apply.

The Production Language

Part 6 deals with the process of the "reading" of the script. Each reading covers a specific area of directing. After this, the checklist is discussed and each point on the checklist is filled out, using *The Raiders of the Lost Ark* script as an example. It is here that the ease of this method becomes clear.

This final section also covers the nitty-gritty: the budget. Armed with the knowledge of how a film is made, it is possible to determine whether a film can be made within the projected budget.

Chapter **2**

THE DIRECTOR'S
PRIME DIRECTIVE

DEFINING THE DIRECTOR

He is the guide, the protector, the dictator, the taskmaster, the sadist, the pain in the ass, the artist, the fighter, the trickster, the lover, the teacher, the comedian, the parent—in short, the director is many different things to many people. His job is often misunderstood not only by the general public and by his peers in the movie industry, but also by the director himself.

Why the director is granted total authority over the production and why this authoritarian position is necessary is at the heart of the process of directing. The director's function is dramatically different from that of the crew, the cast, sometimes the producer, and even the writer. In a way, the expression "The buck stops here" clearly defines the director's position. He transforms all those chicken tracks scrawled across pages into a coherent, emotionally charged piece of film. He has the ultimate responsibility for making the film, but he recognizes that making a film is a collaborative effort. But that is not his primary responsibility. So what is?

The Directors Guild of America states that the creative right of the director is that his cut be presented to the producer. The producer has the right to change or reject the director's cut. The director's cut sets the pattern and is often close to the final cut.

• • • • • • • • • • • • • • • • • •
A SCREENING ROOM ANALOGY

To illustrate the director's primary directive in filmmaking, let's examine this fictitious story.

The director is about to screen his "dailies" for the purpose of selecting the best "take" to make up the director's cut. Those selected shots are then spliced together by the editor, and they become the director's cut.

The director invites the cast and the crew to help her select the takes for the director's cut. The scene in the screening room may run something like this:

The make-up person says the base makeup reads too light in takes 1 and 2. He thinks take 5 is the best.

The wardrobe person excitedly jumps up: "The women's dresses are too hippie. It minimized the poor fitting. Take 2 was the best." She thought the costumes looked very good.

The sound person, before responding to the director's request, asks the projectionist if the sound level was altered during the screening of the dailies. The projectionist hotly assures him that he did not alter any of the levels. Then, without any hesitation, he says his choice is take 3: "It had the cleanest sound."

The director of photography's primary responsibility is to give the picture its "look." She chooses take 4. The "key" was properly balanced, which was the "correct" look for the picture, she said. "In the other takes the lights were too hot," she concludes succinctly.

The production designer agrees with the DP. His reasoning is that "the colors of the set were best rendered in take 4. He smiles sheepishly at the director (who makes the decision on camera placement), and then with a touch of gentle reproach he adds, "Camera placement could have been better"—meaning he did not think his set was showed at its best.

The costume designer diplomatically agrees with the production designer (the boss) but thinks the "silhouette of the costumes" was best in take 4.

The production manager (whose primary job is to bring the picture in on budget) says take 1 is the best. He reminds the director that if he shot only one or two takes, it would save time and money. This would bring the picture right in on budget.

In exasperation, the star explodes, taking the production manager's comment personally. She says her character comes through in take 11, adding in a scathing tone that she was right to insist on shooting those additional takes. The crew members had heard of the star's vindictive nature. They nod their heads in pretended agreement.

The experienced producer rarely views the dailies with the director, let alone with the crew. But for the sake of this story she is there and openly agrees with the star that "take 11 is best." "Yet," she adds, "eleven takes does seem excessive." She knows the front office would approve of her stand.

The experienced editor has survived the wars among stars, directors, and producers by being neutral. But for the sake of this illustration, the editor declares himself for take 8. This startles the director, for no one else has chosen that take. When the director questions him, he confides, "The movement of the actress is easily matched." The editor is secretly thinking that his fellow editors will admire his skill at smoothly matching the scene into the sequence.

The script supervisor is liaison between the director and the editor. She communicates any information the director has for the editor. Her primary responsibility is to make certain that the movements and the costumes of the actors match from shot to shot. She proudly agrees with the editor.

Usually after the final draft is accepted, the writer is dismissed unless he is directly involved in the production. Most directors wish the writer were on the set because instant rewrites are often required (some directors insist upon it, like Milos Forman). The writer, who had worked on the dialogue for hours, succinctly states, "Take 1 is the best. It was the only time the dialogue was spoken exactly as written."

This example is dramatic and it does give us insight into the director's dilemma, but not into his prime directive.

● ● ● ● ● ● ● ● ● ● ● ● ● ● ● ● ● ● ●

THE PRIME DIRECTIVE

At my directing seminars, the first question I ask is, "What is the prime directive of the director?" The answers range from "being a communicator" to "helping the actors" to "camera placement," which are all part of the director's job but are not the prime directive.

The director's prime directive is to capture and control the mind and spirit of the audience. The director has to give the audience members what they want, even before they know they want it. Herein lies the director's paradox.

The Director's Dilemma

In the early nineteenth century, touring theater companies brought stage plays to towns and hamlets throughout the United States. Some stars loved to embellish their roles with displays of acting histrionics that had little to do with the play. The larger their egos, the more "improvements" they added and the more they bored the audiences. Finally, when the stars threatened the very existence of the touring company, drastic action became necessary.

The solution was obvious to the "practical" investors in these stock companies. To avoid these abuses someone in the touring company had to represent the audience. This person also had to have the authority to enforce decisions.

A new job was created, titled simply "director," to serve the interests of the audience. The director was to disregard the whims of stars or producers or even the stock company investors themselves. The director was given carte blanche.

The investors believed they had solved the problem. In a way they had. In another way, they created a strange paradox.

The Paradox

An audience usually views the play only once. Audience members react spontaneously. They only know whether they like it or not. They don't care why. When they buy tickets the play is a hit.

The director, unlike the audience, labors through the production. He rehearses the play for weeks, sometimes months, and even years. It may take a year to make a feature film; it may take longer. But in that case, how can the director represent the audience?

This dilemma is complicated further by the production needs of film and television. Unlike her stage counterpart, the film director does not have an audience in attendance to check herself or the material. She is literally shooting in the dark.

This explains the need for "live audiences" to attend the taping of situation comedies to "test" the material. When the audience has left, the director may have to shoot "pickups" to fix things that did not work.

But this invited audience would never stand around when a film is being shot one-camera style. These films are shot out of continuity, and the picture is seen by only one person on the set. That person is the camera operator. Visitors to the set, after about an hour (or less), cannot wait to move on. They are bored.

This dilemma remains and plagues directors, but there are some answers, which are addressed in the next chapter.

Chapter **3**

THE CENTRAL THEME

You have been hired to turn this hundred pages of chicken tracks into an exciting movie. Now what? The game plan is simple. First, you read the screenplay. (The rules on the "readings" are found in Part 6, Chapter 19, but read this chapter first.)

Second, you decide how the audience is to see the film. Third, you shoot the film. Fourth, give the editing plan to the editor. Finally, go home to something truly boring, like sleeping or eating a meal in peace.

Of course, before your departure you pick up your pay. You never know when the producer may fire you, especially after he has seen your dailies. (It is frightening to consider that someone is looking at all the bits and pieces of a disassembled film.) You are certain that no one understands how you planned to put it all together. You are not really sure it will all go together anyway, but you are afraid to admit that to anyone except God and only in the wee hours of the morning. You become mildly hysterical.

What is worse is that the producer appears to be a nice, supportive person. But every director knows in his heart of hearts that beneath that "nice" exterior is a monster who embodies all horrors and past ignorance, a maniac placed on earth specifically to get you! There is no paranoia here, just the facts of everyday directors' insanity. (These insecurities will be addressed in Parts 3 and 4, the visual sections.

"Whoa!" some of you may say. "Let's go back to the beginning." You wish to know how the director did his magic. How was he able to translate those chicken tracks so blithely into a movie? Certainly he must have done more than just read the script. How did he do it? What was that creative process?

• • • • • • • • • • • • • • • • • • •

THE CHECKLIST FORM

In Chapter 18 you will find the checklist form mentioned earlier. Note that after the title is the central theme, which is the first gigantic step in this creative process. This step becomes the foundation for all the creative work to follow. Don't worry; when you finish reading this book you will wonder why directors get paid so much for such an easy job.

• • • • • • • • • • • • • • • • • • •

WHAT IS THE CENTRAL THEME?

The central theme is the unifying idea that makes a film intrinsically different from all other films. It is the main idea, the concept that makes the story hang together and make sense. To put it another way, each story is unique, and that uniqueness is the central theme. The central theme gives the film unity, purpose, and credibility.

Unity

All works of art demand unity. The cohesive idea gives the work its needed unity, and we call that a central theme. The central theme causes the story to make sense. The other elements, such as cinematic language, picturization, composition elements, camera placement, storyboarding, staging, casting, props, scenery, and all the other details of making a motion picture, are selected to support the central theme.

Purpose

The central theme gives the story purpose. The central theme is the reason for the film's existence and the reason for the audience to view the film. It may have a theme as simple as "love conquers all," or as complicated as that of *Gone with the Wind.*

Its raison d'être (reason for being) is what makes it different from other stories. This does not mean that the film must have some socially redeeming message or must preach a moral lesson like an Aesop's fable. Rather, the purpose is a creative concept. Every story has a theme, or an idea. The central theme is not necessarily a moral or ethical statement or a judgment, though it may be.

Harry Cohn, the movie mogul who built Columbia Pictures, had a caustic response to films with a message: "If you wanna send a message, call Western Union." He favored movies that entertained for the sake of entertainment only. It's an old Hollywood story, but it survives because it says something pertinent. Preaching an ethic, especially a political or moral idea, is not an obligation of the central theme, though in some cases the central theme may be characterized by such ideas.

Credibility

If any story elements contradict the central theme, then the film is compromised. If there is a "credibility" question, it is because there has been some breach of the central theme.

We all have been distressed when some incident ripped the fabric of the reality of a film. We got angry or felt betrayed; something seemed to be wrong with the film, but we did not know what it was. If the audience feels cheated, or questions the story, the people, or the events, this means that the central theme of the film was violated in some way, resulting in a serious question of credibility. The director is responsible for maintaining the integrity of the project.

The central theme is critical and should be understood by the director after the second reading. If the theme is unclear, then the director should not proceed until it is identified. Otherwise, the project is doomed and disaster will follow.

Once the central theme is made clear, then production decisions are easily made. The clarity of the central theme helps to prevent contradiction of the film's creative concept.

Major decisions like rewrites, casting, camera placement, and staging all stem from an understanding of the central theme. In addition, the central theme dictates details like hand props, makeup changes, and so on.

• • • • • • • • • • • • • • • • • • •

FINDING THE CENTRAL THEME

Most of us have been taught to judge or find the moral or ethical lesson in the story. Then we marshal all sorts of sociological/psychological theories and write a treatise using glittering generalities that have little to do with preparing to shoot the film. This kind of critique makes excellent fodder for interviews. Somehow when the film artist spouts theories critics are convinced by her sincerity. I suspect that this approach has more to do with appeasing the "ego" of the critic than with understanding the material. However, it certainly is not the way to find the central theme.

To discover the central theme we must read the screenplay without prejudgment. To take an example, let's examine a popular but dated television series in which the central theme is very easily understood.

Case Study: "Father Knows Best"

Most readers have probably seen a "Father Knows Best" episode (though it is not required for understanding this example). To ferret out the central theme of the series, we examine each episode's plot, seeking the concept that is common to all the episodes. Each episode's plot demonstrates how Father (Robert Young) solves the problems of the family. In fact, every episode proves that "Father knows best." (Often the title will state the central theme or at least point you in the right direction.)

Let's assume you were assigned to direct a "Father Knows Best" episode. You read the script to find that it centers on the teenage daughter, the "Princess" (Father's nickname for her). The question is, should she go to the prom with her "steady" or with a young man who has recently moved to their small town? The Princess finds the new young man attractive and mysterious. Father suggests that her prom is too important to trust to a stranger. But infatuated with him, and against Father's advice, she goes with him to the prom. It turns out badly. Father, with Mother's (Jane Wyatt) support, rescues the Princess, proving again that Father knows best.

The actors in a television series are cast, but the director has a choice of the "guest actor" for the episode she is directing. If she casts the new young man as a villain, it makes Father appear stupid since he picks up on the obvious. But if the young man is charming and fools everyone (even the audience), except, of course, dear old Dad, then that makes Father appear smart, showing that he does know best, and this supports the central theme.

The central theme also dictates camera placement. When he meets this young man who is polite, pleasant, and charming, Father's antenna goes up. This may be indicated to the audience by placing the camera at an unusual angle that suggests Father's inner ability to see the kind of viper this young man really is. In Part 3 we will go into detail about camera placement selection.

How can we be sure we have found the central theme? There is a method of making certain. This method has two names.

One name comes from the actor's language and is called the "beat." The other name is from the screenwriter's language and is called "dialogue linkage." The dialogue linkage forces the writer to make the dialogue, as well as the action, clear and sharp.

The director, being the pragmatist, knows the beat, or dialogue linkage, to mean a group of lines, or a unit of action, which are linked together by a common subject or objective.

Case Study: *Raiders of the Lost Ark*

Another example is the more recent and highly successful film *Raiders of the Lost Ark*. The story concerns the search for the ark that is supposed to contain the remains of the Ten Commandments. The epilogue completes the symmetry of the structure, which starts with the prologue, revealing that the Ark is warehoused, never to be seen again.

The film begins in the year 1936. The prologue foreshadows the conflict of the film. It begins with Indiana Jones entering an Amazon burial ground seeking an ancient gold head. We admire his deftness, his determination, his ability to outwit the traps set for intruders. He evades trap after trap, barely escaping a large boulder, to roll literally into the hands of Belloq, his archenemy, another raider of ancient treasures.

He is forced to turn the gold head over to Belloq but manages to escape from these Amazon natives. The chase is perilous; he makes it aboard a waiting seaplane and escapes, but without however, the treasure.

Then the story of the *Ark* begins. Indiana Jones is teaching at the local university when the government men arrive to tell him the Nazis are seeking the Ark. It is imperative that "the good guys" get the Ark because its mystical power and the belief in its power can give the Nazis the edge in winning the war. They also tell Jones of a special medallion that contains the secret of where the Ark is buried.

Indiana Jones sets off. He arrives in Nepal at Marian Ravenswood's bar, a scene we will later examine in detail to demonstrate the use of dialogue linkage.

At this point, please turn to the Appendix and read the scene from the screenplay of *Raiders of the Lost Ark*. Ideally, you should also view the film; it should be in your local video store.

Because *Raiders* is an action picture, the dialogue was kept to a minimum, while the actions of the characters were short and clear. The script has been broken down into "dialogue linkage" and/or "beats" sections to illustrate how it works. But suffice to say that each dialogue section has a hidden agenda — that is, the objective each character tries to accomplish. Sometimes the motivation of the character is apparent and it may even be directly stated by the character, but often, as in real life, the actions of the characters speak the loudest and we deduce their motivation from these actions.

Each section indicates how each character tries to accomplish his or her objective, and the adjustment each makes to the demands of the other character. If it is written well, then simultaneously the plot is moved forward as well. The characters play out their "objective" in the form of an action. As in life, we have objectives, needs we want met by another person. (The inner process of figuring out the beats is covered in Part 5, Chapter 16.)

First, this scene is described as a "two-for scene," meaning it is a scene between two people. We learned from the previous scene that Indy had come for the medallion. Marian's feelings about him constitute a discovery for the audience.

The first beat sees its conclusion with a surprising blow by Marian (unscripted). It visually expresses her objective, which she stated in the opening line of section 2: "I learned to hate you in the last ten years." (This blow was discovered through rehearsal and/or performance.) For ten years she has been waiting for him to walk through that door (to deliver that blow). This proves how much she still loves him.

The second beat starts with sharp recriminations from Marian, and a defense from Indy. Her feelings are out in the open. Finally, but much too quickly to be truly believed by Indy, she orders him to leave. It's a standoff.

In the third beat, Indy repeats his need for the medallion and implies he will pay her a lot of money for it. Marian grudgingly admits she knows of the medallion he means.

In the fourth beat, Indy doesn't see his mentor and innocently asks of his whereabouts. (Perhaps he thought Abner might be easier to deal with.) Marian, in her abrupt fashion, dumps the fact of her father's death on Indy. It probably is another test by Marian. Indy is earnestly sorry.

The fifth beat is clearly a lament by Marian about her life; she asks for Indy's sympathy. He gives it.

The sixth beat is the payoff. Finally, Indy pitches his form of trust, using the key line, "Trust me." As noted, there was a discrepancy between script and shooting. In the film Marian went to slap him again, but this time he catches her hand and thrusts the money into it. Steven Spielberg's director's touch made the section visual.

The seventh beat has Marian putting Indy off and rejoicing in her control over him. Feeling he has no choice, he departs.

Dialogue in action-adventure pictures like *Raiders* is kept to a minimum. The concentration is on seeing the characters in action. Dialogue is contrapuntal (see the discussion of collision cinema language in Chapter 12, Part 4). Sean Connery's James Bond films are an example.

In the process of breaking the script down into beats (following the plot that forces the director to be clear in understanding the actions of the characters) the clarity of the central theme emerges. The central theme is deduced from the plot by following the beats of the story.

For instance, in *Raiders* we understand it is a story about those who seek the Ark. Indy is the hero and Belloq is the villain. What's more, the best villain represents the "dark side" of the hero. This is classic in story structure. There is an unconscious sense of justice the audience enjoys in the moments when this element becomes clear.

Recently, the *Batman* story structure also used this technique. The Joker represented the dark side of Batman, and their histories were almost identical. This kind of symmetry in storytelling is pleasing to audiences.

Point of View

Whom are we rooting for in a given scene? Whom do we identify with in the scene? This is deduced from the beat. Every scene has a point of view — a key difference between reportorial work and the dramatic form.

In the *Raiders of the Lost Ark* scene we analyzed, whose point of view was represented, Marian's or Indy's? Was it that of both? Was it the view of the writers?

Again, we go back to the beats of the scene. As we analyze each beat, it should become apparent whose point of view was being represented. The point of view implies empathy for that character. (This will be discussed further in Parts 2 and 3.) Clearly, the scene flows from Indy's point of view. Spielberg set the tone from the first shot. Review the video and the script, and it will be clear because the point of view implies the desire to gain the audience's empathy. Every scene has a point of view, even if it appears that it does not.

Help for the Director through Linkage

A further help to the director in breaking down the script into beats occurs when a character enters or exits. This new "scene" gives information pertinent to the story, information that the audience usually knew before and had to be reminded about.

This process by which scenes are indicated through the exits and entrances of characters is called "French scenes." The term was named for the French playwright Molière, who was known for dividing his plays into scenes by the entrances and exits of his characters.

In our procedure, the French scene is then broken into smaller units, the dialogue linkage, or beats. This is the smallest unit. If there is any confusion, refer back to the *Raiders of the Lost Ark* scene in the Appendix. If confusion continues, do not panic; there are additional examples to be found in Part 4, Chapter 10, specifically in the master scene cinema language example of *Big Country,* and in the interpersonal cinema language *Vertigo* example. In both of those scenes, the beats are marked off. The procedure for reading the screenplay is thoroughly explored in Part 6, "The Production Language."

PART **2**

THE LITERARY LANGUAGE

Chapter **4**

RULES OF A SCREENPLAY

The director's first challenge is the screenplay. It is unlike the novel, which is written to be read, or the play, which is written to be performed.

Most screenplays are written only for the eyes of the producer, the studio head, the actor, and the director. Plays are read by laypeople. Their dialogue is studied and enjoyed by many. Many plays are read and studied in high schools, colleges, and universities. But can anyone remember the last time a screenplay was read in school for its literary quality?

Reading a screenplay is unlike reading a novel, short story, newspaper article, or even your own checkbook. Reading a screenplay is not usually done by the average reader.

Screenplays are difficult because they read like a technical document, relying as they do upon the ability of the reader to "see" the pictures. The form requires minimal description and dialogue. The typical novel has from 200,000 to 400,000 words, the play has about 60,000 to 80,000 words, while the typical screenplay has about 40,000 words. It is not a difficult skill to learn, but the layperson not interested in making movies wants to be entertained. Screenplays are not necessarily fun to read, unless you are in the movie business.

"Readers" read screenplays for a fee. They also learn how to write good screenplays, which is usually the reason why many work for minimal fees. They are not necessarily sensitive to the important challenge of a screenplay, whether it would make a good movie, but rather whether it is a good screenplay. These are not necessarily the same thing. A good "reading" screenplay may make a bad film. In the "coverage" given to the producer, the reader sums up the plot succinctly, maybe in a page or two, and then expresses an opinion whether the producer should read it or not, stating reasons.

The difference between the written word and a wonderful film is obvious. That producer or studio head who says the script will make a wonderful film has little to go on. It takes incredible insight to determine which script is going to turn into a wonderful movie.

Sometimes people say in a movie theater, "Why did they bother to make such a bad film?" This is amusing, for no one ever starts out to make a bad film. If the creators had known it would turn out badly, they would not have made the film. But that is the challenge and the fun of the art.

Another area of controversy is the subject of the film. Some people find turtles fascinating and would spend all their time and money viewing turtles. This is no joke; the success of the Ninja Turtles on television, in movies, and more recently in rock concerts attests to this phenomenon.

Others might think a story about a dysfunctional, institutionalized person unable to cope with the world would be impossible to make into a film. Wrong again. View *Rain Man* and experience the insight and growth. The film gives us insight into the human condition.

Subjects can be as various as man going to the moon or a child falling in love with a red balloon. Choice of subject seems to be determined by the personal interests of the filmmaker and the people who put up the money.

It is often amusing to listen to the marketing people tell the creative community what is selling and what is not, implying that the creative community should continue to make the same pictures because they are making money. The marketing people are talking about what the creative community did successfully. Ironically, they talk about history, but it is the creative community, with the help of the financial people, who make the history.

The subject of the chosen story has more to do with personal taste rather than with what is marketable. In spite of gloom projectors, screenplay writers are paid huge sums of money to write stories. Let's start at the beginning and first find out what a screenplay is.

• • • • • • • • • • • • • • • • • • •

DEFINING THE TERM

A screenplay is a series of events told in an organized manner; it tells a story with a beginning, a middle, and an end. Most agree with this definition. But for a screenplay to be taken seriously in the producing community, it must contain the following elements: empathy, central theme, conflict, characters, and structure.

● ● ● ● ● ● ● ● ● ● ● ● ● ● ● ● ● ● ●

EMPATHY

Empathy is defined in the dictionary as "the projection of one's own personality into the personality of another in order to understand him better." This is the heartbeat of a successful film. Without it, you have lost the audience. For the record, the audience will forgive problems with any of the other four elements, but never the loss of empathy.

Empathy won the film *Rocky* an Oscar, made Sylvester Stallone an instant star, and spawned an ongoing series of *Rocky* pictures. In the classic *Gone with the Wind,* the screenplay writer, Sidney Howard, was presented a challenge. The story was about the destruction of the American South. The challenge was to keep the audience sympathetic. This was no simple feat, considering that most of the population lived in the North at the time of the picture's projected release and were not kindly disposed toward aristocratic ways and the keeping of slaves.

Scarlett O'Hara was the answer. The story is told through the eyes of this charming, spoiled child-woman, from a prominent Southern family. If the audience roots for her, then the crushing fall of the South will have the desired emotional impact upon the audience. As the story progresses, we applaud Scarlett's fight for survival, and watch with fascination her stormy maturity during the reconstruction of the South. Empathy has made *Gone with the Wind* one of the most successful films ever.

David Selznick recognized how important it was to find the right actress to play Scarlett. He searched the world for the right one and found her in England. Vivien Leigh brought to the role the correct mixture of innocence, vamp, and vulnerability. It made her a star and the film a classic overnight.

The "antihero" film appears to contradict the theory of empathy. But this is not the case. The audience identifies with the antihero until he makes an unethical choice or commits an immoral act. With mixed feelings, they watch the fall of their "hero" and, if the film is properly constructed, want him to get his just desserts. When the film is over, the audience will feel redeemed, but with a poignant residue of regret as well.

The antihero film pattern is best illustrated by Herman Mankiewicz's screenplay of *Citizen Kane*. It had for its hero a rich and powerful man, Charles Foster Kane. The film starts with his death and is made challenging by the conflicting opinions about his character. Mankiewicz's screenplay used a device found in most dime novel detective stories. The mystery of "Rosebud," the last word Kane spoke before he died, sets up the excuse for examining Kane's life. (Orson Welles's close-up of a pair of lips had become *Citizen Kane*'s signature shot.)

Though the audience was challenged by this device, Mankiewicz and Welles knew they had to gain sympathy for Kane or they would quickly lose the audience. The answer: show Kane as a child, torn from a good home and a loving father and thrust into the arms of the cold, calculating banker, Walter Thatcher—all for the sake of money.

Flash forward: a young Kane has bought a newspaper that he humbly and sincerely dedicates to the principles of truth and justice for all. When the newspaper fails, he drops his principles and buys success by hiring a group of ruthless newspaper people. The audience roots for Kane to win against the corruption of money (the central theme).

The challenge then is to create a screenplay that has empathy. Without audience identification with the hero (or the villain), people will be long gone to their local video store, bar, or even the yogurt palace. In order to win an audience's sympathy, our hero must have one or more of the following characteristics.

Morals and Ethics

First, our hero has to be ethical and moral. Though presently out of vogue, our Western movie heros were honest, ethical, and moral. Gary Cooper, Hopalong Cassidy, Tom Mix, Gene Autry, and Roy Rogers were some of those representing the American Western hero. He was a strong, silent man of few words, but when he spoke, it was with simplicity and humility. Generally, he represented the idealistic American way of life. He protected the innocent, defended the weak, and fought for freedom. He was a moral man who resorted to violence only as a final resort. This is the profile of the classic American folk hero found in most Westerns.

Star Wars followed a similar formula. The Western has the hero joining the downtrodden group, sometimes farmers or sheepherders, against the evil cattle barons. Transpose farmers into rebels, the cattle barons into the evil empire, and you have *Star Wars*.

We tend to dismiss the characters of a past generation as naive, but when we examine them in a more objective light, the formula becomes apparent. The formula is the same; the packaging brings it up to date. When the formula appears as if it were new and current, then the present generation accepts it, though *Star Wars* is just a Western dressed in sci-fi clothes.

Loyalty

Loyalty is another trait used in gaining empathy. In *Star Wars,* for instance, Han Solo (Harrison Ford) abandons his friends for money, but later suddenly turns up and saves his friend Luke from certain death.

In Sam Peckinpah's film *The Wild Bunch,* loyalty was used to glorify the heros and win the hearts of the audience. The final shoot-out is precipitated by a villainous Mexican bandit who had violated, humiliated, and finally killed one of the *Wild Bunch* gang. They gave their lives to avenge his death. Though it was a foolish gesture, the heros were redeemed and were elevated to the level of superheros because they kept their unspoken word to their dead comrade. This suggests the next principle.

Altruism

Altruism is another trait of heros, who help someone or some cause without hope of material gain. This is exemplified by William Holden's character with his Hole-in-the-Wall gang in the *The Wild Bunch*. In *The Wizard of Oz* Dorothy saves her little dog, Toto, and desperately tries to get home, making this film an eternal pleaser of all audiences. Altruism is used in films even today.

Compassion

A compassionate, caring person is an empathic character who is difficult to dramatize. This trait does not lend itself easily to the dramatic form, but it has been successfully done, as can be seen in *Butch Cassidy and the Sundance Kid.*

In William Goldman's *Adventures in the Screen Trade,* the audience had to love his characters, Butch Cassidy and the Sundance Kid, or the film faced failure. Goldman created a Western hero who was a polite, caring, charming, and gentle bank robber. When his authority is challenged by a member of his gang, the hero outwits him in a simple but resourceful manner. Then he turns around and accepts the challenged member's suggestion.

The relationship between Butch (Paul Newman) and the Sundance Kid (Robert Redford) was unique. Each gave to the other the dignity to be his own person. Though Sundance teased Butch, he also followed him. They left the United States and traveled to Argentina so that they could continue to rob banks — together. They simply cared for each other. It was the "super-posse" (the supposed good guys) that drove Butch and Sundance out of the country. Not for a moment did the audience ever doubt who were the good guys.

Butch Cassidy and the Sundance Kid was a different kind of Western, and George Roy Hill, with the support of his stars, was able to fight off the studio people who insisted that it should follow the traditional Western. William Goldman, George Roy Hill, Paul Newman, and Robert Redford were successful. They gained the audience's support as well as forgiveness for the lack of violence, which is usually found in the Western genre.

A Lover

Any story with lovers immediately endears itself to most viewers. For instance, in Shakespeare's *Romeo and Juliet* the youthful lovers kill themselves because of their feuding families. These teenage lovers are full of innocent passion and virginal love. Is there anyone alive who doesn't recall his or her first love affair with fondness?

Many films deal with people in various conditions of love, from out of love, falling in love, being in love, about to fall in love, and the many variations. (This device is also widely used and expertly practiced by daytime drama.) In Sydney Pollack's *The Way We Were*, Barbra Streisand loved Robert Redford, which endeared her to the audience. In *Love Story*, was there a dry eye in the audience when Ryan O'Neal discovered his wife (Ali MacGraw) was going to die?

In *Arsenic and Old Lace*, Cary Grant is about to marry when he is prevented by his crazy brother and tries to kill him. In *Paper Chase*, the law student falls in love with the professor's daughter. In *Love with a Proper Stranger*, the girl (Natalie Wood) is pregnant and seeks the father (Steve McQueen) for help in getting an abortion. These are all examples of creating empathy for characters by having them fall in love, be in love, chase after love.

Underdog Status

Many comedians use the underdog role as part and parcel of their public character. Jerry Lewis has made a lifelong career of playing low-status characters who are silly, as in *The Bellhop* and in *The Nutty Professor*.

Another popular practitioner is Woody Allen. From *Annie Hall* to *Manhattan* to *Sleeper*, the Woody Allen image is always a low-status neurotic character.

Victim Status

When someone is "taken advantage of," the audience's sympathy is engaged. This positioning is the launching platform for many pictures, especially action pictures.

First Blood, Rambo Part II, Rocky, Rain Man, and *Top Gun* are a few films that used the victim format. The hero saves the victim and/or restores his position, or the hero avenges the wrong done to him. *Scaramouche*, based on the famous Sabatini romantic novel of the same name, is a classic that uses this structure. The duel was obligatory and resulted in the longest fencing sequence in the movies. *Rocky* also followed the same structure. In *Star Wars* Luke Skywalker became an orphan, and a victim in an instant. In *The Wizard of Oz* Dorothy became the victim when the twister sent her to Oz, friendless and alone.

Martyrdom

Martyrdom began when the first Christian was thrown to the lions. Self-sacrifice is still used in plots today, as when the brother goes out to work to get a member of his family some life-saving operation, or to put a sibling through college, and so on.

Many World War II films used martyrdom, such as *Sands of Iwo Jima, Back to Bataan, Fighting Seabees, Thirty Seconds over Tokyo*, to name a few.

In Milos Forman's *One Flew over the Cuckoo's Nest,* Nicholson's character sneaks the inmates out of the locked ward to go on a fishing trip. We love him for that, but we know, and he knows, that he is going to suffer the consequences. His punishment, however, is far greater than any could imagine.

In *Firefox* Clint Eastwood plays an emotionally unstable Vietnam fighter pilot who goes to the Soviet Union and steals the fighter plane called *Firefox.* He does it for his country.

Betrayal

When the hero has been betrayed by a friend, lover, or member of his family, he is motivated to retaliate. In *The Godfather* Michael (Al Pacino) discovers that his older brother had betrayed him and he retaliates. Another famous betrayal is that of the Wizard, in *The Wizard of Oz,* who betrays Dorothy by sending her off to perform another chore. In *Splendor in the Grass* the father (Pat Hingle) commits suicide and abandons his son (Warren Beatty). These examples use betrayal to make the hero vulnerable and sympathetic.

Justice

Use of justice ranges from the simplistic, as the *Superman* movies, to the sophisticated, as *The Birdman of Alcatraz.* The pursuit of justice is the raison d'être for many action pictures. Some obvious examples are *Star Wars, In the Heat of the Night, Deathwish,* and *Rambo.* Besides action pictures, there are other "justice stories," such as *Inherit the Wind* (on the famous Scopes trial), *Mutiny on the Bounty, Paradine Case, Wrong Man,* and *I Confess,* to cite some of the films that have used this formula.

As in life, a screenplay changes from moment to moment, and so may empathy identification. For instance, in one section of a film, the audience identifies with a character because he has fallen in love. Later on, he sacrifices his love for his friend or family. This occurs in *West Side Story* and in *Romeo and Juliet.*

There are many combinations of traits and changes. The director must know how these combinations affect the audience. That is the purpose of the experiential graph (see Figure 4.1). The graph traces the desired emotional involvement of the audience members as they view the film.

• • • • • • • • • • • • • • • • • • •

THE CENTRAL THEME

The central theme and the motivation of the hero must be inextricably bound up together for the screenplay to have unity. In *Raiders of the Lost Ark* Indiana Jones illustrates this unity. His character is a compulsive

Figure 4.1 *The experiential graph represents the emotional involvement of the audience as they view a film. If the audience experiences the film as indicated by this graph, then the audience is rooting for the hero. This means the film will be successful.*

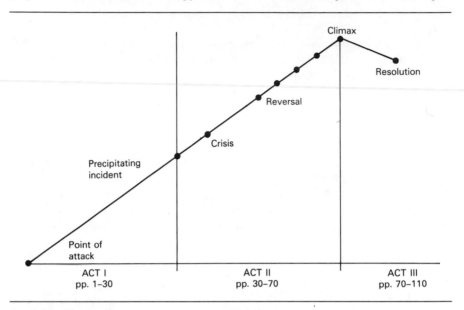

Note: There are other experiential graph configurations. For instance, films like *Nashville, Boccaccio 70,* and Somerset Maugham's *Trio* stories require other types of graphs.

archaeologist who spends his life seeking ancient treasures. That is his prime motivation, and it makes the screenplay credible.

The plot proves it every time. Recall the incident in which he discovers that his girlfriend, Marian, is alive but a prisoner. He is overjoyed and is about to release her. True to his character but to the shock of Marian, however, he reties her, explaining he will return after he has located the Ark, which is supposed to be nearby.

Additional proof is found in the scene in which Indy has a bazooka trained on the Nazis, threatening to destroy the Ark unless they release Marian. Recognizing that Indiana is incapable of destroying a relic from the past, Belloq calls his bluff and tells him to fire away. Indy capitulates and puts his bazooka down, becoming their prisoner.

The sequel, *The Temple of Doom* has a flawed central theme. The premise of finding great treasures from the past was put on hold, while Indy went to save the kidnapped children. Altruism, the writers thought, would excuse not using the original central theme. But rarely does an audience accept a substitute central theme. Usually, they feel cheated. In the third sequel, *The Last Adventure,* the central theme was not only restored, but Indy's father reinforced it and became a foil character for Indy. In some ways, the third film is the best, because it is classic in its structure.

Once the question of the central theme has been addressed, there are two ways of approaching storytelling. They can be best summed up as inductive and deductive.

The Inductive Approach

When a character's needs cause the events, the story is an inductive one. These are also called "people stories" or character-driven stories. Some actors and directors prefer this approach, since it offers creative opportunities to explore the human condition and address some of the enigmas of life. Are we not all seeking some answers to the great mysteries of life and death?

The inductive method is used more often by foreign filmmakers, though there are many such American films: *Annie Hall, Diner, Ordinary People, Rain Man, Driving Miss Daisy, Steel Magnolias, Dad, Citizen Kane,* and *Field of Dreams* are some examples. They are all character-driven stories, in which the events were generated by the desire of the main character.

Terms of Endearment, written and directed by James Brooks, starring Deborah Winger, Shirley MacLaine, and Jack Nicholson, is an excellent example. Basically this is the story of a single mother raising her daughter, their relationship, and finally the impending death of the daughter. It is a touching and loving story and is character driven. The exception is the discovery that the daughter, now a grown woman with a husband and two children, now has terminal cancer.

To set the picture up, James Brooks has the mother (Shirley MacLaine) rushing into the baby's room late at night. She has not gone to help the baby but to see if she is allright. One senses that she is an overindulgent mother since there was no reason for her to tear into the child's room.

The relationship between the mother and daughter is what this picture is about. Though we focus on the daughter (Debra Winger) as she copes with her everyday problems, as does the mother with her crazy boyfriend (Jack Nicholson), the film remains true to its central theme and remains an inductive story. Clearly, the emphasis is on people, not events.

Inductive stories are difficult to get financed. The studio executives, familiar with the world of commerce, contracts, and sales, find it difficult to trust "feelings" or "instincts." This is the basis of the inductive screenplay. The screenplay format does not lend itself to emotional explanation the way a novel does (see Chapter 6 for further explanation on the screenplay format).

The inductive stories to get financed are often based on successful Broadway plays, such as *Driving Miss Daisy* and *Steel Magnolias.* The studio executives are assured that these plays have appeal because of the successful Broadway run. If there is any attack by the stockholders, these executives explain that they chose to do this Broadway play because of its success. The response could be that the Broadway play did not appeal to everyone in the country. This gives the studio executives a reprieve.

The bottom line is that if the studio does not show a profit after a year or two, the executives' jobs are in jeopardy. The expression "You're only as good as your last picture" rings through the halls of the studios as the executives shift and fade in and out of their offices every few years. This applies to the producers, writers, directors, and stars as well. Only rarely will a studio back a creator consistently unless he or she shows some immediate success. That was true back in the days of the major studios, but not today, when the profit return separates the people from their jobs.

Original screenplays are especially intimidating to the studio executives. Reading a screenplay and understanding the underlying feelings are difficult enough for the sophisticated reader, but the process is terrifying for the studio executive. These skills are not taught in the law or business schools, where many studio executives have been trained.

Inductive stories also get supported when promoted by a powerful star, director, producer, or writer, especially if this person has a successful track record in the inductive story.

James Brooks, the successful television producer-writer, wrote the script for *Terms of Endearment* and desperately wanted to do the film. Paramount Pictures' Barry Diller knew that a successful television series generates $60 – $80 million, and with a licensing fee and in syndication it can earn an additional $200 million. Also, it is an asset on the corporate books, the reason for big bonuses. *Terms*'s cost could not exceed $15 million, if that, which is a cheap price to pay for a potential hit television series.

Diller agreed to finance Brooks's *Terms of Endearment* but under the condition that Brooks agree to create another television series. Diller did not know and perhaps did not think it was significant that *Terms* would be successful, but in any case he'd get Brooks to do another television show.

Some inductive screenplays get done outside studios through different means, such as getting the support of relatives. Peter Masterson, a successful character actor and Broadway producer, is a case in point. He had never directed a film before but prevailed upon his cousin Horton Foote, the writer of *Tender Mercies,* to permit him to direct his screenplay, *Trip to Bountiful.* The rest is history.

The advantage of inductive stories is that they give the audience a powerful catharsis. Audiences come out glowing, singing the praises of the film. But for the filmmakers, there is a grand feeling of contributing to a better understanding of the human condition. Certainly this has greater weight and significance than a horror film.

The disadvantage of an inductive story is in its difficulty to structure. This ability to get inside the skin of the characters comes from being "artistic." When dealing with feelings of characters, rather than situations, it is imperative to know when another emotional value has to be added, or when a change of pace is needed. Also required is the ability to predict the reactions of the audience. There is tendency especially in this inductive mode for the beginner to repeat the emotional values in scene after scene. This causes an audience to feel that the story does not go anywhere.

This "emotional" training is mandated in the acting profession, though instinctively many writers pick it up as well. Some successful screenwriters have a background in acting. For example, Clifford Odets, John Huston, Billy Wilder, and Harold Pinter are writers who were trained as actors as well.

The major pitfall in the inductive story occurs when the leading characters do not communicate their "reality" to the audience. Consequently, the audience gets turned off.

The Deductive Approach

When the situation dictates the action, and the character is manipulated to serve the machinations of the plot, the story is a deductive one. Simply stated, this is an event-driven story.

Some obvious examples are *Raiders of the Lost Ark, Rambo, Star Wars,* and *Ghostbusters.* It is the plot, the series of events, that moves the story. The characters are usually one- or two-dimensional, but skill is needed to make the characters appear three dimensional (see the section "Characters" in this chapter to understand how to make this work). Violate the character's major (spine) objective, and credibility becomes an issue. In *Raiders,* the Ark was the star, not Harrison Ford's Indiana Jones. As you may recall from Chapter 3, Indy's character mandated that he be obsessed with finding ancient treasures.

But structuring the events requires clarity. Selecting the correct point of attack that best dramatizes the story is a challenge. Contrasting one event to another, understanding the emotional mood, and maintaining the integrity of the story is the key to achieving a successful deductive story. The selection of the events, riveting the audience to their seats without violating the central theme, takes skill.

The major advantage of a deductive story is that the film moves at a robust pace and is most exciting. The story is horizontal rather than vertical.

The major pitfall in this procedure is that the film may feel contrived. For instance, in *Raiders* when Indiana Jones holds onto a submarine conning tower as it submerges while crossing the Mediterranean Sea, it does seem to stretch the viewer's credibility. Nevertheless, that thought probably occurred to few in the audience. Minor miracles were accepted because everyone was rooting for Indy. Empathy again is the winner.

Inductive versus Deductive

Most screenplays are a combination of both inductive and deductive approaches. The emphasis is dictated by choice of central theme, and empathy point of view.

For instance, when the plot studies the relationship between a mother and a daughter, then the inductive method is implied, as it was in *Terms of Endearment. Driving Miss Daisy, Diner,* and *Annie Hall,* are all inductive stories.

A tale of finding lost treasure requires that plotting come first, then characters to make it work. An excellent example is *Romancing the Stone.* In another example, a band of men protecting a village from bandits, as in *The Magnificent Seven,* mandates the deductive approach.

E.T. is an example of an excellent mixture. The film had two sections: "getting to know E.T.," and "the government is coming after you." The first section was inductive and built incredible empathy for E.T., while the second was deductive.

Robert Zemekeis and Robert Gale's 1985 Oscar-winning screenplay *Back to the Future* is an example of an inductive and deductive mixture. The father's overcoming the bully of his childhood was character development (inductive), while the son's coping the time travel was deductive. But in the sequel, the story became almost exclusively deductive.

Other examples of films are *Ordinary People* (more inductive), *Vertigo* (more deductive), *The Informer* (blend of both), *Guns of Navarone* (deductive), *Stagecoach* (more deductive), *Citizen Kane* (more inductive), *Gone with the Wind* (blend of both), and *The Wizard of Oz* (more deductive).

It is rare that a screenplay is just inductive or deductive. The Indiana Jones films are clearly deductive, but inductive sections are there as well. For instance, the scene in which Indiana Jones and Marian are safely aboard a friendly freighter and in their cabin is inductive. It might have ended differently, though it did end abruptly, but it was motivated by character not circumstances. Marian's accidentally flipping over the mirror and knocking out Indiana was in keeping with their style of romance.

● ● ● ● ● ● ● ● ● ● ● ● ● ● ● ● ● ● ● ●

CONFLICT

All drama films must involve conflict between two or more forces. These forces are named for the empathy positioning of the audience. The heros, the protagonists, have the audience rooting for their victory, while the villains, the antagonists, have the audience rooting against them. Hitchcock believed the more hated and dreadful the villain, the better the movie. Many horror films follow this rule to an exploitable fault.

There are only three basic conflicts. Most films have more than one type of conflict, and usually that makes it a better film. The three basic conflicts are discussed in the following sections.

Man versus Man

Man against man, or against another man (woman), or against himself (herself) are all included in this category. In Shakespeare's *Hamlet,* Prince

Hamlet is the protagonist. His antagonist is Claudius, his uncle, who was also the king, representing authority and the state. His other antagonist is himself. His hesitation, his uncertainty about what course to pursue, represents his inner conflict. His indecision and considering suicide is an indication of that as well.

Dressed to Kill has two basic conflicts, man against himself, and man against man. Michael Caine's schizophrenic character represents the inner conflict, while Nancy Allen, the protagonist, represents the other conflict. She tries to trap the schizophrenic killer Michael Caine.

The Lost Weekend, Days of Wine and Roses, and *Tender Mercies* all represent inductive stories of the inner conflict of their main characters, but they include other conflicts as well. In *Altered States* the hero experiments with mind-expanding drugs, succeeding in changing himself into a primitive man. His success creates the conflict: man against his primitive self. In *Cool Hand Luke* Luke's character had hubris. His pride proves to be his downfall, even his death.

Man versus Society

The individual against the group, the tribe, the town, the college board, the rules, the unfair government—in short, against society—is the second conflict. This dates back to the ancient Greek theater and to the comedies of Aristophanes that poked fun at the Athenian government. In *Lysistrata* the women of both countries banded together, refusing to have sex with their husbands until they stopped making war, an example of "humorous" man versus society conflict.

Several centuries later, the Globe Theatre's playwright dared to make the family the villain. In Shakespeare's *Romeo and Juliet* the teenage lovers were pitted against the feuding families. Their rebellion was against their society. They died for it but live eternally in the hearts of the audience.

In the twentieth century, the movie studios discovered that youth rebellion films were box office winners. These "youth" movies, exhibited during the summer when the young people are free from school, have proved to be a major source of revenue.

Man against society abounds in World War II films. *The Sands of Iwo Jima, Thirty Seconds over Tokyo,* and *Flying Tigers* all tell the story of an individual of the good society fighting against the evil "Axis" society.

The Western *High Noon* followed the plot formula of the Second World War but in reverse. In *High Noon* the sheriff (the hero) abandons the town, the evil society. After bringing law and order to the town, the sheriff, about to retire, learns that the gang of murderers he had put behind bars has been released from federal prison. They are returning to kill the sheriff. He asks the town for help, but they abandon him, leaving him to face the gang alone. Even his bride, a Quaker, begs him to leave with her. He refuses, knowing they will come after him. She leaves (well, not quite). The conflict is the same, except in this case *High Noon* indicts the town, the society. *High Noon*'s author, Carl Foreman, was blacklisted, and this was his way of indicting the McCarthy commission.

Man versus God

The term *God* refers here to conflicts that deal with the metaphysical. Ingmar Bergman explored the relationship, or the lack of it, between God and man, while other filmmakers use it to exploit people's fear of the unknown. This device is used in many horror films.

In *The Exorcist* the plot has an evil spirit take possession of an innocent thirteen-year-old girl. Subsequently, this evil spirit is exorcised and the girl is saved. In *Poltergeist* the spirits are outraged because their final resting place had been disturbed. Revenge was their motivation.

Oh God! (with God played by George Burns in Larry Gelbart's script) is another variation of God versus man. God is represented as a kind, knowing, and compassionately amusing figure. Man is presented as thinking that he knows the way the world is and that is pretty much without a God. God has come to reinforce the message, that *He is!*

The *Star Wars* line "Let the Force be with you" made use of this conflict, focusing more on hardware and special effects in the first two of the series. The showdown in the final film of the trilogy was between the "evil" Emperor and the "innocent" Luke Skywalker. The Emperor's costume and makeup recalled images of the devil himself. The *Star Wars* trilogy included the other three conflicts as well. Man-against-man conflict had the heros pitted against Darth Vader, and the conflict of man against society had Luke joining the rebels against the society, the Empire.

When all three conflicts are in a screenplay, they support the tensions of the story. *Back to the Future* has all three working in the story. First, there is the father who has to overcome his high school bully (man versus man), then the son (in his father's past) follows the rules of that society but is not too successful (man versus society). To return to his own time, he has to follow the rules of time travel (man versus God).

• • • • • • • • • • • • • • • • • • •

CHARACTERS

A character must ring true. A character must be quickly identified by type, social position, status, and relationship, to the other characters in the screenplay. This is called the "shorthand" of identification and is used when introducing a character. This first rule mandates the character be identified as hero or villain, and/or how that character is aligned in relation to the hero or villain. Although main characters are fleshed out as the story progresses, nothing unnerves an audience more than when they are made to feel uncertain who is the hero or villain. Most films set that up at the first fade-in.

Secondary characters are identified by their relationship to the hero or villain. In *Star Wars* the characters were from another time and universe, but their types were quickly identified. This action-oriented movie demands that the characters be identified immediately as friend or foe.

Equally important is the clear statement of what that character wants. In *Raiders of the Lost Ark* Indiana wanted the Ark. This objective is referred to as the "spine" of the character. Indiana Jones, a compulsive archaeologist who spends his life seeking relics from the past, was mandated to pursue the Ark, and the plot proved it every time. This marriage of Indiana's character and the film's central theme made the film credible.

Every character has an objective, a spine. Even incidental characters have a spine or an objective. For instance, a hotel doorman may serve the plot by identifying the main character and by making it clear that he lives at the hotel. He may do that by referring to him by name and holding the door for him. The doorman's "spine" is his job and his relationship to that main character in that capacity.

Contradictions

Character contradiction is the springboard for surprising but necessary changes in the story direction. A contradiction or "flaw" in the character can turn a dull, pedantic person into a fascinating character.

Indiana Jones is unafraid of huge boulders, headhunters, Nazis, airplanes, heights, guns, knives, and submarines, but he can't stand snakes. The scene in the film when Indy is trapped with more snakes than one would see in three lifetimes adds an amusing and interesting character insight.

War Lord is an intriguing film. At the time of the picture's release, Charlton Heston, who played the War Lord, was known as a leading man in action pictures. Consequently the audience expected a sword-and-sandal action picture. The story takes place during feudal times. The War Lord, a veteran of many battles, is given the prize of ruling over a small community. He is a prudent, honest man, known for his valor and loyalty. With his small band of soldiers, he arrives in this hamlet to take up his command. On his way into town, however, he catches a local maiden bathing nude in a small pond. He is taken by her and discovers she is to marry a serf.

Against the advice of his friend and comrade in arms, his younger brother, he insists upon his war lord's privilege to bed the young serf's bride on their wedding night. In the morning, when the bridegroom serf comes to claim his bride, he refuses to give her up.

Suddenly, the story changes from a sword-and-sandal picture to a love story. An honorable man throws over all he holds valuable because he has fallen in love with this young maiden. It spells doom, not only for his love affair but for his life as well. The contradiction is in the character of the War Lord.

Determination

The determination of the hero to get what he wants regardless of the cost is the "locking" device that drives a film to its inexorable conclusion. For example, Indiana Jones had the determination to go after the Ark even when he thought his girl was killed, or when he was buried in a tomb, or when the Ark was aboard an airplane, an armed truck, a submarine. Not even the Ark's awesome power could prevent him from returning it to the United States. His determination drove *Raiders of the Lost Ark* to its conclusion.

The classic *Wizard of Oz* would not have succeeded if Dorothy had not had the determination to get home. It was the reason the film was able to continue. Without her determination, the film would have been over at Dorothy's first encounter with the Wicked Witch. In *Gone with the Wind* Scarlett O'Hara had the will to restore and hold on to her family plantation. It was her determination that drove that film. Clearly, this fierce determination of the heros to get what they want is an essential ingredient in making a good screenplay.

Foil Characters

A foil character contrasts with our hero. Shakespeare employed this device in many of his plays. In *Hamlet* Laertes returns to the castle, his sword raised, demanding revenge. Throughout the play, Hamlet, by contrast, tries to determine what action to take to avenge his father's death.

In *The Godfather* Sonny (James Caan) was the foil to his brother Michael (Al Pacino). When Sonny plotted a course of action as the new leader of the Corleone family, his plan was impetuous and stupidly violent. He failed and was killed by his enemies. Michael's plan, thoughtful and carefully laid out, was effective. It made Michael the godfather.

Raiders of the Lost Ark used Belloq, the French archaeologist who works for the Nazis as a foil to Indiana Jones. Belloq represented the "evil" side of the driven archaeologists.

This foil character concept is helpful not only in providing a contrast to the main character, but in creating subplotting. A subplot is usually designed as a contrast to the main plot, and it uses foil characters to contrast with the main characters. This is done for several reasons, ranging from building suspense to adding texture to the story.

Pivotal Characters

A pivotal character sends the story off in an unexpected direction. For instance, the Wizard in *The Wizard of Oz,* by insisting that Dorothy get him the Wicked Witch's broom, in effect sent the story off in another direction.

The term *deus ex machina* refers to a machine that lowered from Mount Olympus one of the gods who had come down to settle the mortal's problem. This device was popular at the time of Sophocles and Aeschylus but is also used in today's films. When Indiana Jones and his sweetheart Marian are tied to a post, as Belloq and the Nazis open the Ark, the ghost-demons released from the Ark destroy the villains. By default, Indiana wins. It was the deus ex machina device that turned the story around; an old device, but with an appropriate application. A pivotal character turns the story around.

Character Dialogue

Dialogue is written to be spoken by an actor. This seems obvious. But in practice we have both written and spoken languages, and they are different. That is evident in most novels. There are traditions for written dialogue that would never survive in a screenplay. It is literate, designed to be read, not heard or interpreted by an actor.

In a screenplay, the dialogue is written for the character and with the understanding that an actor will say those words. In this way, it is similar to plays. Indeed some playwrights write dialogue as if their screenplay were the same as a play script.

Dialogue indicates the education, environment, and status position of the character. Obviously, a college professor does not talk the same way as a construction worker. Syntax, vocabulary, and slang expressions are quite different from each other. To illustrate, let's say a bright, sunny day has changed to a sudden rain shower. If they are caught on the street without any rain gear, their dialogue might go something like this:

```
                    PROFESSOR
                    (To himself)
          Damn, you certainly can't trust
          the weather report, can you?


                CONSTRUCTION WORKER
          Shit! The TV weather man
          screwed up again!
```

Good dialogue expresses the feelings, thoughts, and relationship to other characters, and it gives us insight into the character. Equally important, it must give us the back story (exposition) and still advance the story. A tall order!

There are two theories about dialogue in films. One says that dialogue informs, talks about actions, explains the actions, verbalizes insight, and in fact serves the film much as it does a play. The pitfall is that the picture can get too "talky." Generally, episodic network television and especially situation comedies rely heavily on this concept. Most of Neil Simon's films, like his *Heartbreak Kid, Goodbye Girl, California Suite,* and *Barefoot in the Park* illustrate superior use of dialogue. The Academy Award – winner *All about*

Eve bristles with "smart" dialogue and insights into characters, all the while being delightfully entertaining.

The other theory is that dialogue should be minimal and should take second place to the picture. It is better to show something than "talk" about it. The philosophy is that an audience goes to see a movie, not to hear a lot of talking. This concept is supported by filmmakers who follow the silent movie tradition. They believe a picture is worth a thousand words.

For instance, Hitchcock's films emphasize the visual, placing dialogue in second place and at times using dialogue to support the visual (see "Collision Cinema Language" in Chapter 12). In contrast, Robert Altman neutralizes the picture by selecting the master scene cinema language so that the audience "listens" to the dialogue.

Linkage

Generally, when a writer has a character enter, it is because there is new information pertinent to the film being given to the audience. This was covered in Chapter 3. You may recall that using entrances and exits of characters as play division is called French scene, in honor of the French playwright Molière.

Chapter **5**

STRUCTURE OF A SCREENPLAY

Plotting the development of "empathy" characters within a cohesive story, following a central theme, and telling the story in an organized form is what we mean by structure. When a story has a point of attack, a series of incidents leading to a rising action, crisis after crisis, followed by complications and reversals, and is resolved in a final confrontation of the two opposing forces, then the screenplay has structure. For instance, *Raiders of the Lost Ark* is an action-adventure picture. Though a weighted deductive story, its events are full of action and suspense, with rising action, crisis after crisis, unexpected complications, surprising reversals, and a final resolution; in other words, the film has good structure.

The prologue places Indiana in the jungle about to get the golden head. He outwits the traps and, taking the golden head, barely escapes with his life. Belloq appears with his headhunters and demands the golden head. Indy, desperate, gives him the head, makes the final bid, and escapes with his life.

The prologue has set up the "raiders" story. The "Ark" story begins with the appearance of the government men at the university. They tell Indy about the Ark and start him on his quest. Act I concludes with Marian declaring herself a partner in exchange for the medallion that Indy needs to find the Ark.

Act II begins with Indy fighting off the hordes of villains who are trying to kill him and Marian. Marian appears to be killed. But Indy pushes on. He discovers the Ark, and then to his delight, that Marian is not dead. The second act concludes when Indy recaptures the Ark and successfully escapes with Marian. With the help of his good friend Omar they leave aboard a freighter.

The third act begins with Indy and Marian in their stateroom. In the morning, a Nazi submarine seizes their vessel. Belloq captures the Ark and makes Marian his prisoner again but is unable to find Indy. Indy follows Marian and the Ark. He is captured. Belloq and his Nazis open the Ark and are vanquished. The epilogue concludes the film with the star of the film, the Ark, being warehoused into oblivion.

Hitchcock, with a writer, spent months structuring his screenplays. As good a filmmaker he was (and he was one of the best) he knew that structure was the foundation of a good film.

• • • • • • • • • • • • • • • • • • • •

POINT OF ATTACK

Choosing the point of attack means selecting the beginning of the story. History, actions, and decisions made prior to that point then become the "back story," referred to, in playwright's parlance, as the exposition. The point of attack is determined by the point of view of the story. This is ascertained by asking the following questions: Whose story is it? From what point is it best to begin to tell the story? Why?

In *Raiders* the prologue showed Indiana in action, though he lost to Belloq. It foreshadows the Ark story. That was the point of attack. In *Ordinary People* screenwriter Alvin Sargent begins with the daily acctivities of the family. The film begins with scenes of peace and beauty, shots of a peaceful lake, a pier, trees wearing fall colors; this is followed by the singing choral group, where we discover Conrad. Sargent could have begun the picture with the boat accident, the death of the brother, or Conrad's attempted suicide. But, with director Robert Redford, Sargent decided against the obvious. They understood how to make Conrad's viewpoint work.

Empathy Viewpoint

Generally, most stories set up the hero's viewpoint on the first page. *Ordinary People*'s structure was no exception. (Incidentally, the power of that empathic story created a new star, Timothy Hutton.) The point of attack was obligatory. The audience had to experience Conrad at home. The interactions between him and his mother, then his father, and finally his school friends were essential in positioning him in the story. The choice of structuring successfully gained empathy for Conrad and reinforced the central theme.

The Central Theme

Conrad had to discover that he had done his best and was not to blame for his brother' death. He learned to approve of himself, and he faced the terrible recognition that his guilt feelings were fostered by an angry, hateful mother.

Conflict

Conflict is created by selecting events that have inherent conflict which serve the story and dramatize the forces hitting against each other. The rule is, the more conflict there is, the better it engages the audience. In *Ordinary People* Conrad's struggling to maintain his grades, dating his choral girlfriend, and fighting with his inner fears adds up to high drama.

Creating "ambient" conflicts, such as catching a bus and hurrying to finish breakfast to make the bus—the usual conflicts we experience in everyday life—reflect "real life" while keeping the story vital and interesting to the audience. In Herbert Ross's film, *Steel Magnolias,* the wedding included the father's shooting off his pistol to scare off migrating birds nesting in the trees, delivery of broken champagne glasses, repairs on the front of the house, young brothers planning to "condom" the departing automobile, the pink nail polish demand of the bride—all ambient tensions that added to the drama of the wedding. Though many of these events were unrelated to the basic conflict of the film, they added to the tension of the film. In real life, we struggle to reach our goals by overcoming everyday obstacles. The audience accepted these incidents, which added texture and humor, and kept viewers actively involved.

• • • • • • • • • • • • • • • • • •

THE OBLIGATORY SCENE

The obligatory scene is mandated by the central theme. When the obligatory scene is omitted, a structural flaw is created that impairs audience acceptance of the film. Unfortunately, this error is made by both beginning and experienced writers, and by directors as well. Most obligatory scenes are found in the third act. Sometimes these obligatory scenes are referred to as the "payoff" scenes.

In *Rocky,* a deductive story, the fight between the champion and Rocky had to be seen by the audience. It could not have occurred offscreeen. Another obvious example is the showdown fight in *Star Wars,* another deductive story. Skywalker had to make the final run to drop that bomb to destroy the death star.

Inductive stories also include obligatory scenes. In *Ordinary People* the confrontation between Conrad and his mother was required. Mother and daughter facing death together was obligatory in *Terms of Endearment.* In *Steel Magnolias* the graveyard death scene was obligatory so that the audience could witness the bonding of the characters. This sharing of their grief was essential.

An example of a film that failed by omitting the obligatory scene was Bud Yorkin's film *Second Chance*, with Gene Hackman and Ellen Burstyn. The obligatory confrontation scene between the husband and wife was left out. The plot has a man fall in love with another woman after thirty years or so of marriage. Though his daughter verbally attacks him, he knows his relationship with his wife (Ellen Burstyn) is terminal. The event of their daughter's wedding could have offered the excuse for a final confrontation between Hackman and Burstyn, but it never happened. The concluding shot has Hackman walking away from the church to meet his girlfriend. End of story, leaving the audience cold.

• • • • • • • • • • • • • • • • • • •

RISING ACTION

By *rising action*, we mean the twisting and turning of events, rising in intensity to the climax (see Figure 4.1) *The Wizard of Oz*, a "rising action" story, is classic in its structure. Each event gives rise to the next. The tension is increased by adding doses of "threat." To be effective, rising action must include the following features.

Threat

There must always be a threat to the hero in order to keep the audience actively involved.

Complications

The story must take unexpected twists. For instance, in *The Wizard of Oz*, when Dorothy sneaks out in the middle of the night and meets a medicine "snake oil" salesman, he recognizes her dilemma and encourages her to return home. The surprise is that the snake oil man is kindly.

Crisis

Crisis must occur at frequent intervals. When Dorothy returns home, she runs into a tornado, which catches her and her dog and almost kills them by whirling them out of the world.

Reversal

A surprising event sends the story off in an unexpected direction. An event is to be made credible by foreshadowing. This is called a "plant." In *The Wizard of Oz*, the tornado is planted. The story takes place in Kansas where tornadoes are common. Dorothy's being thrust into the land of Oz is an example of a story reversal.

Climax

The rising action, through a series of events, compounded by crisis and reversals, increases the tension and must lead to the final confrontation, the climax (see Figure 4.1). The climax of *The Wizard of Oz* is the confrontation between the Wicked Witch and the little girl.

Resolution

The resolution is the settling up between the hero and the villain. When the conflict is resolved, then the film is over. Dorothy victoriously returns to Oz for her reward. The Wizard (another reversal) is revealed as a phoney. But in another reversal, it is discovered that he has wisdom. He solves everyone's problems, including helping Dorothy to get back home. The epilogue concludes with the central theme of the film, "There is no place like home."

• • • • • • • • • • • • • • • • • • • •

THREE-ACT STRUCTURE

Most dramatic films follow a three-act structure. This formula has evolved from ancient Greek theater, the ancestor of all modern drama. The three-act structure is the basic form. Even if there are four or five acts, the drama still follows the three-act form (see Figure 4.1).

Act I

Act I sets up the story, the past events (exposition), the hero, the heroine, the villains, and the conflict. Since our attention span has been shortened by television, a strong event capturing the viewers' attention must occur in the first five pages. Act I totals about one-third of the screenplay, or roughly 30 – 40 pages.

Act I is easier and the most fun to write. Most writers know the beginning of their story and the ending. It is the middle, the second act, where they may get into trouble.

Act II

This act is trickier because it must build through crisis after crisis, event after event, with lots of surprises and twists, yet it must follow an inner logic and adhere to the central theme. The events must frustrate the hero. This is the longest of the three acts and should constitute about 40% of the page count. The difficulty is in structuring the events, maintaining integrity, keeping the events logical, and continuing to engage the audience's empathy, especially for the hero.

At the conclusion of Act II, a switch in the story is required which sends the story off in a surprising and unexpected course of action but which, with hindsight, is quite logical. It is imperative that the audience believe in the event. With a "plant" correctly structured into the story, the audience will accept the change. A major setback for our hero should conclude the act with a cliffhanger. This assures the audience's continued emotional involvement and will heighten suspense. Again, study the experiential graph in Figure 4.1.

Act III

This is the shortest but most exciting act. It is the payoff of the film. The length should not exceed 25% of the page count. If the third act is too long, then it relieves the tension and softens the climax. The third act always contains the climax and the resolution, though on occasion the resolution may be attenuated in the form of an epilogue.

If the film ends with a victorious hero, then it is a comedy. If the hero loses, then it is a tragedy. The tradition of happy endings makes American films popular throughout the world.

• • • • • • • • • • • • • • • • • • •

MISE-EN-SCÈNE

The selection of an event that best dramatizes the story is what we mean by a mise-en-scène. This is meant for every scene and/or event selected by the writer. Well-selected mise-en-scènes make the difference between a pedestrian screenplay and an exciting one. This is the most challenging aspect of writing and directing as well.

Case Study: *To Catch a Thief*

A retired, well-known jewel thief has paid his debt to society and presently earns his living growing flowers. He lives a quiet life, enjoying the pleasure of some wine, an occasional woman, and the peace of his own place. The hero is a man of charm and wit, living the good life. This graceful ambience is built into the screenplay.

Suddenly, a rash of burglaries, duplicating his style, occurs. The police are sure he has come out of retirement and seek him out. The hero decides that flight is better than protesting his innocence. He meets with an old friend whose aid he enlists in proving his innocence. That is the premise of the story.

We need to invent mise-en-scènes that dramatize the crime, but the hero's manner is charming so the burglary must be committed with charm, wit, and style. To further this concept of charm and suggested sensuality, the hero sneaks into the boudoirs of women and steals their jewelry as they sleep, thus earning the nickname "The Cat." A black cat is an excellent image because of its mysterious ambience.

The mise-en-scène begins at night. The camera glides across the rooftop like a cat, moving down and into the boudoir of a sleeping woman. A black-gloved hand reaches into the jewel box and plucks out twinkling gems. Then, with the suddenness of a blazing morning, accompanied by cries of hurt disbelief, the awakened lady stares at her empty jewel box. Her scream is heard way down the street.

We then dissolve to another rooftop at night, as a black cat is seen gently padding across it. Instantly, it is morning and a middle-aged woman is screaming her indignation as she holds an empty jewel box.

Once again it is night, and the black cat moves across the rooftop. We cut to the police station during the day as the three pairs of staunch, square-looking men pile into waiting cars. They depart, raising clouds of dust, reminding the viewer of the famous Keystone Cops of silent film days.

With some variation, these series of mise-en-scènes succinctly made the statement of the picture while artfully engaging the audience. Many will recognize the opening of Hitchcock's *To Catch a Thief*. Note that the points of attack in the scenes were precise and told the story visually and clearly; they captured the essence of the scene and the action in a short span of time. In short, this is what creates an excellent mise-en-scène. This example is cited in Chapter 12, in the "Symbolic Cinema Language" section.

To sum up, a screenplay must have conflict, structure, and characters who engage the audience while giving us insight into the human condition. This is the kind of screenplay that should make a superior motion picture.

Chapter 6

SCREENPLAY FORMATS

When the motion picture business began, there were no screenwriters. The production team gathered to make a film, and the director and/or the producer usually had a story idea but rarely a script. Sometimes the actors joined in the process.

Plots were simple. Nonstop action enchanted the audience. Cast and crew made up the story and shot the film as they went along, with silent film stars like Charlie Chaplin, Fatty Arbuckle, Buster Keaton, and the famous Keystone Cops. The bottom line was that there was no screenplay format.

As silent films became popular and the need for product grew, a method of keeping track of the story was needed. This form was dignified by the name *scenario*. It was in fact no more than a series of notes. There was just one page at first, and then it began to grow. This scenario became the granddaddy of the format we will look at next.

TREATMENT

The treatment tells the story briefly. Ideally, it is no longer than a few paragraphs, a page if really necessary. Today, the purpose of a treatment is to sell the story. If it is successful, then the next phase is to write a screenplay

47

or a longer treatment. The challenge of writing a treatment is to give the reader the belief that he or she was viewing the film.

Rules

A treatment is written in prose, paragraphed to look like a short story, but it is not. (Some writers fall into that trap.) An acceptable treatment makes the events of the story visual. In a novel, the writer might describe a place in the following manner:

> John felt the hairs on the back of his neck rise as he studied that lonely house. He remembered how the house was filled with hate and despair. He knew he could not change that as much as he desperately wanted to.
>
> He longed for peace. Somehow without solving that feeling about the house he could never know true peace.
>
> He bit down on the pipe in his mouth, took a long drag, and with the crowbar firmly in his hand walked to the doorway.

If this had been written as a treatment, it would fail because it did not indicate the pictures the audience would see. In addition, there is no way a designer can make a house "filled with hate and bitter despair." Specific time and date is necessary. This subjective kind of writing works in a novel. As with the mise-en-scène, the skill of writing a visual presentation applies equally to the treatment; perhaps even more so.

To convert this prose into a film, another point of attack has to be taken. One way to solve the static quality of the story is to create an event to dramatize the inner life of the main character.

> John stares at the Victorian house with its high spires and dull, gray paint. His eyes fill with pained remembrance.
>
> Suddenly a voice calls out, "John Wittaker, is that you?"
>
> John turns to face a middle-aged woman with a rather large hat and a warm smile.
>
> John greets her shyly, "Mrs. Milhouse."
>
> She nods. "It's been a long time, Johnny." She embraces him.
>
> John looks into her kindly eyes. "This place always gave me such pain, it always made me feel . . . unloved."
>
> "With good cause, Johnny." Mrs. Milhouse continues, "It was amazing to me that you survived."
>
> John smiles, drily adding, "I left as soon as I knew there was a door that led out."

The "event," someone from John's past, is an expository character who becomes the platform for his character to express his feelings. The scene was written from John's point of view. Information was communicated through dialogue. This approach is acceptable.

Joseph L. Mankiewicz, writer and director, believes in the power of dialogue, as he demonstrated in his Academy Award–winning film *All about Eve*. Hitchcock represents the opposite viewpoint. He regarded dialogue as a way of reinforcing plot points or of adding humor.

Another way of solving this plot point is to invent another kind of scene, which in a way may be more suitable to film since it does not rely on dialogue.

> John stares at the Victorian house with its high spires and dull, gray paint. His eyes fill with pained remembrance. He jams the crowbar between the door and the chain and yanks it with all his strength.
>
> The chain snaps. He swings the door open to reveal the interior.
>
> The room is as if it were a century ago, even to the faded pictures on the mantle, musty and cobwebby, filled with dead air.
>
> A picture of a grim-faced man with a child on his lap is held by John. John's face is filled with fierce recollection. We hear the voices from his past screaming their condemnation.
>
> John violently throws the picture across the room. It lands in a corner. The glass webs across the face. Tears stream down John's face.

This incident tells the story pictorially. Note the sentence structure. The sentences are slipped and moved around to be dramatic, placing the pictures in a specific sequence so the reader will see the pictures on the movie screen inside his or her head. For instance, the following line suggests a close-up of the still picture.

> A picture of a grim-faced man with a child on his lap is held by John.

Another rule is that treatment prose should be terse. Without flowery prose, writing that gets to the point is appreciated. Careful and precise selection is desired. Hemingway's writing style is an excellent model for treatment and screenplay writing as well. Writing a treatment in an informal style, using phrases such as "then we would see," is acceptable and in some cases preferred in the next variation of the treatment form. These direct statements serve to inform the reader, inviting participation in the growth process of making the film. This frequently means putting aside the literary aspirations some writers may have.

A third rule is that the central theme must be apparent and clearly spelled out. Do not beat around the bush, but state it clearly and plainly. People in development appreciate candor.

Treatment Outline

The outline is an abbreviated form of a treatment. The rule here is that less is best. A paragraph or two is all that is asked for. After a story has been pitched to a producer, the treatment outline may work as a reminder. But it must be written clearly and must stand on its own. The producer may elect to give it to a third party.

• • • • • • • • • • • • • • • • • •

TYPES OF SCREENPLAY FORMAT

The screenplay format was created as a result of sound movies. In the late 20s and early 30s playwrights were brought out to Hollywood to write for these newfangled "talkies." Some of these writers did not honor or understand the tradition of silent films, and to them writing dialogue for the movies, as opposed to writing dialogue for the stage, was a mystery. In truth nobody knew how to write dialogue for films. Many movie producers were as lost as the writers. The producer only had to think of the "billboards" as the written dialogue words. (Billboards were the words that were flashed on the screen representing the dialogue of the characters. This approach was more expository.)

These writers were used to writing plays, and indeed they ushered in a phase of film style that charmed its way into the world of cinema. These wonderful human comedies with snappy humanistic dialogue reached their zenith in the late 30s. The crazy, zany chases of the silent films were banished. Lubitsch and Preston Sturges's romantic comedy films became the kings of Hollywood. Their equal in high comedy has not been seen since.

The writers settled down and claimed responsibility for the story and dialogue. They stated, much to the relief of directors, that the "pictures" were the director's domain. The screenwriters felt comfortable since they looked upon the directors as they did the directors of their plays; and the film directors accepted this. But they also knew they wrote in another language, the picture language. Good producers who understood this process understood it as well as the directors. Finally, as the talkies were accepted, everyone knew where he or she belonged and who did what to whom.

Master Scene Screenplay

It was natural for these ex-playwrights to write in this new form, and as a result the master scene screenplay was born. Everyone who has read a play can see the similarity between master scene screenplay format and play scripts. In Hollywood, it has become the accepted format for feature films.

The master scene screenplay format is used for feature films, and for the MOW (movie of the week) as well. *Raiders of the Lost Ark* was transcribed from the film. It too fits into master scene format.

In contrast, look at the format of the scene from *Raiders* titled the "Whip and Gun" sequence in Chapter 11, "Fragmented Cinema Language." Notice the difference in the format. This was written to list the various shots, which is closer to what the audience viewed. It certainly is closer to what was seen than is the master scene screenplay.

Some screenwriters use paragraphing with capitalization of key words to imply certain pictures as an aid to the reader in visualizing the picture. But some writers fear the director's anger to react territorially and resent visualizing.

Most directors, however, welcome the input and encourage the writer's participation. In the past, Hollywood traditions worked against this alliance. With the new WGA (Writers Guild of America) contract, the writer is now encouraged to be on the set and to share in the process of production. It is to be hoped that this will diminish the antagonism between the director and writer and that they will work together as a team.

The Basics of the Screenplay

The screenplay is written in plain, simple language, as is the treatment. The instructions are direct. The descriptions of the set are without detail since the set will be designed by the art designer. But any essential information should be clearly noted in the script. Critical information for the set designer is part of the script, such as style and age. Basically, the screenplay is a guide for the art director, the director, the producer, and the production manager.

A page from the screenplay *Kiss of Venus,* written by the author and Cindy Dickinson, follows as an example of this type of format. An analysis follows the page. In reading the script, note the simple language, the shot description, and especially the paragraphing. The arrangement of paragraphs is a tool that subtly suggests the cutting of the picture.

<u>Kiss of Venus</u>

<u>MASTER SCENE SCREENPLAY</u>

*(Scene #122, cont'd)

1   TONY
          You surely were. Like hell.

                     MARIE
          Jason, would one vial help us?

                     JASON
          This is one dose.

2   John pulls a sheet of paper out of the box.

                     JOHN
          The formula. Can you make
          more?

                     JASON
          In about a week—in a lab.

                     TONY
          Isn't there any way to do it
          faster?

> JOHN
> Yeah. You're supposed to be some
> kind of fucking genius. Do some-
> thing.

> TONY
> Damn it, Jason. You should've
> protected the box better.

* 3   EXT: CRASHED HELICOPTER   123
        SITE—DAY

Another helicopter comes out of the sun, like an ominous black bird of prey. It swoops down, bowing the bushes and scattering the debris as it finally squats down.

PARKER and the LIEUTENANT followed by Dr. DiGANG step out and walk to:

4   THE PILOT

who is sitting alongside the crashed helicopter. He is being treated by some medics. Parker goes over and gives him a supportive nod and then turns to the Lieutenant.

The LIEUTENANT comes rushing over, his face flushed with excitement.

Here is an explanation of the numbers and terms used in this example of a master scene screenplay:

- * Note this number at the top of the page indicating that this scene was continued from the previous page. The scene number is not written by the writer but by the assistant director and/or production manager at the time of production. It is foolish for the writer to write in scene numbers.
- 1 Character names are centered and put in caps, while the dialogue is written below skipping only one space.
- 2 Descriptive action or an event is paragraphed, implying the need for a cut. This paragraphing alerts the reader.
- 3 Master scene is indicated by the titled line, and, as in the play script format, each scene setting is described in detail. The new scene always starts with the line EXT:, which means exterior, or INT:, which

means interior. Then this is followed by a specific description of the set like this:

EXT: CRASHED HELICOPTER SITE—DAY

- CRASHED HELICOPTER SITE is the specific set description. This site had been seen earlier in the film, therefore, there was no need to describe it in detail. This line precedes the scene each time it is intro-duced into the script. The structure of cutting back and forth between two different locations implies that they are happening simulta-neously. These are referred to as parallel scenes. When this scene appeared in the script for the first time it read as follows:

EXT: CRASHED HELICOPTER SITE—DAY

The remains of the Helicopter were smoldering. Smoke spiraled into the air, clearly marking the site.

The LIEUTENANT was lying down against a large rock. He was alive.

- "DAY" is an important designation since single-camera style films are shot in bits and pieces out of sequence, and therefore it is important to repeat the time of day of the scene. This indicates whether the action is ongoing or whether time has elapsed. This is extremely helpful during the shooting. When the location is changed, it gen-erates another descriptive line in the same format and a *new scene number*.

- 4 The obligatory camera shot is the one that must be there to make a story's point. The paragraphing and titling suggest to the director that the shot of the PILOT is an obligation. It is written without any camera description, such as "The PILOT is seen in a close-up." This is a shot suggestion by the writer to the director, who appreciates the writer's help. Also note that when this shot description is included and is included with EXT: CRASHED HELICOPTER SITE, this means that this is a close shot within that set and is not a change of location place or time.

Next, we will examine a *Doctor Zhivago* sample page from the original shooting script written by Robert Bolt and David Lean. The difference between the American shooting script and the European has to do with shots written in detail and listed with progressive scene numbers.

When the *Doctor Zhivago* shooting script was compared to the film, it matched consistently. When changes occurred they were dramatically dif-ferent. My guess is that David Lean did not settle for a substitute, but rather invented other scenes or situations that would serve the film equally well.

Doctor Zhivago

Shooting Script Page by Robert Bolt

1522   CLOSE SHOT   KOMAROVSKY stares up at him;
loses his temper:

> KOMAROVSKY
> Stay here then and get your
> desserts! Your desserts, do you
> hear me?

The light goes off him. The sitting room door slams.

> You think you are—immacu-
> late! . . .

He has made a violent gesture, which sets him off
balance, and he goes flying, clattering down the
stairs.

EXTERIOR LARA'S HOUSE   STUDIO   NIGHT
SNOWING

1523   MEDIUM SHOT   At the foot of the stairs a few
rats scuttle across the porchway.   KOMAROVSKY
lurches into picture and collapses on the floor,
momentarily stunned. A rat darts over his hand
and runs out into the falling snow. He heaves himself up.

INTERIOR LARA'S APARTMENT   STUDIO
NIGHT

1524   MEDIUM SHOT   YURI stands motionless inside
the sitting room, turned away from LARA, who is
still seated at the table where the bottle stands.
Hesitantly she lifts a shameful face and looks at
him. KOMAROVSKY's voice comes up the stairs:

> KOMAROVSKY (SOUND)
> You are not immaculate!

They turn to the door, listening.

> I know you! . . . Do you hear me?
> . . . I know you!

EXTERIOR LARA'S HOUSE   STUDIO   NIGHT
SNOWING

1525   CLOSE SHOT   KOMAROVSKY has mounted the
first two stairs; his face is flushed and hateful, but
oddly, also tear-stained. He bawls passionately:

                    KOMAROVSKY
            We're all made of the same clay
            you know! . . . CLAY!!

INTERIOR LARA'S APARTMENT   STUDIO
NIGHT

1526   MEDIUM CLOSE SHOT   LARA, in foreground at
the table, looking at YURI, his back to her at the
door. He lowers his head. She turns to the table as
if having had sentence justly pronounced against
her.

Television Screenplays

Most episodic, hour-long television programs are shot in a single-camera style similar to that of feature films. The script format is the same as that of master scene except for these differences. Episodic scripts have less detail because each episode has the same characters, locations, and sets. The staff is familiar with the format of the show.

Incidentally, directors in this episodic world lack weekly continuity. A week of preparation, several exhausting days to shoot the picture, and a couple of weeks to cut the show makes it impossible for any one person to direct an episode every week.

Videotape script formats have a history dramatically different from that of feature or episodic films. The videotape script formats are based on the radio format of the 1930s and 40s. In the early days of "live" television most of the people came from radio, and they adapted the radio format for television. Television programs were done "live" like radio drama, as opposed to the stop-and-go of a motion picture. It seemed natural to use this type of script format for videotaping programs. This format is commonly referred to as "tape" script.

As most people know, daytime drama programs ("soaps") appear on television during late morning and early afternoon every day of the work week. The stories are ongoing, continuing from day to day, week to week, month to month, year after year. It is remarkable the loyalty they command. It is also a wonderful training ground, providing regular employment for actors, directors, writers, producers, and the many technical people. It is also another type of programming, and there are some very successful producers, writers, directors, and actors who have earned a consistent living in this medium. Many of the star writers, directors, and actors have worked in soaps.

Some creative people in daytime drama abhor the term *soap*. They think it suggests a lack of respect of the work they do. Indeed, turning out a one-hour quality dramatic program in a day is remarkable. The quality of the acting, the directing, and the writing, plus the technical support, is a tribute to these people. They truly perform a daily miracle. This type of program is the closest thing to dramatic "live" television and to the feeling of theater.

Daytime drama uses the "tape live" format. Daytime dramas (as well as situation comedies) have cameras shooting while the actors perform the scene as if they were onstage. Of course, they play it differently for the camera.

The "cutting" is done while the actors are performing. This selection process is done by the director in the control room, which is adjacent to the shooting stage. With the script in front of him, the director is seated at a long table facing a row of monitors (television sets) that show the pictures from each camera and the "line" monitor. Also with script in front of her, seated alongside the director, is the associate director. Her function in the control room is to ready the camera and time the show.

The technical director is seated on the other side of the director, also with a script in front of him. The TD, or "switcher," is seated in front of an electronic device called the "switcher." It has several rows of buttons and toggle levers, sometimes as many as three but at least one. The purpose of the switcher is to switch from camera to camera, placing a different picture instantly into the "line" monitor.

When the technical director, at the director's command, presses a button, the picture is switched to the "on line" monitor. The pictures on the line monitor are recorded on videotape. This becomes the "cut" picture. Cuts, in videotaping control room parlance, are talled "takes," and are represented in handwritten script with a *T*.

The television videotape script page is divided in half. The left side contains all the information about the set, dialogue, and essential action written by the writer. (The dotted line running down the center of the page and the underlined titles of "Writer's side" and "Director's side" put into the script by the author are not found in the normal video script.)

The right side of the page is left blank. The director writes in the camera shots. These camera commands, which indicate the switching of cameras and sound sources, are given over the intercom as the actors perform the scene.

The sitcom uses "tape" technique and usually uses four cameras, as opposed to three for soaps. Sitcoms often change the shot every eight to nine seconds. This amounts to more than 200 shots in about 24 minutes of running time. This frequency of switching cameras requires hard-edged discipline in a language that must be precise. Those camera switches happen at the snapping of the director's fingers.

Included here is a sample of a sitcom, a "What's Happenin'" episode titled "The Play's the Thing," written by Saul Turtletaub and Bernie Orenstein, directed by the author, and originally aired on ABC (See Figure 6.1).

First, note the miniature floorplan—that is, the diagram of the camera placement and the actors on the living room set in the upper-right-hand corner of the page. Generally the director needs to have a sketch of the new set. This helps staging and camera placement logistics and avoids unreasonable camera moves. This earns the respect of the crew.

- F.I. stands for "fade in" (see "Transition Cinema Language" in Chapter 12 if you are uncertain what this means).
- T# alerts the director that the next number is the one assigned to the camera to avoid the confusion with the other numbers.
- The circled number 1, above the camera #2 is the number of the shot. That is the number given to the shot list handed to the camera person running camera #2. On that list, drawn up by the associate director (AD), is the other number 3. According to this page, the camera #2 shot list has only two shots, shots 1 and 3. Camera #4 has shots 2, 4, and 6. Camera #3 has one shot, 5. Camera #1 only has one shot, numbered 7.
- (MCU of Rog.), written below "F.I. #2," is the description of the shot. MCU of Rog. stands for "medium close-up," meaning a shoulder shot, of Roger. The picture shows Roger with the cut-off being at his shoulders. Note that everything in parentheses below the camera shot number is descriptive of the expected shot. "MS Mama" means a medium shot, usually a waist shot, of Mama. "CU" means close-up, a head shot, then followed by the subject, as in shot 3 for camera #3, which is the close-up of Roger.
- (OS Raj to Mama) means that camera #4, shot number 6, is an over-the-shoulder of Raj to Mama. Mama's size in the shot is determined in camera-blocking rehearsal.

Figure 6.1 *Videotape Format, "What's Happenin'."*

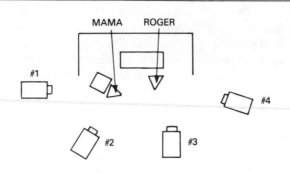

"What's Happenin'

VIDEOTAPE FORMAT

ACT ONE

WRITER'S SIDE   DIRECTOR'S SIDE

[This is written in
pencil so it can be
erased. There is a
shorthand system of
marking a script; some
directors might find it
helpful to know]

FI   #2
(MOV of Rog)

FADE IN:

INT: THOMAS LIVING ROOM

(MAMA SITTING ON COUCH,

APPARENTLY BEING ATTACKED   (Below Sofa)

VERBALLY BY ROGER. MAMA IS

HOLDING AN UNIDENTIFIABLE

PIECE OF PAPER.)

WRITER'S SIDE   DIRECTOR'S SIDE

RAJ

I mean it Mama—I've had it. I'm   T #4   ②

not a kid anymore, I don't need   (MS MAMA)
                                             T #2   ③
you to tell me what I can do or   (CU ROG)
                                             T #4 ④ ⓪
what I can't do. You messed up   (CU MAMA)

your life, but you're not going to

mess up mine.

                MAMA
                                               T #3   ⑤
My goodness. ─────────────────
                                            (2 MS)

        RAJ

How do you like the scene, Mama?
                                             T #4   ⑥
Wasn't that great? ─────────────
                                           (OS RAJ TO MAMA)

                MAMA
                                             T #1   ⑦
It's good, son. It's darn good writ- (2 L.S. POV DOOR)

ing. Now, go on, finish it.

─────────────────────────────────────

- (2LS POV Door) means that camera #1, shot 7, was a full-figure shot of
  Raj and Mama from the point of view of the door. Note the position of
  camera #1 in the diagram.

The urgency of giving commands while shooting the scene is the cause of this system. The lines drawn below each take are for emphasis and mark the precise point in the dialogue for the cut to happen. Some directors do not bother with the lines. Teamwork is the key to success.

Know that this is the system used when directing in the tape format. It is not the standard in the videotape format only because there is none. Every director and production company develop a special system of notation. To avoid confusion, be aware that all the other variations are just that, variations. But what we have presented here is an overview pattern that is understood by most who work in the videotape format. Once this format is understood, adapting to the other variations should be no problem.

The Shooting Script

The shooting script basically is the master scene screenplay but with many other contributions from the production departments. First, when it is declared a shooting script, this means it has gone through a series of revisions, and the director, the producer, the studio heads, the production manager, the art director, and the assistant director have all read the script and have added their expert knowledge. The script how has become a technical document. This includes all kinds of notes and is the script that the director and everyone else uses to shoot the film. This does not mean it is not changed during the shooting process; it simply means that it is the best representation and guide of what the picture looks like. At this stage there is the most growth.

Scene numbers are added, and the production heads get a copy to read prior to production meetings. The writer has little to do with this script unless there are rewrites of the content or the writer is the producer or associate producer. It is not uncommon for more than a few writers to work on a film. This works to the advantage and to the disadvantage of the property, giving it both continuity and a breath of fresh air.

The Director's Cinematic Script

The director's cinematic script translates the screenplay into the final vision of the film, the director's vision. This blueprint of what the film will look like includes sets, costumes, locations, special props, storyboarding, photographic equipment—in short, everything that is needed for shooting the film. It indicates where and in what scenes these things will be required. The director's shooting script is complete, and the production manager is able to be precise in her budget projections; now that would make the studio heads feel quite secure and happy.

Unfortunately, this script format is rare. With the advent of storyboarding and sophisticated computer graphics programs, it will not be long before scripts are written in pictures with dialogue noted below. Presently this format is used when doing an animated film or when there are special effects that require detailed coordination. What we are referring to is the practice of writing a script into pictures. We are almost there as of this writing.

Soon, a computer program will automatically translate the script into the various cinema languages. The director will have the opportunity to see her movie before she shoots it, and so will the producer. H'mmm. . . .

PART **3**

THE VISUAL LANGUAGE— UNDERSTANDING THE CINEMA LANGUAGE

Chapter **7**

THE SHOT

Understanding the composition and picturization rules of the shot is the purpose of this chapter. The shot is the smallest basic unit of the cinematic language.

A feature film is made up of thousands of pictures organized into shots. By *shot* (referred to as a "scene" in motion picture parlance) we mean photographing the event until the camera is stopped. The shot may last as long as there is film in the magazine of the camera, or it may be as short as a blink of an eye. Alfred Hitchcock's *Rope* had each shot run ten minutes. The maximum load of a 35-millimeter 1000-foot magazine was ten minutes at that time.

• • • • • • • • • • • • • • • •

COMPOSITION

A composed shot is made up of a rational arrangement of elements, including emphasis, stability, sequence, and balance. The goal is to achieve a picture of satisfying clarity and beauty. The shot also has structure, form, and design, and expresses feeling and mood through the use of color, line, mass, and form. Composition does *not* express *meaning* or tell a story. It is the technique, not the conception. Picturization tells the story.

Rules

To use composition correctly we need to know the rules of emphasis, stability, sequence, balance, structure, design, color, line, form, and mass so that we can apply them to support our picturization.

Line   The "line" of a picture is determined by outlining the subjects and/or objects in the picture that would give its line content. For instance a picture of a sunset usually has a horizon, which communicates peace and harmony. The principal line is a horizontal. All things being equal, different lines express different emotional qualities:

Horizontal lines create a restful, oppressive, calm, distant, languid, or reposeful feeling. The viewer feels stability, heaviness, monotony, restfulness, and peacefulness.

Perpendicular lines express height, grandeur, dignity, regal or forced impressiveness, frigidity, or spiritual, ethereal, soaring, or aspiring qualities.

Diagonal lines express a sense of movement, or an unreal, artificial, vital, arresting, bizarre, or quaint quality. This line is often found in the climax.

Curved lines express femininity, naturalness, intimacy, quiescence, freedom, gracefulness, flexibility, and coziness.

Straight lines express strength, sternness, formality, severity, simplicity, neatness, and regularity.

Broken lines express informality and disorderliness.

Zigzag lines express craziness, unpredictability, uncertainty. Depending upon how the line is rendered, it could be light or heavy in feeling.

Circular lines are comedic and exasperating.

Perpendicular lines may be straight or curved; horizontal lines may be straight or broken. Broken perpendicular lines give a feeling of defamed violence; broken horizontal lines give a casual, informal feeling.

Form   By *form* we mean anything that has a shape. The structure of form is a fundamental understanding that everything is either form or space, and like the ying and the yang neither can exist without the other. Forms may be symmetrical, asymmetrical, shallow, deep, compact, or diffused.

Symmetricalness   A symmetrical form implies formality, grace, and rigidity.

Asymmetricalness   An asymmetrical form implies flexibility, casualness, and a lack of order. Contemporary sets for example use asymmetrical design to suggest modern times.

Period pictures constantly use symmetry in their design and the composition. With *Tom Jones* Tony Richardson brought the period piece film into contemporary time. One of his principle devices was asymmetrical design. This also enhanced the feeling of the film's reality.

Depth   Depth expresses warmth, richness, mellowness, sincerity, and realism. This feature was characteristic of the films of John Huston. Study some of his shots and discover how many shots are designed with a great deal of depth.

Shallowness   Shallowness expresses quaintness, artificiality, effectual, shallowness, excitement, and alertness. This is a popular choice when doing period pieces; for instance, *Dangerous Liaisons* started with shallow pictures, but as the film progressed the seriousness and threat of reality came crashing in and the shots were designed with more depth.

Compactness   Compact form expresses warmth, force, horror, and power.

Diffuseness   Diffused form expresses indifference, coldness, turmoil, defiance, and individualism.

Mass   Mass is the weight in the picture. It is either light or heavy. The practical use is in shots where the director may wish to create the feeling of threat or abandonment. For instance, having several characters surround a single character may give the feeling that the character in the middle of the circle is being threatened, or, by changing body attitude through turning away, that the character is being abandoned.

Texture   Texture can be rough or smooth. Rough is masculine, strong, varied, and mottled. Smooth is usually feminine, surfaced, casual, and indifferent. The use of texture can be as simple as giving the hero a two-day-old beard. This textures his face and makes him appear tough, more worldly. Don Johnson used this device in the "Miami Vice" series.

Unity   All things being equal, there should be a sense of unity in the picture. That means an organization of the elements so they suggest a feeling of togetherness.

Stability   Stability is the element that ties the picture down. The picture feels anchored, and gravity is not violated. An example of a violation of stability is found in Hitchcock's film *Vertigo*. Through the use of a "trick shot" (see *Hitchcock*, by François Truffaut), the audience is made to feel a form of vertigo. Hitchcock achieved this disorientation by having the camera move into the staircase while he zoomed back. In this way the bond of empathy between the audience and the hero is strengthened as the audience shares and understands his vertigo.

Balance   A picture that seems to adhere to gravity looks balanced. The set designer is aware of this when she designs the sets. Depending on its needs, the set will have balance in symmetrical or asymmetrical terms. The placement of the set pieces (furniture) and the dressing (drapes, lamps, and such) supports the balance selected by the set designer.

Color   *Hue* refers to color. In painting it is called pigment. An example of a hue is red or blue. Hue is either primary or secondary. Primary color is pure pigment—that is, there are no other colors mixed with it. The painter's primary hues are red, blue, and yellow. In the electronic world of television the primaries are red, blue, and green. But in the film world, the labs use chemical processes that follow the secondary color system—that is, the chemicals bathe the film in such a way that the negative appears in secondary colors. Secondary colors are orange (a mixture of red and yellow), green (a mixture of blue and yellow), and purple (a mixture of red and blue).

The intensity scale has to do with the amount of pigment. If a color has a great deal of red pigment, then it is called saturated red.

The amount of white or black mixed in with the pigment is another scale referred to as "value." If a red pigment has a great deal of white in it, the resulting hue is pink; if there is more black mixed in, then it appears dark red. This scale has a strong impact on black-and-white television. Today it is used in design. In commercials the hue can be turned off so that everything is seen as black and white except the product, which is seen in rich, blazing color.

The creative use of hue can be seen in John Huston's films *Reflections in a Golden Eye, Moby Dick,* and *Moulin Rouge.* In *Reflections* Elizabeth Taylor's costume was deliberately enhanced to give the audience a special insight into her character and the actions. In *Moby Dick* Huston had the colors darkened, muted, to represent the evil Captain Ahab, and he added more white to represent the wonderful spirit of Moby Dick. In *Moulin Rouge* Huston did the reverse; he had the colors saturated, capturing the Parisian era and suggesting powerful use of color made famous by Toulouse-Lautrec.

Michelangelo Antonioni's manipulation of color in *Blow-up* and in his other films, especially *Red Sails,* is extraordinary. His use of color is consistent throughout his films.

Quality of Light   Lighting is classified as either soft or hard. By "soft light" we mean a light that has a soft edge, creating a world of warmth and softness. Hard light is hard-edged and is associated with "reality" or a documentary feeling. The choice is up to the director, but the director of photography is responsible for its execution. In practice, a creative DP is a gift and often a treasure, making a major contribution to the film.

The other area of lighting has to do with the ratio of front lights on the subject to that of the back lights. The higher the ratio, the more contrasting the picture.

Comedy requires a bright picture. The contrast of front to back light is modest, more like one-half to one. This is sometimes referred to as "flat lighting." Sitcoms usually are light in this manner. Dramatic contrast lights are seen in feature films, as in *Flashdance*. This is an excellent way for the director to communicate the quality of light, knowing that DPs think of light in this manner.

Area The area of a shot is divided in the following manner. There is the point closest to the camera (the foreground), the farthest point from the camera (the background), and the third section, in the middle (the middle ground). If the area of the frame is divided into thirds, then the center area is the one that gets the emphasis. Most sujects fall into that midthird area of the frame. In television, because of the curvature of the picture tube, plus the various adjustments on home sets, CBS set up a circle of information guide — that is, keeping the subject within the center of the frame, like the CBS eye logo.

This type of placement is not the only way to play around the area of a shot. Because of the various formats, the critical area will vary. Presently, U.S. broadcast standards dictate the format, but that may be changing because of high definition and digital video.

Generally, though, the subject is assigned to an area of the frame consistent with the cinema language and with the emphasis design, which usually means that it falls into the center of the area.

Space The more space a subject is given, the more emphasis it gains. For instance, say we compose a shot of a person sitting in a meadow, while in the other half of the frame, among some trees, sits another person. Obviously, the person in the meadow will have the emphasis.

Plane All other things being equal, the foreground is the strongest position because it is the closest to the audience. For instance, a subject closer to the camera looking past it has more emphasis than another person who is standing in the background. The plane is divided into three parts: the foreground, the strongest; the middle ground; and the background, the weakest.

Level The tallest person has emphasis — this is an excellent example of what we mean by level. In stage tradition, the hero was always the tallest person on stage. In film, the use of apple boxes and the digging of trenches to accommodate for the hero's height is not uncommon.

Repetition Repeating subjects gives emphasis. A subject repeated by another subject, or a subject placed in the foreground is made stronger by repetition.

The use of furniture can reinforce the subject. Stationing a character next to a fireplace mantle or near a sofa reinforces his position through the lines of the furniture. This is an example of the use of repetition. In a musical, if the lead character is in the chorus and we wish to give him emphasis while watching him in action, we do so by using repetition. By placing the subject in the background, but with the repetition of other chorus line figures whose faces we can't see, we give emphasis to the figure at the end of the chorus line.

Movement   Movement is emphasis. Chapter 13 deals with it in detail. Suffice to say here that almost any movement commands emphasis.

Sequence   "Sequence" refers to arranging the subjects in a particular order so they connect in a pleasing manner. By directing the eye of the viewer using sequence, we may give the subject emphasis, as was demonstrated in the chorus example just cited. A pleasant picture is also created.

Contrast   Contrast makes a picture pleasing and gives the subject focus. For instance, if several people are looking off in the same direction, except for one, that one obviously gets our attention and becomes the primary emphasis.

Emphasis   It is the director's responsibility to control the viewer's focus. Every shot should draw the viewer's eye into the picture and should focus on the person, object, or thing the director wishes. This is called the primary emphasis. A director knows what he wishes the audience to see when the shot appears on the screen.

"Line of interest" is the look exchanged between two players. For smoother cutting, this line of interest should match position from shot to shot. For instance, if the line of interest is going right to left in one shot and then switching to a reverse shot, it must match the look by going from left to right. A close shot of a character, seeing both of his eyes from a front position, has the strongest line of interest.

Secondary emphasis is created by having the viewer's eye shifted by the primary throwing focus to the secondary. A common method is to have the primary person look to the other, secondary person. This secondary device is frequently used in mystery or horror films in order to shock or surprise the audience.

An imaginative use of secondary emphasis to demonstrate the central theme was made by the director Michelangelo Antonioni. The central theme of *Blow-up* is "what you see is not necessarily what truly exists." Through secondary emphasis the director reinforced the theme. His plan was simple. As you viewed the primary object, at the last moment, often unexpectedly, the focus was suddenly thrown to the secondary object. At that moment you realized that what you thought was true was not. Sometimes it happened so fast you caught yourself thinking, Did I see what I thought I saw? And that was exactly what Antonioni wanted us to think, keeping with the central theme.

The line of interest is observed from three basic camera positions. These three camera positions are the same for film and for multiple camera shooting. The pattern remains the same. (See the diagram of *Big Country* in the "Master Scene Cinema Language" section, Chapter 10.)

The Rule of the Triangle   The three basic camera positions are built on a right triangle, with the camera being at the corner. The line of interest is parallel to the baseline of the triangle of the three camera positions. This line has to match in shots and position. Again, see the diagram of *Big Country* in Chapter 10 to examine the three camera positions.

The line of interest is altered by repositioning the camera. For instance, a low-angle shot changes the line of interest to an oblique line, which heightens the tension of the shot. This may be accomplished by cutting in a shot with the camera shooting from a low angle (nearer to the floor) so the line of interest is shifted.

Body Views   The arrangement of the characters to create a straight line in the frame is another way to gain emphasis. This is done by lining up the bodies in relation to the camera so they form a straight line. The emphasis is shifted by the eye contact of the primary person or by having the others look at whatever the director wishes the audience to look at.

The right angle is another body position and is more interesting than the straight line. The face-to-face and back-to-back, and various combinations are used to throw emphasis. In battle scenes, where the action is suddenly sent off to another area of the same action, this technique is very useful.

Multifocus   "Multifocus" means that several people in the shot have equal emphasis. Focus is thrown by one or more of the people looking at that other person (line of interest). A multifocus scene occurs in group scenes, such as dinner parties, conference rooms, mass meetings, and so on.

Cinematic Language   Arrangement of the shots is another way of gaining emphasis. This idea will be examined in detail in the following chapters on the visual cinematic languages.

Image Size   The size of the subject in the frame is another form of emphasis. Obviously the closer shot has more emphasis than the long shot, and the close-up gives more emphasis than the medium shot.

The rule of thumb is, the larger the subject in the frame, the more emphasis. In order of emphasis are the following: (1) The close-up (head shot), (2) the medium shot (bust shot), (3) the medium long shot (full figure usually filling the frame), and (4) the long shot (this covers the entire scene and may be referred to as the establishing shot).

• • • • • • • • • • • • • • • • • • •

GRAMMAR OF THE CAMERA

The camera is the tool by which the director's vision is expressed. To understand the camera and the way it sees the world with its limitations and peculiarities is the purpose of this section. Through this understanding we can create the pictures we need to tell the story by using the power of the camera, lens, lights, and the various tripods and support materials.

The Frame of the Picture

In the same way a painter selects a frame size, the director chooses a format. Television has its aspect ratios, and film has its formats designated as camera apertures. Reduced to simplicity, this is just another way of setting up the parameters—the "frame" of the picture—just as artists select different frame sizes to suit different designs.

Since we do not have the choice of changing the frame size for every shot, there are other ways we can creatively alter the frame size. The size may be altered by placing objects around the outer edges of the frame. For example, we can place a branch or leaves from a tree or bush in the foreground of the shot while we view the subject in the center of the frame. Effectively what this does is alter the shape of the shot and of the square frame. This is an interesting device and is used to accomplish all kinds of emotional changes. The oval-shaped frame, for instance, is considered a classic for portraits; the cinemascope aperture is considered panoramic. Scenic vistas work well within the cinemascope frame size.

Presently television 3 × 4 aspect ratio is the only format available. The discussion here will be limited to feature films. Curiously, these films all end up on television anyway. (This problem may be resolved by high-definition television and digital pictures, which will open the way for various other formats.)

Matching   The rule of the triangle applies here, as does the principle of matching size and area from shot to shot. To ensure matching, the area must remain constant. If the subject is established in the right section of the frame, she must remain in that area even when you are cutting to another angle. When it is a reverse shot, logically one might think the placement of the subject in the reverse area is necessary. But this is not the case. In fact it tends to confuse the audience. The simple theory is that the shifting of the viewers' eyes from one area to another confuses them. Let's say that subject "A" is in the right center; then a cut to subject "B" in left center is acceptable. This minimizes the viewer's eye shift and makes the cut acceptable.

The second concern is that the look has to match from shot to shot. If subject "A" is looking frame right, then her look must remain consistent. She must continue to look in that direction, and then, when cutting to subject "B," she has to be looking frame left.

But if the desire is to do a complete reverse and have the "A" subject now looking frame left to right, the tendency is to reposition the subject to another area of the frame to indicate a change. But the rule of minimizing the viewers' eye shifts supersedes all other theories of perception, meaning that subject "A" should stay in the same area. This makes the cut less jarring and more acceptable.

Examine Marian's Barroom scene from *Raiders* and note the consistency in the placement of Marian and Indy, even on reverse angles. The dynamics occur as a result of unorthodox camera placement. Our acceptance of the cuts results from keeping the figure in the same frame area.

The Lens

The lens may be thought of as the eye of the camera. The lens transfers the image to the recording medium, be it tape or film. The director needs to understand the creative applications of the lenses and how to use them. The focal lengths of the lenses vary according to their angle of view. The confusion is that the same-numbered lens will be designated as wide angle in one format and as standard in another.

To clear up this confusion, you should understand that the significance of the creative use of the lens has nothing to do with its format, but only with its classification. The format dictates the lens size, but its classification as wide angle, standard, or telephoto is most important for its creative application.

Each format or film size has a lens designated as the standard lens, meaning that the lens delivers a picture that represents the normal view as if it were seen through the naked eye. For instance, a 35 millimeter (mm) film registers the 2-inch lens (the 50 mm) as its standard, while 16 mm film registers the 1-inch (the 25 millimeter) as its standard lens. Lenses have different focal lengths, indicating their angle of view.

The significance to the director is that when the standard lens is known, then the other focal lengths are either wide angle or telephoto and they have the same common creative characteristics.

Depth of field refers to the area in which the subject can move while remaining in focus. The depth of focus means that the subject remains in focus with no need to adjust the camera's focus knob.

Creative Applications   The long lens, also called the telephoto or the close-up lens, is quite selective. Its angle of view is narrow; hence it registers movement minimally. It has a narrow depth of field and a shallow depth of focus, which presents a problem of holding focus. More light for telephoto shots increases the depth of field and helps to alleviate the problem.

Telephoto lenses intensify the action, making a subject appear larger than life, while movement appears to be nonexistent, futile, or difficult to accomplish. If a telephoto shot is taken of a runner as he races across the field toward the finishing line, he will appear to be running slowly, gaining no ground, when in fact he may be leading the pack.

A good practical example of many creative uses of a long lens is found in a popular television series. The producer Steven Bochco mandated that movement in cover shots be shot with a telephoto lens whenever it was practical. The Emmy Award – winning series was exciting, with blurred backgrounds, and larger-than-life characters moving across the television universe into our lives under the guise of the ironic title "Hill Street Blues." The narrow depth of field restricted movement, but it worked well because it supported the exciting creative concept. The Hollywood inside joke was that the director had to be outside the studio, across the street, to get some of the shots. Those 300 – 500 telephoto lenses need a great deal of distance from the subject to keep everything in focus.

Richard Donner's *Lethal Weapon* used telephoto lens shots consistently. The violence of the action was often staggering because of Donner's adroit use of these lenses.

In contrast, the wide-angle lens registers movement at a shocking rate. If the director wishes to impress the audience with the speed of the action, then she will shift to a wide-angle lens, which expands depth, making a subject appear as if it were moving two to three times faster than its real speed. It is a wonderful lens for shooting car chases. Cars will zoom, tear around corners, and do all those magical things one expects from car chases, which have been with us since silent film days.

Another application of the wide angle is distortion without tricky opticals. A subject placed very close to the lens has his or her features appear larger than life. The nose protrudes, thrusting forward like the beak of a bird, while the forehead recedes at an alarming angle, moving from the foreground to the background. Wide-angle lenses may be used to indicate emotional states. The depth of field in the wide-angle lens is greater than that of the telephoto lens. It is easier to keep the subject in focus. The variations of mixing these lenses creatively adds to the excitement of making wonderful pictures.

Focus   Another wonderful tool is the camera's ability to force the viewer's attention on a specific subject in the frame. This is done through the use of focus.

We have the ability to focus selectively. We can focus on the subject and make the background soft and impressionistic while keeping the subject sharp.

Some examples of forcing emphasis can be seen in some of the movies from the 1970s. The technique of "racking focus" was popular then. For example, the shot may show the softness of a flower in the foreground, when suddenly the focus is shifted back and another image appears out of the impressionistic background. The viewer's attention is controlled in an obvious manner. This is called "racking the focus." This is another tool for the director to use.

Focus can also be pinpoint sharp or soft edged. A soft edge suggests a romantic image and may be accomplished by putting Vaseline on a lens or gauze around the lens. This was a favorite choice of leading ladies who were a little older than the character they were playing. In fact some stars had their own favorite director of photography for this reason.

Camera Placement

Some directors tend to think in a one-shot scenario structure. The placement of the camera is rarely decided on a shot-by-shot basis. But the bottom line is that the "storyboard" in the director's mind dictates the camera placement. This technique will be discussed further in the following chapters, and in Chapter 18 in relation to the checklist.

But there are camera placement considerations that the director should be aware of. When the camera is placed low, looking up to the subject, this has the psychological effect of making the viewer look up to the subject. The story content can vary the reactions, from intimidation to admiration for the subject. This needs to be taken into account when structuring the selected cinema language.

Conversely, the camera looking down on the subject makes the audience feel sorry for the subject. The theory is that the viewer feels superior to the subject. Further, this positioning works well for comedy. The camera is placed at eye level or above eye level. It should not draw attention to itself. Howard Hawks used this technique. His films look simple and ordinary, but his skill with camera placement has been overlooked by many critics. In fact, like Ford he was a master of invisible camera placement. He frequently stated that the camera should be an unintrusive observer.

Perspective Unity   The horizontal, vertical, and sloping lines that deal with one-dimensional aspect and are concerned with vanishing points and creating depth—this is what we mean by perspective unity. This perspective unity can be either symmetrical or asymmetrical. Presently we deal with a picture that is flat. In fact, every picture needs perspective, which adds to the quality and texture of the picture. As mentioned earlier, depth creates a feeling of warmth, but knowing that the film is two-dimensional should sensitize the director to seek depth in his picture and request the DP to light for it. The choice of symmetrical or asymmetrical perspective has more to do with the emotional content and follows the composition rules already discussed.

• • • • • • • • • • • • • • • • • • •

PICTURIZATION

Picturization is the visual interpretation of each moment as the picture unfolds. The correct placement of characters and things to suggest their emotional states or attitudes toward one another so the situation is understood by the viewer, without dialogue or previous viewing, is what is meant by picturization. Composition, on the other hand, supplies the rules in order to make picturization work.

Picturization Procedure

What is the procedure to come up with the correct picture? This is probably the first question every director asks herself. It is not complicated or difficult. The central theme is the reason for selecting the particular picturization. The selection process is predicated on understanding the impact of the composition elements.

Labeling the Scene   Begin by reading the screenplay, doing the beat breakdown, and deducing the central theme as described in Chapter 3. The next step is to label the scene. The emotional content of the scene needs to be stated in a word or two. This helps the actor and the director to remain in contact with the emotional needs of the scene. This clarity always helps the actor and the director to get a handle on the scene. Labeling forces the director to use correct composition elements to support his picturization.

Emotional relationships break down into the following categories: love, fear, hate, fight, anger. The label stays with the basic emotions. If the label is dislike, apprehension, bitterness, or depression, then that is difficult to act, let alone direct. The actor as well as the director needs a positive emotion to make the scene work. Depression, apprehension, and bitterness are passive emotions. The scene works better if depression is changed to angry frustration, apprehension changed to fear, and bitterness changed to hate or anger. The elevation of the emotion is the next choice.

In "action" scenes, the director needs to determine whether it is a main or secondary scene. A main action moves the story forward, and it is directly related to and inextricably wound up in the story, dealing directly with the principal players.

A secondary action label means it is a subplot. Then the director needs to understand how it relates to the main story. The secondary story has a direct correlation to the main story. The director must make certain that the connecting plot point is given emphasis.

Labeling also helps the director to remember the mood and to use correct composition elements to support picturization. Background atmosphere can be controlled and used as part of the picturization. In *The Wizard of Oz*, when Dorothy first went to see the Wizard, the local people made us realize that the Wizard was not someone to fear.

The term *incidental action* describes scenes that add local color or give an insight or foreshadow the action of a major scene. The prologue of *Raiders of the Lost Ark* is classic in its configuration. It foreshadows not only Indiana losing to Belloq, but also the massive snake attack in the climax of the film when Indiana discovers the pilot's pet snake in the seaplane's cockpit and screams how he hates snakes. Everyone knew that was not going to be the end of snakes in this picture.

Cinema Language   The shot's picturization needs to flow into the cinema language. Turn to the analysis of *Big Country* in Chapter 10. On the camera pattern diagram (see Figure 10.2), note that the "B" master camera position sets the position for picturization.

Remembering the composition rules of the triangle and that the frame is divided into thirds, "B" camera position has Gregory Peck on frame right (the Mexican is ignored and never included in any of the shots, except at the beginning and end of the sequence), and on frame left is Burl Ives. Between them is the prize, Jean Simmons. This is correct picturization since she is the person that Peck and Ives are fighting about. Simmons is further threatened by the massive, tall Chuck Connors, who hovers alongside her. She is caught between the two forces, the hero Peck on the right side, and on the left the villain Ives. She is further threatened by Connors's proximity.

This picturization reinforces Peck's problem of rescuing Simmons. With Peck occupying only one-third of the frame, put in profile, in the sun, below Ives's eye level, Peck's position is weakened, though he continues to gain the audience's empathy. The oblique line of interest increases the tension in the classic composition of a face-off. Ives is not only physically larger than Peck, but standing on the porch, the structure reinforcing his figure, while poor Peck sits on his horse in the hot sun. This picturization is also a graphic image, meaning it not only makes dramatic sense but at the same time has caught the essence of the scene.

This picturization enabled William Wyler, the director, to sustain a static scene for a long period of time. Obviously the cutting that paced the scene was done in the editing room, though it was made easier because of the excellent picturization.

Picturization, supported by correct composition, gave a scene that could have been melodramatic, bordering on the silly, taste and sensibility, and built the tension of the film. Wyler is one of the best in using the master scene cinema language. He rarely explored the other cinema languages, but what he did, he did with restraint and style.

The principle of composition and picturization are used to support the shot, which is the basic unit of the cinema languages. These principles give the director support for the selected cinema language.

Chapter 8

CINEMA LANGUAGES

Every film lover and filmmaker owes David Warwick Griffith an eternal debt of gratitude. By simply moving the camera he created one of the most dynamic tools of the twentieth century and turned film into the first twentieth-century art, becoming the father of "editing."

In the twenties, the moving picture camera, hand-cranked by the operator, photographed events from a stationary position. Some thought of film, as simply a recording device, much like audio recordings. A method of "saving" the performances of artists. Certainly, no one envisioned the power of the medium nor even today, is this power fully appreciated.

THE DEVELOPMENT OF CINEMA LANGUAGE

The creative process of editing needed a name. To distinguish it from the mechanics of editing the Russians chose the term *montage,* from a French word.

In the late 1920s, Kuleshov, the Russian experimentalist, demonstrated the theory of montage. He joined a shot of a man to a shot of a loaf of bread. The audience knew the man was hungry.

When Kuleshov replaced the bread with a shot of a woman, the viewers' perception was changed quite dramatically. Viewers were certain that the man was deeply in love with that woman. Some viewers claimed the man's face expressed a degree of love that was rarely seen in films. This was in spite of the fact that the shot of the man was exactly the same as in the sequence with the bread. This demonstration proved that arranging shots in a particular sequence is a very powerful tool. Obviously, further exploration was necessary.

The term *montage* has many other meanings today, so to avoid confusion, a new term, *cinema language* will be used here instead. *Cinema language* is defined as the planned creative series of shots put into a particular arrangement and run for a selected period of time, causing the audience to react in the desired manner. The shot captures the action of the event and in effect breaks two of the constant unities of life: it captures space and controls time.

TIME

The technology to record events on film or videotape gives the filmmaker the unique ability to control time. There are four categories of time that can be controlled:

1. *Audience time* is the time it takes for an audience to view a film. Today the average feature film runs about 90 minutes to 2 hours. A director knows when a sequence may be too short or too long by knowing the planned overall running time of the picture.

2. *Story time* is the time period of the story dictated by the plot. For instance, *Gone with the Wind* takes place in the nineteenth century, while *Ordinary People* takes place in modern times.

3. *Plot time* refers to the time covered within the story. In George Lucas's *American Graffiti* the story takes place over a 24-hour period. James Brooks's film *Terms of Endearment* details the relationship between mother and daughter over a 20-year period. In sharp contrast, *The Wizard of Oz* takes place in the mind of Dorothy. Only when she awakens, back in her bed in Kansas, do we learn the "real" time her dream (her visit to Oz) took place in.

4. *Cinema language time* gives us the ability to control time. In this instance, the artist can use time as an artistic tool. For example, in a popular TV commercial, a child seated in his high chair tosses a plate of food from his tray. The food floats in the air, flying in slow motion. After slowly landing on the floor and then bouncing for another second or two, the food finally comes to rest, demonstrating that the carpet is stain-resistant. In real time, the action would take a fraction of a second. In filmic time the commercial ran for 30 seconds.

Instant Change

In Stanley Kubrick's *2001* a young man becomes an old man in seconds, in the next instant an infant, and finally a "star-baby" of the universe a few dozen seconds later. In Sam Peckinpah's *The Wild Bunch,* a man is shot and he dies in slow motion. He explodes, in all directions—slowly. His death is endless. In real time, he dies instantly.

Peter O'Toole, when viewing the final cut of *Lawrence of Arabia,* tells the amusing story that he saw himself age 2 years—instantly. He explains that it took David Lean 2 years to shoot the film, so when he spliced a shot done at the beginning of the schedule to a shot done at the end of the schedule, O'Toole appeared to age two years in an instant.

Expanding or Contracting Time

Cinema language time requires that the actors' acting and reacting be adjusted to the needs of filmic time. For instance, in Brian DePalma's *Dressed to Kill,* the elevator sequence stretched time to a stressful length.

Future Time

Film can also flash the viewer forward to the future, as in *The Getaway.* For example, Steve McQueen watches some action offscreen; suddenly he is seen jumping into a lake, and then Peckinpah returns to the same shot of a dry McQueen watching people swimming in the lake. On the next cut, he is wet as he enters the apartment. You realize suddenly that it was the future you were viewing. This is an example of flashing forward to the future. All edited film controls time. Selecting the arrangement of shots alters time.

Camera Time

There are two other "camera" methods of controlling film time: frame speed and special effects.

Frame Speed   Photograph a scene at 48 frames per second and it appears slow when projected at the standard 24 frames per second. Conversely, photograph a scene at 12 frames per second and when projected it appears to move twice as fast.

Optical or Special Effects   These techniques are used to change time. There are two procedures.

1. Superimposition means combining two or more pictures into one composite shot. Paris, or a Tibetan mountaintop, or whatever background is needed for a film, can be projected onto the screen, and by using the "blue matte" process it appears as if the characters are in that place. Though this procedure is given different names with each new technical improvement, it still remains a form of superimposition.

2. In stop motion, the motion of an object or thing can be stopped by photographing it a frame at a time. This technique is used in live action films like *Star Wars, 1941, E.T.,* and *Ghostbusters.* TV commercials use it to make the product move. The product is placed in one position, a few frames of it are shot, then the product is moved to its next position, and some more frames are shot. Eventually, when these shots are spliced together the product appears to be moving. When this stop motion technique is used with a series of drawings, it is called animation.

• • • • • • • • • • • • • • • • • • • •

SPACE

A picture takes space, which limits the picture by its format. The formats in motion pictures fall into two categories: the wide screen (1:85 ratio), and the standard square (2½ x 2½).

The Screen

It is believed that the wide screen lends itself to spectacle films, while the standard is for "people" pictures. This theory appears to be academic. Most films today are eventually seen in the 3 x 4 format on television. A feature film director may wish to compose his picture for the television format, even while shooting it for theatrical release.

Within the Screen

A painter can alter the parameters of the frame by placing objects around or near the frame; the director may do the same. This procedure varies the composition of the shots. Director Sidney J. Furie used this technique in *Appaloosa,* giving that film a unique look.

Recognizing that time and space are manipulable in the medium of recording images makes it imperative to know and understand the rules that govern the cinema languages.

Chapter 9

RULES OF
CINEMA LANGUAGE

In the study and practice of directing, filmmakers have determined 12 cinema languages. It is quite possible there are others that are not yet discovered or yet to be born as a result of new technology. At this juncture, however, we will examine all the cinema languages known today.

Many are woven together, making them appear to be different, new, and unique. But when all is said and done, there are 12 cinema languages, with the thirteenth being a combination of the other 12.

In his *Big Country* (which is cited as an example in the "Master Scene Cinema Language" section in Chapter 10), William Wyler uses interpersonal cinema language within the master scene cinema language configuration. In Chapter 10, look at the *Big Country* analysis.

The following sections describe the general rules used by all the cinema languages, except when an exception specifically is mentioned.

REPETITIVE SHOTS

Shots are repeated throughout a sequence, frequently in groups. The repetitive image technique achieves several goals.

Assurance

The audience members greet the recycled shots like a friend or an enemy, depending upon their relation to the story line. The viewers, however, always do this with a sense of "knowing" the shot because it is familiar.

Anchorage

A repetitive shot gives the audience a feeling of stability. They know where they are, who is who, what the character is expected to do, and so on. This is particularly true in the master scene cinema language, the workhorse cinema language of Hollywood episodic television.

A Cyclical Pattern

The shots are cyclical. The shots are repeated in a specific pattern, which is dictated by the specific disciplines of the cinema language being used. The pattern must usually be repeated at least three times within the sequence. The master scene cinema language pattern generally starts with an establishing shot, followed with a medium shot, and then a closer shot. This is called an A-B-A series of shots. This pattern is followed in *Big Country* master scene cinema language. (See the *Big Country* analysis in Chapter 10.) The scene starts immediately with shots 1 and 3, representing "A" (shot 3 is merely a closer view of 1), then 4, the "B," and then the payoff is shot 5, the "C." This cycle of shot pattern is repeated throughout the sequence.

Payoff

The classic Carl Foreman and Freddie Zinnemann Western *High Noon* used this payoff technique by designing cycles of repetitive shots (parallel cinema language) of the outlaws at the railroad station waiting for their leader, as the sheriff (Gary Cooper) desperately tries to round up a posse. He fails; no one wants to help to fight the outlaws he sent to jail. He is made to appear pathetic through the use of repetitive cyclical shots. The payoff results in the obligatory gunfight, the climax of *High Noon*. When studied, the classic configuration of the film's payoff shots heightened the tension. The shots of the clock showing the countdown to "high noon" were part of the cyclical pattern of shots that was repeated throughout the film.

With *Big Country*, analysis will demonstrate how the A-B-A, A-B-A, A-B-A pattern was used. The following groups of shots used this payoff technique: 3, 4, payoff shot 5, then 6, 7, and 8, with shot 9 as the payoff. This is especially true in interpersonal cinema language. Examine the discussion of *Vertigo* in the "Interpersonal Cinema Language" section of Chapter 10.

• • • • • • • • • • • • • • • • • • • •

REVEALMENT

To reveal an event, an action, or a thing that the audience has not seen before is another rule of cinema language. It is often done with a camera movement, a push in or more often a pullback. As the camera moves back, it suddenly reveals a gun, or a bouquet of flowers, or a man doing . . . something.

The revealment is dictated by the story, the environment, or a pictorial statement. It works best when it is done in one unbroken shot. It works using a cut, but not quite as well as in the unbroken move.

• • • • • • • • • • • • • • • • • • • •

ORCHESTRATION

Selecting the cinema language technique by understanding its relation to the whole film is what is defined as orchestration. To select, mix, and combine the cinema languages so the film will have hills of excitement and valleys of "rest," properly balanced, matching the emotional needs of the story, is what we mean by orchestration. It may be thought of as similar to the way in which an arranger arranges his music and treats the themes in various sections.

Climax

In planning the orchestration of a film, the climax sequence is dealt with first. This makes certain that the highest point of the film is uniquely different from any other part of the film. Once the cinema language for the climax has been selected, then orchestrating the balance of the film is easier. A number of devices are used to orchestrate the climax.

A Combination of Cinema Languages   Francis Coppola's *Cotton Club* climax is an excellent example of the marriage of six different cinema languages in a complicated mosaic that creates a climax and concludes the various stories and the film at the same time. Coppola used constructive, interpersonal, symbolic, collision, and fragmented cinema languages in an extraordinary piece of film. It is worth taking out from your local video store. The foregoing terms are explained in the following chapter.

Compositional Devices   An example of selecting oblique lines plus collision cinema language (contrapuntal sound) is found in Martin Scorsese's *Raging Bull* as Jake LaMotta fights and wins the championship. It was not so much a fight as a requiem for the "champ" as the antihero, Jake LaMotta, brutally beat his opponent and to his amazement easily took the crown. (See Chapter 12 for an explanation of collision cinema language.)

Location   Selecting a location not seen in the film before heightens excitement and is an excellent tool for the climactic sequence. There are many existing examples, but the best is the climactic sequence on Mount Rushmore: Hitchcock's *North by Northwest*.

These are the operational rules of the cinema languages. These rules are to be used as a guide when the director is choosing and implementing a cinema language. Like all rules they are not written in stone and are meant to guide, not dictate.

PART **4**

THE VISUAL LANGUAGE— THE 12 CINEMA LANGUAGES

Chapter 10

THE MOST-USED
CINEMA LANGUAGES

The master scene and interpersonal cinema languages are the two most common ones in use today and have been around since the beginning of filmmaking. Both are natural and easy to conceptualize. If you have a camera and can edit, you can use these languages.

• • • • • • • • • • • • • • • • • •

MASTER SCENE CINEMA LANGUAGE

Historically, D. W. Griffith developed the master scene cinema language technique. It was a natural step for him. The technique was essentially a master cover shot of the action. When Griffith moved his camera, he moved it closer to the action. Then he began to experiment with medium shots, then closer shots, and so on.

The theory that deliberately repeating portions of shots because this made it easier for an audience to follow the action was quickly abandoned. Each shot then began an add-on and continued telling the story.

By definition a master scene is the one shot that records all the action or events in one shot. Usually it is a long shot that establishes the environment and the people, and records the event or action in its entirety.

Then the action is repeated for the master shot in a series of closer shots from varying positions. This is referred to as "overlapping" the action. In effect, the director masters the action from several angles. Selecting the shots and their final arrangement is done in the cutting room. The director has a vision of how the pieces go together but this cinema language allows flexibility in the cutting room unlike some others, which will be discussed. This procedure is called the master scene cinema language.

For example, say a man enters his office, sees a note from his wife that says he must call home at once. He telephones as his secretary enters, telling him they are waiting for him to attend the board of directors meeting.

The master scene cinema language plan starts with a long shot of all the action, including the note on the desk, the phone call, and the entrance of the secretary. This is referred to as the master scene or master shot. This is then followed by a series of close shots, such as the man at his desk, a close shot of his picking up the note, an even closer shot of the note so the viewer can read it, a shot of the man dialing the phone and the entrance of the secretary, a closer shot of the secretary as she tells him of the waiting board members, his reactions to her information, and so on. The choice of these closer shots and point of view would be the next concern. But there are some specific rules for master scene cinema language one needs to know before proceeding to use it.

A Popular Approach

Master scene cinema language is the most popular in Hollywood because it uses the team approach to filmmaking, as opposed to the European auteur concept. This language is favored among most of the episodic television producers. It gives choices other than being locked into the director's cut. Editors prefer it because they can show alternative ways of cutting the scene. Many directors prefer it. It allows them the freedom of making final decisions in the cutting room.

Creating Order and Stability

Master scene cinema language has a calming effect upon the audience. It leads an audience into and out of tense situations. It gives the viewer a feeling of order and stability, since the event and the people are clearly placed and stated.

Building and Releasing Tension

The flip side is that this approach can also build and release tension. The example chosen, *Big Country,* is at the climax of the film. The physical action is put on hold while the tension mounts through master scene cinema language. This was a courageous choice since it was an action movie, and suddenly to have all that dialogue at this close point of the climax was a breach of the Western cowboy tradition.

Establishing the Shot The establishing shot sets up the geography of people, place, and things, leading to lessening or building of tension. It is usually the first shot of the sequence.

Magnification

After the master shot has been shot, then the same action is repeated in the medium and close shots, resulting in the impression that the viewer is merely watching a magnification of the action. This leads to the myth of the invisible cut.

The Invisible Cut *Invisible cut* means the viewer is not aware of the change of camera angle. The audience members feel they are watching a continuous story rather than a series of shots spliced together. This rule is more true for master scene cinema language than for all the other cinema languages.

Repeated Shots Repeated shots follow this pattern: long shot, then medium shot, then back to the long shot. The *Big Country* analysis demonstrates the pattern, which can be expressed as A-B-A, A-B-A, A-B-A.

The second pattern is this: medium shot of two people, then reverse medium two-shot, followed by a single shot, which is usually the close-up, the payoff shot. This configuration is classic for master scene cinema language, giving emphasis. The rhythm of the cuts determines the weight of the payoff close-up.

Camera Placement

Camera placement is normal. There are no sharp angles to draw attention to the camera angle. The placement that seems natural, that does not draw attention to itself, is the best for this cinema language.

A master of natural camera placement who went for decades without recognition, not only in the Hollywood community but among the critics as well, was Howard Hawks. He had an uncanny ability to place his camera as if it were in the most natural position. His placement was always thought of as being invisible. Viewers always had the feeling that they were eaves-dropping in his movies.

John Ford was certainly another master in objective placement. In later years, he abandoned the master scene cinema language technique and almost exclusively shot in constructive cinema language, unlike Hawks and Wyler, who stayed with the master scene cinema language. (See page 135 in Chapter 11 on constructive cinema language.)

Interfaces

Cinema languages comfortably interface with other cinema languages. Examples abound in features, episodic films, situation comedies, and daytime drama (soaps).

Comedy, Romance, Musicals

These screenplays prefer the master scene cinema language. Traditionally the material is written for the stage. This type of screenplay has more emphasis on the play element than on the screen element.

Comedy   Comedy requires a relaxed type of presentation. The philosophy is that in order for audiences to laugh at the jokes, they must feel relaxed, superior to the characters, and yet sorry for those involved in their plight.

Comedy has other faces as well, and indeed comedy is not limited to the master scene cinema discipline, though traditionally comedy uses master scene more often than the other languages.

Romance   Romance requires putting aside the tensions of the everyday and being relaxed to enjoy the lovers in the drama. Master scene cinema language is preferred. This type of gentle configuration encourages the sharing of the romance with the viewer.

1. *The romantic close-up* presents actors in an intimate way, with the strong possibility of making them into movie stars. Frequently viewers carry away with them the romantic image, becoming movie fans without understanding the process. In fact this "romantic image" shot, when properly cut in, somehow ends up seeming to control the sequence.

2. *The lingering romantic shot* encourages fantasies that have little to do with the story. The viewer will remember long after she has forgotten the movie. The movie studios in their day of building stars recognized that master scene cinema language had this affinity and insisted this discipline be used for their stars.

3. *The viewer's lack of awareness.* That romantic image, when properly placed in a pay-off position and when the cut-ins are gracefully made using those invisible cuts, causes the viewer to drift in and out. It is a trancelike state because the master scene cinema language discipline lulls the conscious mind into a passive state, allowing the unconscious to be accessed. Then that romantic image may be planted without the viewer's being aware. In *Big Country* the Gregory Peck close-ups are a shining example; the picture did reinforce Peck's stardom.

Musicals   The big MGM musicals of the 40s came out of the theater tradition and almost always used master scene cinema language. Music leads the picture and composites nicely. The music of the 40s had the gentleness and clarity required for this type of genre of musical comedy.

More recently, rock videos have burst upon the musical scene, and though occasionally they use master scene, most of them use constructive cinema language that blends into dynamic applications of fragmented and transitional cinema languages (see Chapters 11 and 12). Music videos have brought an exciting and challenging approach to musicals.

The Sound Track

The sound track may neutralize the picture. Robert Altman, an extraordinary contemporary director, neutralizes his pictures by emphasizing the sound track. His *Long Goodbye,* starring Elliot Gould, is an example. Ultimately, the master scene cinema language's integrity is in the close-up and this should never be compromised. The sound track support makes the close-up's impact greater.

A Dominating Sound Track When music, or part of the sound track, needs emphasis, then the master scene cinema language lends itself to that design.

Disguises for Pictorial Changes Whether music, sound effects, or even dialogue, the sound track will divide the attention of the viewer; consequently the picture changes will go unnoticed. This sound track device is frequently used to ease picture cuts if they are not quite as invisible as desired.

Dialogue Dialogue scenes are most comfortably handled by the master scene cinema language. Cinema language procedure for shooting dialogue makes it easy to handle in the cutting room.

1. *Expository lines* can be emphasized. In *Raiders of the Lost Ark* some expository lines were lost during the action of the story. In this procedure, expository lines may be accentuated and given emphasis.

2. *Gag lines* are written for an audience's reaction. This language allows for corrections and improving the comedic timing. A character's reaction to a gag is easily handled in this language. Situation comedies use an invited audience's reactions to guide the editing of the length and loudness of the laughs in the final "air" show.

Many of the sitcoms are videotaped in a continuous performance as if they were on the stage. The placement of the three to four cameras simultaneously shooting the performance may not seem appropriate to master scene cinema language because the format implies a one-camera set up and overlap of each individual shot. But this is not the case. It is generally true that most of these videtaped programs are cut by the director as he views the cameras shots on their individual monitors in the control room. But the rules of master scene cinema languages apply. The major difference is that the cut is made by the director.

The master scene cinema language works well in this environment. As a matter of fact, the videotape director has to be thorough and familiar with the various cinema languages because she is cutting the picture without the aid of an editor or time to review the cut. The videotape director has to cut cameras on the fly since the actors usually perform in front of a live audience and may not wait for the camera change. Conversely, this type of director has more control over the editing than does the episodic television director. The episodic directors present a "director's cut" to the producer. But in the world of episodic programs, where shows are often a day late and a dollar short, moving on inexorably to meet the schedule for network showing, time for cutting is limited.

Cutting comedy or gags has more to do with capturing the reaction to the gag. Hence, the ability to move the image around, playing off the actions and reactions, works best in this cinema language.

3. *Preference by actors.* Actors prefer master scene cinema language because they perform the scene in a continuous performance as if it were on the stage. The scene seems to have a beginning, a middle, and an end. Playing the scene with a responding actor gives the actors a chance to react. Television stars, especially those in soap type dramas like "Dallas," insist that directors and producers use the master scene format. They are absolutely correct—it helps their performance immeasurably.

4. *Dialogue linkage (the beat).* Dialogue is written in cycles, which are grouped together by a common objective or subject. (Please refer to Part 1, Chapter 3, and Part 6, Chapter 19, "Second Reading.") These beats are more controlled in this master scene language because of the overlap technique. It gives control over dialogue scenes that the director never has in the theater.

5. *Tempo and pacing.* Because of the overlap procedure of the master scene, the director and the editor have a great deal of control over the tempo, pacing, and rhythm of the scene. Perhaps some of the best dialogue cutting is done in Hollywood. The editors are masters of building a dialogue scene.

6. *Emotional information.* Getting emotional information about the inner life of the screenplay's character is supported by this cinema language. The repetitive procedure, which is similar to that of stage acting, encourages the actor to seek inner truth. Part 5 focuses on actors and will deal with this inner truth and film acting in specific detail.

7. *Sync dialogue* means that the lip movement matches exactly the words being spoken. This discipline demands that all the dialogue be in sync. Violating this rule destroys this cinema language. Though in the cutting the dialogue may be placed over a picture of another character who is listening, when returning to the speaking character the dialogue must be exactly in sync. Being off by just a frame is enough to cause a violation and break in viewers' concentration.

Time

Time demands in the master scene cinema language are clear and definite. The scene must appear as if happening moment to moment. The scene cannot be moved or compressed; it must appear to be happening, in real time, then and now. Violate this rule and credibility goes out the window.

Continuity   Since the event must appear to be happening in real time, several guidelines must be followed:

1. *Sets, costumes, props.* The sets must match from shot to shot, as must costumes, set props, and hand props. All must maintain the illusion that the event is happening as it is being viewed. One of the main functions of the continuity script supervisor is monitoring the shoot and making certain that all things, like costume, hair, and so on, match from shot to shot.

2. *Actors match.* The actors must match themselves from shot to shot. In other words, the actor repeats his dialogue and actions from shot to shot. As a result, when cutting to other shots, the illusion of the moment-to-moment reality is maintained.

3. *Overlapping action.* Actors are required to repeat their actions exactly from shot to shot, but in addition they must repeat the action for every shot. For instance, say the actor picks up a cup of coffee with his right hand and switches to his left hand when he takes a cookie. The camera shots the action from one angle and sees his right hand only. When the camera placement is now on his left side, the actor might think it is not necessary to repeat the action. This is incorrect. There may have been a shifting of body or shoulder that would not match in the new shot. Repetition is safe.

The actor is required to do the complete action so there is overlap. By repeating the entire action, the actor gives the editor the opportunity to match the movement and action into the new incoming shot. This continues the myth of no camera shot change.

Lighting

Lighting must match from scene to scene because a mismatch draws attention to the new shot. The director of photography (DP) is responsible for lighting and is sensitive to motivated light sources and to mismatches.

The DP gives the feature film and the episodic shows their look. In the latter case the DP has more control over lighting than does the director because the DP usually works on the show every week. The episodic director, needing time to prepare, is unable to direct every week's show. In feature films, the director has more control over everything because there is time to prepare for the project.

Shooting Ratio

The shooting ratio refers to the ratio of all film exposed in shooting the film to the running time of the completed picture. For example, a feature film that runs 90 minutes uses a total of 9,000 feet of film. A shooting ratio of ten to one means you plan to expose 90,000 feet to shoot the picture. In theory this means every scene will be shot ten times.

This ratio is one of the principal ways of cost controlling a production. The production manager, whose primary responsibility is to bring the show in on budget, asks about the ratio. She knows that every foot of exposed film means so much production and postproduction time and that if more film is exposed than planned then the production could be going over budget.

Master scene cinema language is a great user of raw stock (unexposed film). This cinema language, compared with the others, uses more film. Since it is used for dialogue and to cover for overlap from shot to shot, quantities of film are used. Many of the editing decisions are made in the cutting room. Technology for electronic editing has speeded up the editing process. Ultimately, master scene cinema language requires a higher ratio of film than most of the other cinema languages.

John Ford exposed a scant 68,000 feet to shoot the classic film *The Informer*. Other directors, like Hitchcock, carefully plan their cinema language to minimize the amount of film needed to shoot their picture; as a result, though they limited their choices in the cutting room.

Case Study: *Big Country*

To demonstrate the master scene cinema language as practiced in Hollywood, a sequence has been selected from William Wyler's *Big Country*. Wyler's cinematic master scene cinema language configuration is deceptive in its casual design. Wyler is a master filmmaker and artfully tricks us.

The *Big Country* story takes place in the late 1800s. Jim McKay (Gregory Peck), a former seacaptain, arrives out West to marry Patricia Terrel (Carroll Baker), the daughter of the powerful rancher "Major" Henry Terrel (Charles Bickford). Terrel is feuding with another powerful patriarch, rancher Hennessey (Burl Ives). They are fighting for control of the valley, and the one who controls the water wins. The Hennesseys had been using the water from Clem Maregone's Big Muddy ranch. Upon Maregone's death, the ownership of the ranch was passed on to his daughter Julie (Jean Simmons), and she has continued his policy. But the Hennesseys are afraid that she may not continue to do so because of her personal relationship with Patricia Terrel.

Convinced by his son (Chuck Connors) that Jean Simmons is in love with Connors, Ives commands his son to bring her to their ranch so he can get them married. Simmons cannot stand the cowardly Connors but is attracted to Peck. Unknown to all, she sold the ranch to Peck because he promised to continue the practice of free water.

It is Terrel's plan to use Simmons's kidnapping as an excuse to attack the Hennesseys and wipe them out. He marshals his men and surrounds the Hennessey ranch.

To avoid an open range war, in which many men would die, and with the hope of effecting Simmons's release, Peck, guided by a friendly Mexican, Ramon, rides through Terrel's men, into the Hennessey camp where this sequence begins (see Figure 10.1).

The following abbreviations and terms appear in shot descriptions.

- L.S.—long shot.
- M.L.S.—medium long shot.
- C.S.—close shot.
- M.C.U.—medium close-up.

Figure 10.1 Big Country, *Master Scene Cinema Language. This scene takes place right after the Cinema Master scene described in detail. Connors and Peck are about to duel.* (©1958, renewed 1986 Anthony-Worldwide Productions. All rights reserved.)

- C.U.—close-up.
- POV—point of view.
- B.G.—background.
- F.G.—foreground.
- X's—A character moves in some direction.
- HEAD, SHOULDER, WAIST, HIP, THIGH, SHOT means the bottom frame line cuts the subject's body at the designated part. It is written as HEAD SHOT, SHOULDER-SHOT, WAIST SHOT, and so on.

The number of people in the shot is indicated by the number that precedes the abbreviation, for example, "2 L.S." means two people in a long shot.

New and established shots will repeat in a pattern. Though the pattern is dictated by the beat (dialogue linkage), the new shot is the signal of another cycle. To indicate a new shot an additional space was skipped.

Big Country

MASTER SCENE CINEMA LANGUAGE

Shot	Description	Time
1	L.S. (ESTABL. SHOT) POV SIMMONS X's IVES standing on porch. In B.G. PECK comes riding up with RAMON alongside. CAMERA POSITION A.	4.7
2	2 L.S. SIMMONS FOLLOWED BY CONNORS . . . POV PECK. CAMERA POSITION B. They X's into the Foreground.	1.8
3	2 M.L.S. (CAMERA POSITION A.) Shot is identical to Shot 1 EXCEPT magnified. PECK rides up to the Porch as IVES positions himself frame left. RAMON is dropped from the sequence until end. This is a deep focus shot.	4.2

> PECK
> Hello, Mr. Hennessey . . .

| 4 | 2 SHOT . . . PROFILE OF PECK, TO MEDIUM SHOT OF IVES | 1.4 |

> PECK
> I'm Jim McKay.

| 5 | WAIST SHOT OF IVES . . . POV PECK. He watches him in amazement. | 11.5 |

> IVES
> I know who you are. This is a dif-
> ferent kind of party we're hav-
> ing here today. Not as elegant as
> the Major's shindig but it's goin'
> to be a lot more livelier.

6   4-SHOT. PECK frame right F.G., IVES frame   18.6
     left. SIMMONS & CONNORS stand on the porch in
     B.G. (CAMERA POSITION B.)

BEAT _____ <2>

                    IVES
          Now may I ask what brings you
          here—uninvited?

                    PECK
          I've come to take Miss Maregone
          home.

                    IVES
          Mister, you've got more gall than
          brains. You just rode by a parcel
          of guns and you got a couple on
          you right now. Now just what is
          your notion of why Miss Mare-
          gone is here?

7   CHEST SHOT OF PECK . . . POV IVES (MASTER   4.2
     CAMERA POSITION A . . . ROMANTIC SHOT)

                    PECK
          We both know why Miss Mare-
          gone is here, Mr. Hennessey.

8   CLOSE-UP OF IVES (MASTER CAMERA POSI-   7.3
     TION C)

                    IVES
          My cows are watering on the Big
          Muddy again. And pretty soon
          I'm gonna have Henry Terrel
          right where I want him if that's
          what you mean.

9   CHEST SHOT OF PECK . . . POV IVES   6.3
     (Repeat #7)

> PECK
> Then you got no more reason to
> hold her here. I own the Big
> Muddy now . . .

10   SHOT PECK IN PROFILE IN F.G., IVES IN B.G.   5.8

> PECK (OFF-SCREEN)
> Then I give you my word. You
> can have all the water you want.

11   WAIST SHOT OF IVES . . . POV PECK   8.3
      (Repeat of #5)

BEAT _____ <3>

> IVES
> N'you got any proof of that, boy?

12   2 M.L.S. OF IVES WITH PECK ON HORSE   8.4
      (Repeat #1, MASTER CAMERA POSITION A)

> PECK
> Right here . . .

He turns to get it out of his saddlebags.

> IVES
> Hold onto your seat.
> (LOOKS LEFT) Buck?

Turns back to PECK as CONNORS (Buck) enters
X's B.G. above horse.

> IVES
> Buck will do the looking.

13   SHOULDER SHOT OF SIMMONS . . .   3.

She moves and then looks frame right looking
concerned.

> CONNORS (OFF-SCREEN)
> Well . . .

14 2 M.L.S. OF PECK WITH CONNORS (Repeat #3)   7.9

> CONNORS
> . . . What have we got here?

> PECK
> The deed is in my coat.

Connors takes out a large wooden box, which
he opens.

> CONNORS
> Now ain't that really pretty?
> (X's to IVES) Now look, Pa . . . Toy
> pistols . . .

15 MEDIUM SHOT OF IVES ON PORCH . . . BUCK   8.4
    X's INTO FRAME The box contains a matching
    pair of dueling pistols.

> IVES
> Gentlemen's weapons. (TAKES
> PISTOL OUT OF BOX . . . THEN TO
> PECK) You've come loaded for
> bear, didn't you, boy?

16 CHEST SHOT OF PECK (Repeat #7)   2.6

> IVES (OFF-SCREEN)
> What did you expect to do with
> these?

PECK looks to SIMMONS, silently asking, are
you OK?

17 CLOSE SHOULDER SHOT OF SIMMONS (Repeat   1.9
    #11) She is about to say something but decides
    against it.

18   CHEST SHOT OF PECK (Repeat #7)   2.1
      He looks concerned.

                        IVES (OFF-SCREEN)
                    Buck, look in his coat.

19   M.L.S. OF PECK ON HORSE (Repeat #3 MAS-   11.1
      TER) CONNORS X's back and searches his coat
      and takes out paper. He looks up at PECK ques-
      tioningly:

                            PECK
                    It's been recorded.

CONNORS X's off to:

20   M.S. OF IVES ON PORCH. BUCK X's TO HIM   29.0
      (Repeat shot #6, MASTER CAMERA POSITION
      B)

      CONNORS X's to IVES, gives him the deed and
      then steps above him as he reads over IVES's
      shoulder. Satisfied it is the deed, he X's back to
      SIMMONS. ENDING IN SAME MASTER SHOT.
      IVES holds the deed in his hands:

                            IVES
                    Now ain't this frosty Friday. I've
                    been tryin' to get ma hands on
                    this deed since Clem Maregone
                    died.

He hands the deed to PECK.

21   4 L.S., PECK IN MIDDLE, RAMON IN F.G., CON-
      NORS & SIMMONS IN B.G.

BEAT _____ <4>

                            PECK
                    Now what about my promise? All
                    the water you want. Just as long
                    as you want it.

22   SHOULDER SHOT OF IVES (NEW SIZE, SAME   19.6
       "C" CAMERA)

IVES
You got the looks of a man that
means what he says, but this
ain't just a matter of water. The
Hennesseys will have no peace
until the bones of Henry Terrel
is bleaching in Blanko Canyon.
Now he started this blood spill-
ing and I aim to finish it.

23   2 L.S. SIMMONS & CONNORS   2.9

IVES (OFF-SCREEN)
. . . his way.

They are looking at Ives, worried. They shift
their eyes to:

24   CHEST SHOT OF PECK (Repeat #7, ROMANTIC   23.1
       SHOT PAY-OFF)

PECK
You had me fooled for quite
awhile, Mr. Hennessey, with
your self-righteous talk. What is
the difference between his way
and your way? How many of
those men out there know what
this fight is really about? This is
not their war. This is nothing
but a personal feud between two
selfish, vicious old men.

25   2 SHOT WAIST SHOT OF IVES. PECK IN   4.1
       PROFILE (Repeat #4)

PECK (OFF-SCREEN—Cont'd)
. . . Henry Terrel and you.

CONNORS (OFF-SCREEN)
(TO IVES) You gonna stand . . .

26   3 L.S. PECK IN F.G., CONNORS AND SIMMONS   8.5
      IN B.G. (Repeat #5 MASTER & end position of
      #18)

                    CONNORS
            . . . here and take that.
            (TO PECK) I've had enough of . . .

BEAT _____ <5>

                    SIMMONS
            You're mistaken, Mr McKay. I
            came to visit for a few days.
            There is no need to worry.

27   C.S. OF SIMMONS & CONNORS (Same Camera   8.2
      Axis matching PECK's POV)

                    SIMMONS
            I suppose . . . (LEANS AGAINST
            CONNORS) I should've left word
            with somebody . . .

      CONNORS picks up on her and puts his arm
      around her.

28   CHEST SHOT OF PECK (Repeat #7)   4.4

      He is startled. He turns and looks harder at:

29   TIGHTER 2 L.S. OF SIMMONS & CONNORS   4.
      (Repeat #27)

                    SIMMONS
            I don't care what you think.

30   CHEST SHOT OF PECK (Repeat #7)   2.2
      He is uncertain.

31   3 SHOT. PECK IN F.G. & SIMMONS & CON-   5.2
      NORS IN B.G.

SIMMONS
(X's STEP TO PECK) I didn't ask
you to bother about me.

PECK
Julie, you've got to come with
me.

32   CHEST SHOT OF PECK (Repeat #7)   4.5

PECK
If you don't show yourself at the
entrance to the canyon a lot of
men are going to be killed.

33   SHOULDER SHOT OF SIMMONS   5.0
Her dilemma is acute. She finally looks down.

34   2 L.S. SIMMONS & CONNORS   7.6

SIMMONS
I can't help that. There's nothing I can do about it.

35   CHEST SHOT OF PECK (Repeat #7)   1.7

36   SHOULDER SHOT OF SIMMONS (Repeat #33)   4.8

SIMMONS
This trouble is not about me It's
. . . why don't you just go away.

37   CHEST SHOT OF PECK (Repeat #7)   2.1
He shifts his look at CONNORS.

38   2 L.S. OF SIMMONS & CONNORS (Repeat #34)   2.4
She looks petrified and CONNORS is alert and
menacing.

39   2 L.S. PECK & MEXICAN POV SIMMONS   5.5
PECK understands.

BEAT ——————————————————————————— <6>

He winds his reins around the saddlehorn and:

40   4 L.S. MASTER   14.2

He dismounts. CAMERA PANS dropping the
Mexican from the frame. CONNORS counter X's
frame left coming between SIMMONS and
PECK.

PECK
What is it you're afraid of?

SIMMONS
Nothing . . . Nothing . . . I'm not
afraid.

———————————

When Peck dismounts, it concludes the master scene cinema language section. Wyler begins a new section that we would label the "SHOOT-OUT,"
which is the duel between Connors and Peck.

Big Country

BEAT—SHOT SUMMARY

Shot	Shot Description and Business/Action	Time
BEAT ————— Setting the Stage —————		<1>
1	L.S. POV SIMMONS. Over of IVES, stand-ing on porch, in B.G. PECK comes riding up with RAMON alongside. MASTER CAMERA A.	4.7
2	2 L.S. SIMMONS followed by CONNORS. X's to F.G. CONNORS stands above her. MASTER CAMERA B.	1.8
3	2 M.L.S. REPEAT OF CAMERA A. PECK rides up to the porch, as IVES ends up frame left. This is a deep-focus shot.	4.2

4   2 SHOT OF PECK PROFILE OVER TO IVES ON   1.4
        PORCH

5   WAIST SHOT OF IVES   11.5

6   4 SHOT. PECK RIGHT FRAME IN F.G., IVES IN   18.6
        LEFT FRAME IN B.G. SIMMONS & CONNORS.
        MASTER CAMERA B.

BEAT _____ PECK declares his intention _____ <2>

7   CHEST SHOT OF PECK. POV IVES (MASTER A   4.2
        C.S. romantic shot plays throughout sequence)

8   CLOSE-UP OF IVES (MASTER CLOSE SHOT   7.3
        CAM C.)

9   CHEST SHOT OF PECK; POV IVES (Repeat #7)   6.3

10   2 SHOT PROFILE OF PECK TO THIGH SHOT   5.8
        IVES

11   WAIST SHOT OF IVES (Repeat #5)   8.3

BEAT _ Is he the legal owner of the Big Muddy? _ <3>

        IVES: N'you got any proof of that, boy?

12   2 M.L.S. OF IVES WITH PECK ON HORSE   8.4
        (Repeat SHOT #1 MASTER "A")

13   SHOULDER SHOT OF SIMMONS   3.

14   M.L.S. OF PECK WITH CONNORS   7.9
        (Repeat #1 MASTER "A")

15   M.S. OF IVES ON PORCH. BUCK X's UP TO HIM   8.4
        (MASTER CAMERA POSITION "B")

16   CHEST SHOT OF PECK (Repeat #7)   2.6

17   SHOULDER SHOT OF SIMMONS (Repeat #13)   1.9

| 18 | CHEST SHOT OF PECK (Repeat #7) | 2.1 |

| 19 | M.L.S. OF PECK ON HORSE OVER IVES. MAS-TER "A" POSITION. CONNORS X's, searches his coat and takes out paper. | 11.1 |

| 20 | MEDIUM SHOT OF IVES ON PORCH. CONNORS X's TO HIM CAMERA POSITION "B." | 29.0 |

| 21 | 4 SHOT RAMON IN F.G., PECK IN MID-GROUND, SIMMONS & CONNORS IN B.G. | 6.3 |

BEAT _____ Are you taking my proposition? _____ <4>

PECK: Now what about my promise? All the water you want. Just as long as you want it.

| 22 | SHOULDER SHOT OF IVES (MASTER CAMERA "C") | 19.6 |

| 23 | 2 L.S. SIMMONS & CONNORS (MASTER CAM-ERA "B") | 2.9 |

| 24 | CHEST SHOT OF PECK (Repeat #7) | 23.1 |

| 25 | 2 SHOT PROFILE OF PECK TO SHOT OF IVES (CAMERA POSITION "B," Repeat shot #4) | 4.1 |

| 26 | 3 SHOT PECK IN F.G. CONNORS & SIMMONS IN B.G. (Repeat #6 MASTER CAMERA "B") | 8.5 |

BEAT SIMMONS afraid PECK is going to be killed <5>

SIMMONS: You're mistaken, Mr McKay. I came to visit for a few days. There is no need to worry.

| 27 | CLOSE SHOT OF SIMMONS & CONNORS. (Same camera axis as POV PECK CAMERA "B.") | 8.2 |

| 28 | CHEST SHOT OF PECK (Repeat #7) | 4.4 |

29 TIGHTER 2 L.S. OF SIMMONS & CONNORS   4.
   (CAMERA "B")
   SIMMONS: I don't care what you think.

30 CHEST SHOT OF PECK (Repeat #7)   2.2

31 3 L.S. PECK IN F.G., SIMMONS & CONNORS   5.2
   IN B.G. (Repeat #6 MASTER CAMERA
   POSIT. "B").

32 CHEST SHOT OF PECK (Repeat #7)   4.5
   PECK: If you don't show yourself at the entrance to the canyon a lot of men are going to
   be killed.

33 SHOULDER SHOT OF SIMMONS   5.0

34 2 SHOT SIMMONS & CONNORS   7.6
   SIMMONS: I can't help that. There's nothing I
   can do about it.

35 CHEST SHOT OF PECK (Repeat #7)   1.7

36 SHOULDER SHOT OF SIMMONS (Repeat #31)   4.8

7 CHEST SHOT OF PECK (Repeat #6)   2.1
   He shifts his look at CONNORS.

38 2 L.S. OF SIMMONS & CONNORS (Repeat #31) 2.4

39 2 L.S. PECK & RAMON, NEW POSITION   5.5

BEAT __ PECK has to beat CONNORS to win her __ <6>
    release.

40 4 SHOT MASTER   14.2

   PECK dismounts. CAMERA PANS dropping the
   Mexican from the frame. CONNORS counter X's
   frame left coming between SIMMONS and
   PECK.
   PECK: What is it you're afraid of?

   SIMMONS: Nothing . . . Nothing . . . I'm not
   afraid.

The sequence runs approximately 4 minutes, 22 seconds. Wyler then begins a new sequence, resetting the camera positions for the new sequence.

Big Country Analysis   This sequence is classic in its master scene cinema language configuration. William Wyler follows past traditions and raises the level of excellence of the master scene language. When viewing his films, one senses his precise cinema language design, though at first viewing he appears to be an "invisible" director. His camera placement and staging support the emotional content of the scene (picturization).

Repeated shots are greeted like old friends, for they give the audience a feeling of knowing where they are and where the main characters are placed, thus permitting them to be absorbed into the content of the story rather than in superficialities. It also permits the audience to luxuriate in emotional involvement with the characters. This is especially true for Peck, whose image evokes an aura of romantic strength throughout the entire sequence. Audiences have no greater empathy for a character than when they witness a hero save his lover and fellow man from destruction.

The shots are simple and congruent, following the beat of the scene. The master camera position follows the traditional, basic, three-camera pattern (see Figure 10.2): A and C are the reverse positions, while the B camera covers all the action. This economical placement pattern is designed to be repeated throughout the sequence, making it efficient.

Shot #1 follows the traditional pattern by opening the sequence with an extreme long shot. This establishes the geography for the entire sequence. Shot #3 is simply the closer shot of #1 and is repeated throughout the sequence, weaving into the A-B-A pattern. Wyler's efficient camera place-

Figure 10.2   Big Country, *Camera Pattern Diagram. Diagram A.*

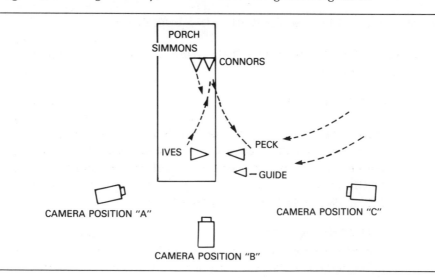

ment ensures good coverage and plenty of overlapping for matching the action into other shots. Considering that Wyler was at the zenith of his career, he could have elected to use many other camera positions, but he chose not to.

His control over the rhythm and pacing of the scene was exacting. (Bryan Forbes also exhibited this extraordinary ability to pace a scene, which can be seen in such films as *Deadfall*.) Jean Simmons is worried that Peck is going to get himself killed unless he leaves without her. She decides to try to convince him that she is in love with Connors. Her beat is re-enforced by the cuts as pauses are deliberately used in an interruptive rhythm. The result is that Simmons's motivation is readily apparent. This arrangement of shots, though the precise detail is worked out in the cutting room, is the earmark of master scene cinema language. But there are other cinema languages that preplan the cutting prior to shooting which brings up the next category.

• • • • • • • • • • • • • • • • • • •

INTERPERSONAL CINEMA LANGUAGE

Interpersonal cinema language (I-P), like master scene, is one of the most used cinema languages, but also most often abused, due to ignorance. Audiences love I-P because it gives them the opportunity to participate vicariously in a relationship without personal intimacy or personal risk. It creates a hypnotic bond between subject and viewer. Ostensibly, it places the viewer into the relationship that exists at that moment and in fact coerces the viewer's participation and empathy.

The methodology is pedestrian. It requires single shots of each subject. By arranging those shots into a particular pattern, the viewer gains insight into the feelings of the participants, as well as the experience and knowledge of the shifting relationships between the parties. What in fact happens is that the viewer is placed in the position of the offscreen character. He receives the onscreen character's persona, which gives him the chance to experience the relationship firsthand. This procedure forces identification and personalization.

The pattern of shots is dictated by the content, usually the beat of the script. The sequence selected to illustrate I-P is from Hitchcock's *Vertigo*, a remarkable tour de force of I-P cinema language. It is a 6-minute expository scene, and it uses I-P exclusively, which is unusual and daring for an "action" movie. Nevertheless, Hitchcock pulls it off. (Incidentally, the *Big Country* master scene sequence cited also includes some I-P as well which were close-ups between Ives and Peck.) The I-P camera pattern configuration is as follows:

1. *Point of view.* The participants are established, usually by a wide shot that shows the location and/or set, the placement of the subjects, and their

Figure 10.3   Vertigo. *This was the last shot just before I-P cinema language begins.* (Copyright © by Universal Pictures, a Division of Universal City Studios, Inc. Courtesy of MCA Publishing Rights, a Division of MCA, Inc.)

physical relationship to each other. This is an objective shot. Then it shifts to single shots of the participants. Camera placement is dictated by the emphasis wanted. The shots are varied but with no regard for point of view. Emphasis dictates when to simulate the offscreen point of view. Examine shots 15, 35, 37, and 43 in *Vertigo* and you will realize that Hitchcook never simulated POV. Some beginning directors slavishly follow "point of view" camera placements and seriously limit their creative use of I-P.

2. *Size of the subject.* This is dictated by the emphasis needed. Emphasis is determined by the emotional and story content. In *Vertigo* Barbara Bel Geddes's "unspoken" love is made clear visually in shots 25, 36, and 38. Hitchcock dramatically changes the size of the subject, giving us insight into the moment of the changing relationship.

3. *The five-degree rule.* Five degrees off the sightline of the participants in the close shots is the strongest camera position. It also is referred to as an "internal" camera setup. The camera has taken the audience inside the proscenium, adding to the feeling of intimacy with the onscreen character.

When content dictates the need for emphasis, then the five-degree camera placement should be used. This type of close shot is the payoff of the beat.

4. *Repetition.* Repetition of the same shot establishes relationships and emphasizes the emotional shift in the scene. The shots are usually repeated in groups of threes. This repetition builds the intimate emotional relationship and encourages the viewer's participation. *Vertigo*'s analysis illustrates this.

5. *Time.* I-P cinema language, like master scene, requires that all the events happen onscreen and appear to be happening at the moment and in "real" time. Violation places this cinema language in jeopardy. In *Vertigo* all the events occur on camera except for one minor jump in shot #32. But this becomes evident only after the viewer has seen the sequence several times. The sequence appears to be happening in "real" time and from moment to moment.

6. *Pacing, tempo, and rhythm.* Pacing, tempo, and rhythm is dictated by the beat of the scene and is most easily controlled in I-P. Hitchcock turns a deadly 6-minute expository scene into a fascinating scene of a personal relationship.

Case Study: *Vertigo*

The film begins with James Stewart chasing a criminal across the rooftops. He jumps, miscalculates, and ends up hanging on to the gutter, his feet dangling over a drop of several stories (see Figure 10.3). A policeman comes back to help him. Stewart, frozen, is unable to grab the proffered hand. The policeman leans over too far and goes hurtling down. The last shot is of Stewart's face, full of fear, as he desperately holds on.

The following sequence is taken from the edited film. For explanation of abbreviations and terms in the shot descriptions, see the case study of *Big Country*.

Vertigo

INTERPERSONAL CINEMA LANGUAGE

Shot	Description	Time

FADE IN:

1   INT. MIDGE'S APARTMENT IN SAN FRAN-   4.2
      CISCO . . . DAY

      ESTABLISHING SHOT. This is the apartment of
      an artist who works at home. MIDGE (BAR-
      BARA BEL GEDDES) is busy drawing at her
      easel, while seated in an easy chair is JOHN
      FERGUSON (JAMES STEWART), balancing a
      cane on his finger. He loses its balance:

2   MEDIUM LONG SHOT OF STEWART.   7.7

      He stretches out and catches it and winces:

                    STEWART
            Ouch! . . . Ouch.

               BEL GEDDES (OFF-SCREEN)
            I thought you said no more aches
            and pains.

                    STEWART
            It's 'cause of this darn corset. It
            binds.

3   MEDIUM LONG SHOT OF MIDGE AT EASEL   3.8

      She's drawing.

                    BEL GEDDES
            No three-way stretch—how very
            unchic.

4   INSERT OF MIDGE'S DRAWING OF A   2
      WOMAN'S BRA

                    STEWART (OFF-SCREEN)
            Y'know those police department
            doctors . . .

5   REPEAT OF SHOT #3   2.7

STEWART (OFF-SCREEN)
. . . have no sense of style.

6   REPEAT OF SHOT #2   3.3

STEWART
Well, anyway, tomorrow will be
the day.

7   REPEAT OF SHOT #3   1.5

BEL GEDDES
Why, what's tomorrow?

8   REPEAT OF SHOT #2   14.7

STEWART
Tomorrow? The corset comes off
tomorrow. I can scratch myself
like anybody else tomorrow.
(HOLDS UP CANE) And this mis-
erable thing, throw it out the
window. I'll be a free . . . man.
Midge, do you suppose many men
wear corsets?

9   REPEAT OF SHOT #3   2.4

BEL GEDDES
More than you think.

10   REPEAT OF SHOT #2   3

STEWART
Really, do you know that from
personal experience?

11   REPEAT OF SHOT #3   9.7

BEL GEDDES
Please.

BEAT _____ <2>

BEL GEDDES (CONT'D)
What happens after tomorrow?

STEWART (OFF-SCREEN)
What do you mean?

BEL GEDDES
Well, what are you going to do
once you've quit the police force?

12   REPEAT OF SHOT #2   4.4

STEWART
You sound disapproving, Midge.

BEL GEDDES (OFF-SCREEN)
No, it's your life . . .

13   REPEAT OF SHOT #3   2.4

BEL GEDDES
You were the bright young
lawyer that decided . . .

14   CHEST SHOT OF STEWART (NEW SHOT!)   3.7

BEL GEDDES (OFF-SCREEN)
. . . you were going to be the chief
of police someday.

STEWART
I had to quit.

15   CHEST SHOT OF BEL GEDDES (NEW SHOT!)   1.7
      ¾ HIGH ANGLE

BEL GEDDES
Why?

16   REPEAT OF SHOT #14   9.1

          STEWART
Because of this fear of heights. I
have this acrophobia. I wake up
nights and see that man fall
from the roof and I try to reach
out to him . . . I just . . .

17   REPEAT OF SHOT #15   1.6

          BEL GEDDES
It wasn't your fault.

18   MEDIUM LONG SHOT OF STEWART (NEW   15.8
    SHOT!) X's AWAY FROM CAMERA

          STEWART
I know that's what everybody
tells me.

BEL GEDDES (OFF-SCREEN)
John, the doctors explained
everything to you . . .

          STEWART
(X's) I know . . . I know I have
acrophobia which gives me vertigo and I get dizzy. Boy, what a
moment to find out I had it.

BEL GEDDES (OFF-SCREEN)
Well, you've got it and there's no
losing it.

19   MEDIUM SHOT OF BEL GEDDES (NEW SHOT!)   2.4

          BEL GEDDES
And there's no one to blame, so
why quit?

20   L.S. OF STEWART (NEW SHOT!)   16
    (Note: CAMERA was shifted right to her POV)

STEWART
You mean sit behind a desk.
Chairborne.

BEL GEDDES (OFF-SCREEN)
Where you belong.

STEWART
What about my acrophobia? Suppose I (SITS DOWN) am sitting in
this chair. And a pencil falls
from the desk . . . Here's (IN-
DICATES WITH CANE) the desk.
And I reach down to pick up the
pencil and bingo—my acro-
phobia is back.

21   REPEAT OF SHOT #19   5.2

BEL GEDDES
(LAUGHING) Oh, Johnny . . .

BEAT _____ <3>

BEL GEDDES (CONT'D)
Well, what do you do . . .

22   L.S. OF STEWART (SAME CAMERA SETUP   8.5
      #20)

STEWART
(RISING X's) Well, I'm not going
to do anything for a while. Don't
forget I'm a man of independent
means, as the saying goes. Fairly
independent . . .

23   REPEAT OF SHOT #19   3.4

BEL GEDDES
Well, then why don't you go
away for a while?

24   REPEAT OF SHOT #22   2.7

STEWART
You mean to forget . . .

25   CLOSE-UP OF BEL GEDDES (NEW SHOT!)   2
          STEWART (OFF-SCREEN)
Oh, Midge, don't be so motherly.

26   REPEAT OF SHOT #22   2.1

STEWART
I'm not going to crack up.

27   REPEAT OF SHOT #19   1.1

BEL GEDDES
Have you had any dizzy spells . . .

28   REPEAT OF SHOT #22   3.1

STEWART
(STEPPING DOWN) Yes, I'm having one right now.

29   REPEAT OF SHOT #19   0.9
Reaction of concern

30   REPEAT OF SHOT #22   3.1

STEWART
Midge, the music! Don't you . . .
its sort of . . .

31   M.S. OF BEL GEDDES. SLIGHTLY BEHIND THE   43
EASEL (NEW SHOT!)

She X's to background while he enters the
picture.

BEAT _____ <4>

He is looking at a brassiere hung on a pedestal above her
easel.

STEWART
What's this do-hickey?

> BEL GEDDES
> It's a brassiere. You know about
> those things. You're a big boy
> now.

> STEWART
> I've never run across one like
> that.

CAMERA MOVES INTO TIGHTER 2-SHOT IN-
CLUDING the brassiere.

> BEL GEDDES
> It's brand new. Revolutionary
> up lift. No shoulder straps. No
> back straps. But does everything
> a brassiere is suppose to do. It
> works on the principal of a can-
> tilever bridge.

> STEWART
> It does.

> BEL GEDDES
> Uh-huh. An aircraft engineer
> down the peninsula designed it.
> He worked it out in his spare
> time.

> STEWART
> Kind of a hobby . . . A do it
> yourself type of thing.

HE X's away into a SINGLE SHOT at 39.4 in
scene.

_____ BEGIN INTERPERSONAL CINEMA LANGUAGE _____

> STEWART
> How's your love life, Midge?

32   MEDIUM SHOT OF BEL GEDDES (NEW SHOT!)   2.8

(She has been repositioned to in front of her

easel chair, a minor violation of the "real"
time I-P.)

                    BEL GEDDES
               (SHE SITS)
               That's following a train of
               thought.

33   MEDIUM LONG SHOT OF STEWART   2.4

                    STEWART
               (SITTING LEANING ON SOFA)
               Well?

34   REPEAT OF SHOT #32   7.2

                    BEL GEDDES
               Normal.

               STEWART (OFF-SCREEN)
               Aren't you going to ever get
               married?

                    BEL GEDDES
               There's only one man in the
               world for me, Johnny-O.

35   MEDIUM PROFILE SHOT OF STEWART (NEW   2.8
      SHOT!)

                    STEWART
               You mean me. We were engaged
               once though.

36   CLOSE-UP OF BEL GEDDES (NEW SHOT!)   3.4
      (Note: This shot reads as I-P continued but it is
      really a break from its pattern. Hitchcock gives
      us an insight. We learn from this shot and the
      way it's cut in that Midge is still secretly in
      love with Johnny. This reinforced by repeat-
      ing this shot.)

                    STEWART (OFF-SCREEN)
            . . . weren't we?

                    BEL GEDDES
            Three whole weeks.

37   REPEAT OF THE SHOT #35   5.1

                    STEWART
            Yeah, good old college days.
            But you were the one that called
            off the engagement.

38   REPEAT OF SHOT #36   3.3

                    STEWART (OFF-SCREEN)
            Remember? I'm still available.

39   REPEAT OF SHOT #35   6.1

                    STEWART
            Available Ferguson.

BEAT _____ <4>

                    STEWART (CONT'D)
            Oh, Midge, do you remember a
            fellow in college by the name of
            Gavin Elster?

40   M. LOW ANGLE TO BEL GEDDES (NEW SHOT!)   4.9

                    BEL GEDDES
            Gavin Elster?

                    STEWART (OFF-SCREEN)
            Yes, funny name.

                    BEL GEDDES
            You think I would. No.

41   REPEAT OF SHOT #35   6

> STEWART
> I got a call from Gavin today.
> Funny, he sort of dropped out of
> sight during the war. Somebody
> said . . .

42   REPEAT OF SHOT #40

> STEWART (OFF-SCREEN)
> . . . he went east. I guess he's
> back.

43   M.S. OF STEWART (NEW SHOT!) HI ANGLE   2.1
Leaning forward scrambling for a piece of
paper in his pocket.

> STEWART
> It's a mission number.

44   REPEAT OF SHOT #40   1.6

> BEL GEDDES
> Well, it's skid-row, isn't it.

45   REPEAT OF SHOT #43   11.4

> STEWART
> Yup, could be.

> BEL GEDDES (OFF-SCREEN)
> He's probably on the bum and
> wants to touch you for the price
> of a drink.

> STEWART
> Well, I'm on the bum. I'll buy
> him a couple of drinks and tell
> him my troubles. But not to-
> night. How about you and me go-
> ing out for a beer?

46   REPEAT OF SHOT #40   3.2

> BEL GEDDES
> Sorry old man, work.

47   MED L.S. OF STEWART (NEW SHOT!)   1.02

                 STEWART
          (GETS UP FROM SOFA)
          Well, then, I think I'll go home.

     He X's to the door and the CAMERA PANS IN-
     TO 2 LONG SHOT

BEAT _____ <5>

____ END INTERPERSONAL CINEMA LANGUAGE ____

                 STEWART
          Midge, what do you mean there's
          no losing it.

                 BEL GEDDES
          What?

                 STEWART
          The . . . the acrophobia . . .

                 BEL GEDDES
          I asked my doctor. He said only
          another emotional shock could
          do it and probably wouldn't.
          You're not going to be diving off
          another roof top to find out.

                 STEWART
          I think I can lick it.

                 BEL GEDDES
          Well, how?

                 STEWART
          I have a theory. I have a theory.
          I think if I could get use to
          height. Just a little bit at a time
          . . . just a little. (RAISES CANE)

                    STEWART (CONT'D)
            like that . . . progressively. Here,
            I'll show you what I mean.

He goes to the stool.

                    STEWART
            Here. (PICKS UP STOOL.) Here
            you start with this.

                    BEL GEDDES
            That?

                    STEWART
            What do you want me to start
            with, the Golden State Bridge.
            Now watch. STANDS UP ON
            STOOL) Watch this. There . . .
            there, I look up. I look down. I
            look up. I look down—there's
            nothing to it. There's nothing to
            it.

                    BEL GEDDES
            You're kidding. Wait a minute.

She X's off to:

48   LONG SHOT OF KITCHEN AREA. (NEW SHOT!)   13.3

She enters picks up a kitchen step-stool. She
X's back to him, into a 2 LONG SHOT.

                    BEL GEDDES
            Here.

                    STEWART
            That's a good girl. We'll use that.
            Put it right there.

She places it in position. He takes the first
step.

STEWART
Alright there's the first step.
There.

_____ BEGIN INTERPERSONAL AGAIN _____

49   MED. SHOT OF BEL GEDDES (NEW SHOT!)   2.9

She watches him with loving care.

BEL GEDDES
O.K. Now step number 2.

50   SHOULDER SHOT OF STEWART (NEW SHOT!)   2.2

STEWART
Alright, step number two coming
up.

51   CLOSE FOOT MOVING TO THE SECOND STEP   1.6
       (NEW SHOT!)

52   SAME AS SHOT #50   9.4

STEWART
(FINISHING STEPPING UP)
Now there we are. I look up . . .
look down . . . I look—I'm going
out and buy myself a nice tall
stepladder.

53   SAME AS SHOT #49   1.5

BEL GEDDES
Now, take it easy now.

54   SAME AS SHOT #50   1.6

STEWART
Alright, here we go.

55   SAME AS SHOT #51   5.5
       He's stepping up to the top.

STEWART (OFF-SCREEN)
No problem.

56 CLOSE-UP OF STEWART (NEW SHOT!) LOW   3.5
ANGLE. He steps up into the frame at the top
of the ladder.

STEWART
Well, it's a cinch. Here.

57 SAME AS SHOT #49   2.4
Watching him.

STEWART (OFF-SCREEN)
I look up . . . I look down.

58 MEDIUM CLOSE-UP OF STEWART (NEW SHOT!)   2.8
LOW ANGLE.

STEWART
I look up . . . I look down.

He looks down and sees:

59 EXT.: LONG SHOT OF STREET BELOW HI   2.7
ANGLE

NEW SHOT BUT HAD BEEN SEEN EARLIER
WHEN HE WAS DANGLING FROM THE ROOF.

60 SAME AS SHOT #58   2.9
PANIC has set in. He is beginning to pass out.

61 SAME AS SHOT #49   1.3

She isn't reacting with the elevated concern
the situation seems to warrant.

62 M.C.U. PROFILE OF STEWART. (NEW SHOT!)   5.3

Collapsing and falling.

__ END OF INTERPERSONAL CINEMA LANGUAGE __

CAMERA PANS STEWART FALLS INTO   1.4
THE ARMS OF MIDGE.

BEL GEDDES
Oh, Johnny, Johnny . . .

His experiment ends in dismal failure as he desperately
holds onto her.

FADE OUT

_____

SUMMARY

Vertigo

Shot	Shot Description & Business/Action	Time
*1	INT: MIDGE'S APARTMENT IN SAN FRAN-CISCO. DAY LONG SHOT OF JAMES STEWART & BARBARA BEL GEDDES	4.2
*2	MEDIUM LONG SHOT OF STEWART in easy chair with cane. He plays with his cane, groans and complains about his strap he is wearing.	7.7
*3	M.L.S. of BEL GEDDES at drawing board . . . dialogue "Unsheik"	3.8
*4	INSERT OF DRAWING OF BRA. POV BARBARA (NEW SHOT!)	2
5	SAME AS #3 (Note: no jump in action. It matches exactly as was seen in the previous shot.)	2.7
6	SAME AS #2 No jump in action, matches exactly as was seen in the previous shot.	3.3
7	SAME AS #3	1.5
8	SAME AS #2—Lines "Throw away the cane and get out of corset."	14.7
9	SAME AS #3 "More than you think."	2.4

10	SAME AS #2	3
11	SAME AS #3 "Quit the police force" <u>BEAT</u>	9.7
12	SAME AS #2	4.4
13	SAME AS #3 "Chief of Police"	2.4
*14	CHEST SHOT OF STEWART (NEW SHOT!) "I had to quit."	3.7
*15	MEDIUM CHEST SHOT OF BEL GEDDES ¾ HI ANGLE (NEW SHOT!) "Why?" Concern playing in her look.	1.7
16	SAME AS #14. "Dream to reach out."	9.1
17	SAME AS #15. "It wasn't your fault."	1.6
*18	MED. L.S. STEWART (NEW SHOT!) X's AWAY FROM CAMERA, LEANS ON CANE "Acrophobia . . ." Lines.	15.8
*19	MED. SHOT OF BEL GEDDES (NEW SHOT!) "No blame . . . Why quit?"	2.4
*20	L.S. STEWART (NEW SHOT!) (CAMERA WAS SHIFTED TO RIGHT POV OF BEL GEDDES.) He sits and describes desk work, making a joke.	16
21	M.S. BEL GEDDES SAME AS #19	5.2
22	L.S. STEWART X's UP "Independent means" SAME CAMERA SET-UP #20	8.5
23	M.S. BEL GEDDES SAME AS #19	3.4
24	L.S. STEWART SAME AS #22 SAME CAMERA SET-UP #20 "means to forget . . ."	2.7
*25	CLOSE-UP BEL GEDDES (NEW SHOT!) ". . . motherly" off-screen shows concern . . .	2

26   SAME AS #22. He X's a step . . . reaction.   2.1

27   M.S. BEL GEDDES SAME AS #19. "Any dizzy   1.1
       spells?"

28   MED. L.S. STEWART X's DOWN SAME AS #22   3.1
       "Having one right now."

29   MED BEL GEDDES SAME AS #19 Reaction.   .9
       Look up.

30   SAME AS #22 Line "It's the music."   3.1

BEAT CONCLUDES INTERPERSONAL CINEMA _____
       LANGUAGE

*31   MEDIUM CLOSE SHOT OF BEL GEDDES. S.L.   39
       BEHIND HER. (NEW SHOT!) She X's to the
       background turns off the music while
       STEWART X's into the frame becoming a 2
       shot. Dialogue about this new bra

____ BEGIN INTERPERSONAL CINEMA LANGUAGE ____

BEAT: Stewart X's. CAMERA PANS HIM INTO   44
       SINGLE SHOT. He asks: "How's your love life?"

32   MEDIUM SHOT OF BEL GEDDES SITTING   2.8
       DOWN AT HER STOOL (NEW SHOT!) (Note:
       Unusual to have a jump of action. BEL GEDDES
       sitting down. Actually she was on other side of
       her easel. It is not noticeable but usually not
       done in interpersonal cinema language.

33   SAME & CONTINUED #31 STEWART SITS ON   2.4
       SOFA. "Well . . . er. . ."

34   SAME AS #32 "One man for me, Johnny-O"   7.2

*35   MED. SHOT OF STEWART. PROFILE SHOT   2.8
       (NEW SHOT!) Reclining on sofa. "We were
       engaged . . . you broke it off"

*36   CLOSE-UP BEL GEDDES (NEW SHOT!) HI   3.4
      ANGLE. She looks up. There's love in her eyes.
      "Three whole weeks"

37   SAME AS #35 STEWART: "You called it off."   5.1

38   SAME AS #36 He says he is still available.   3.3
      She looks up over glasses—love in her eyes.

39   SAME AS #35 "Remember Gavin Woods?"   6.1

*40   MED. LOW ANGLE ACROSS EASEL TO BEL   4.9
      GEDDES (NEW SHOT!) Response. "No, I would
      remember such a name."

41   SAME AS #35 History of Gavin.   6

42   SAME AS #40 She is listening as she continues 2.1
      to work on the drawing.

*43   MED. SHOT OF STEWART. HI ANGLE.   2.1
      (NEW SHOT!) He leans up from sofa into a
      closer shot

44   SAME AS #40 BEL GEDDES listening.   1.6

45   SAME AS #43 "Go out for a beer."   11.4

46   SAME AS #40 "Sorry . . . work."   3.2

*47   MED. L.S. OF STEWART (NEW SHOT!) Gets up   1.02
      from sofa. X's to door into 2 SHOT

BEAT: END OF INTERPERSONAL CINEMA LANGUAGE

Then he says he has theory how he can lick his acrophobia
. . . then X's near window and climbs on the stool to
demonstrate. CAMERA STILL holding it all in a 2 SHOT.

*48   MED. L.S. BEL GEDDES. (NEW SHOT!) X's to   13.3
      Kitchen area gets stepladder and X's back into
      2 SHOT. He takes step:

___ BEGIN OF INTERPERSONAL CINEMA LANGUAGE ___

*49   MED. SHOT OF BEL GEDDES (NEW SHOT!)   2.9
       Watching STEWART climb up first step of
       stool.

*50   SHOULDER SHOT STEWART. LOW ANGLE   2.2
       (NEW SHOT!) Gives impression POV BEL
       GEDDES.

*51   CLOSE SHOT OF STEWART'S FOOT STEP UP   1.6
       LADDER. (NEW SHOT!)

 52   SAME AS #50 He continues taking that step.   9.4

 53   SAME AS #49 Line "Take it easy . . ."   1.5

 54   SAME AS #50 pick-up from #52 continuing   1.6
       the action moment to moment.

 55   CLOSE SHOT OF LADDER SAME AS #51.   5.5
       Stepping up to final level of the ladder.

*56   CLOSE-UP OF STEWART. (NEW SHOT!) LOW   3.5
       ANGLE. Steps up into the frame. "Cinch."

 57   SAME AS #49 Watching him very closely.   2.4

 58   M.C.U. OF STEWART. (NEW SHOT!)   2.8
       ¾ FRONTAL SHOT LOW ANGLE. He looks down
       and sees:

 59   EXT.: LONG SHOT OF STREET BELOW HI   2.7
       ANGLE

NEW SHOT BUT HAD BEEN SEEN EARLIER WHEN HE WAS
DANGLING FROM THE ROOF.

 60   SAME AS #58 Panic and begins to pass out.   2.9

 61   SAME AS #49 BEL GEDDES watching
       concerned.   1.3

*62   M.C.U. PROFILE OF STEWART. (NEW SHOT!)   1.4
       Collapsing falling down . . .

____ CONCLUSION OF INTERPERSONAL CINEMA ____
       LANGUAGE

_____

*new shot

... into the arms of Bel Geddes resulting in a 2 shot. 5.6
His experiment has ended in dismal failure.

_____ END OF SEQUENCE _____

***Vertigo* Analysis**   There are three interpersonal cinema language sections in this sequence. These sections are divided by scenes #31 and #47 and scene #62.

The first shot establishes that the apartment is hers and suggests her occupation. The fourth shot confirms her occupation, and prepares for the brief but amusing discussion (though dated) in shot #31, which concludes the first I-P section.

All the shots in the sequence are single shots, with the exceptions of #1 and #31, which follow a similar design pattern. The final shot #62 concludes the sequence with a powerful visual statement about Stewart's emotional state. The I-P section signals its beginning and ending with a two-shot. This is the standard I-P configuration. This section begins with shot #2 and continues through #13 (#5 and #3 are the same shot split by insert #4), forcing the viewer to play the off-screen character.

Shots #2 through #13 are loose shots and are the most repeated two-shot in the sequence. After shot #13, the audience expects repetition but is surprised by the new shot, #14, which gives it emphasis. This is followed by another new shot, #15, then #16 repeats #14, while #17 repeats #15, which completes the new cycle and the purpose of the entire beat. New shot #18 gives us insight into his phobia, and #19 asks the question we would ask. Shot #20 is a new shot, and is closer to the 5-degree camera placement representing Barbara's POV, and #21 completes the cycle by repeating #19 and starts a new beat. The pattern of repeating shots has been altered to a three-count cycle.

The pattern is consistent from here on. The introduction of a new shot gives emphasis to the beat and is either followed by another new shot or by a repeat of a shot from the previous cycle. Shots #14 and #15 are new shots, which are repeated by shots #16 and #17. The cycle repeats over again, with shots #18 and #19 setting up the pattern for #20, and #19 establishing a repetition pattern for groups of twos. This pattern reinforces the nonverbalized relationship between them which was established by the similar shot configuration of shots #3 through #13. In addition, the audience has been unconsciously prepared to share a private insight into Barbara's feelings through shot #25. Shots #26 to #30 are repeats.

The size of the subject is dictated by the emphasis needed to make the point of the beat. In the opening sequence beat 1 is limited to medium and medium-long shots. The ambience of the environment and the characters' relationship is established.

Using incisive and memorable close-ups, which have a strong recall for the viewer, is characteristic of this type of cinema language. (This is also found in the master scene cinema language.) These memorable close-ups are achieved through appropriateness of content and by contrast to surrounding shots.

The characters' warm relationship is apparent, but her deep affection is emphasized by close-ups #25 and #36 and #38. Though close-up #25 is repeated only once, with his offscreen voice saying, "Oh, Midge don't be so motherly . . ." reveals her concern for him and has some story foreshadowing.

In scene #36 she reacts to Stewart's comment about their brief engagement, which reveals to us how she still is in love with him. (Collision cinema language using dialogue as its counterpoint.) In the case of shots #36 and #38, her feelings are shared only by us, and we know she has been in love with him since college. The contrast between the close-up and the medium profile shot (#35 and #37) gives it its additional emphasis.

Shot #47 begins with a single shot of Stewart when he crosses to the exterior door, the camera pans into a two-shot, which concludes the second section of the I-P cinema language. Shots #31 and #47 are similarly designed, and each begins a new beat while setting up the overall pattern for each section. Shot #62 follows the same pattern, except it concludes the sequence. It is more like a poignant coda with Stewart desperately holding onto her for help.

Scene #31 is the first break in the I-P cinema language. When Stewart crosses away, the camera pans him into a single shot (still part of scene #31), which begins the second section of the I-P cinema language. Though it is the second-longest running scene in the sequence, it follows the pattern of the other two transition shots that break the I-P pattern.

Note that the choice of a frontal view in every shot is not necessary. Shots #15, #20, and #25 are clearly not POV shots, but the audience perceives them as such. The rule is that the audience will accept almost any single shot as long as the onscreen character addresses the other character as if they were offscreen.

Distance between the two subjects has little influence upon the size of the subjects. For instance, the exchange of an intimate look between principals dozens of yards apart has audience acceptance as well. The emotional content of the scene overrides practical objections.

Hitchcock repeats shots two and three times, but he only changes the size of the image when emphasis is needed. For instance, shots #14 and #16 are used for essential plot information, and shot #25 foreshadows the character's mental breakdown, giving us insight into the character's feelings (it is also used for a change of beat).

I-P is one of the more powerful cinema language techniques; it is exclusive to film. It should be used and reused as often as necessary; as long as the rules are not compromised, it is rare that this technique can be overused.

Chapter 11

CONTRASTING
CINEMA LANGUAGES

Constructive and fragmented cinema languages are seemingly very different forms of cinema language which share many similar characteristics. Each is used to create a specific, albeit opposing, mood. Each leaves the viewer out of the action. Each requires a great deal of advance planning and consideration. Fragmented cinema language is in many ways a version of constructive cinema language.

Constructive cinema language is highly ordered and methodical. Its tempo and organization result in dynamic, fast-moving shots. Fragmented cinema language seems, on the other hand, to be random and disjointed. Its strength, although not its only use, is to provide emotional electricity in a scene.

CONSTRUCTIVE CINEMA LANGUAGE

Constructive cinema language is a series of planned shots designed to be placed in a particular order with a specific time given to each shot. Every shot is planned in its placement scheme by its movement, composition, and picturization, anticipating its screen time and its tempo rhythm of the cutting. Detailed floorplans, exact camera placement, and staging patterns, with all the details necessary to execute this plan, are worked out prior to shooting.

• • • • • • • • • • • • • • • • • •

ADVANTAGES

Dynamic Sequences

Each shot is precisely planned into a pattern that is strong in composition, stressed with picturization, and results in a series of dynamic shots.

Climactic Sequence

The constructive cinema language discipline lends itself to a structure that builds to a climax. It accommodates the integration of other cinema language disciplines as well. Fragmented and Vorkapich use constructive cinema language as a tool. This is not obligatory since constructive may be used for neutral content as well as for the purposes of orchestration.

An Economical Approach

There are few if any wasted shots. Hence this approach is economical, and it is certainly more efficient than master scene cinema language. When multiple cameras are used, then this rule may be modified.

Continuity

There is a liberal disregard for "matching" picture and sound. Depending upon the story's need, the violation of "time" is accepted by the audience since this language sets its own precedent. In this cinema language, time violation is acceptable, but the filmmaker should avoid confusing the audience for a length of time, to keep the audience from becoming irritated and losing empathy.

Sync Sound

Sound is impressionistic. Sync sound is not necessary. If sync dialogue is required, then it is acceptable through dialogue or through a voiceover.

Rhythm and Tempo

Rhythms and tempos are part of the design and are manipulated in strong rhythmic groupings. Music videos explore and exploit this area.

Repeated Shots

Shots appear not to repeat, but the viewer senses a natural progression of the action. Without consciously being aware of it, the viewer is oriented by shots that are congruent and are progressive. Congruent shots work from the same placement and logically follow the action of the sequence, though the viewer thinks there are no repeat shots. In all probability, the shots are from the same camera position but using different lenses. This repetition keeps the audience involved and challenged but without the security of master scene cinema language.

• • • • • • • • • • • • • • • • • • •
DISADVANTAGES

The disadvantages are quite dramatic. If an error is made, it is difficult to correct without some major financial costs. Consequently, some common sense in this usage is needed. Careful planning is the key to success.

Action

Constructive cinema language may make the action appear to be jumpy, jerky, or unreal. This staging of the action and the manipulation of time and space in this language require capsulizing reality as opposed to documenting it.

Mistakes

In the elevator sequence of Brian DePalma's *Dressed to Kill,* Nancy Allen sees Angie Dickinson stretching a bloodied hand for help, while, in the elevator's corner mirror, she spies the killer (Michael Caine) moving a straight-edge razor down toward her outstretched hand; simultaneously, the automatic elevator door closes, knocking the razor to the floor.

Every shot was planned and executed without attempting to simulate "real" time. The tempo was slow, bordering on laborious, though the humor of the chambermaid's shrieking an indictment of the innocent Nancy Allen was not lost on the Hitchcock aficionados. Here DePalma stretches time to its limits, making it border on being incredible.

Meticulous Planning

Meticulous planning is necessary for this language to work. In the case of "time," did DePalma make an error? Did his planning fail? In fact, DePalma's films are all in the construction language as are Hitchcock's. Rarely does DePalma shoot in master scene cinema language.

• • • • • • • • • • • • • • • • • • •
HOW TO PLAN

Planning the use of constructive cinema language requires breaking the sequence into sections. Each section has an action, or subject (plot point), that ties it to the next section and an overall scheme of the sequence. Each section contains transitional and repetitive shots. In the final section, all the repetitive shots help to build to the payoff climax of the sequence.

Case Study: Eisenstein's *Potemkin*

The mother and baby Odessa steps sequence is classic in constructive language and runs 1 minute and 15 seconds. The 55 shots break into three constructed sections, with the concluding sequence and the final payoff shot of a woman bloodied. The observing student sets up our point of view as we witness the payoff shot.

The sequence starts with the introduction of the mother and baby:

- Section 1
  - ☐ soldiers
  - ☐ mother
  - ☐ baby carriage and baby
- Section 2
  - ☐ baby carriage and baby
  - ☐ soldiers
  - ☐ mother's death
  - ☐ crowd on the steps
- Section 3
  - ☐ the watchers
  - ☐ woman with pince nez
  - ☐ baby and baby carriage
  - ☐ the soldiers

By design the shots repeat in different patterns in each section and also act as transitional shots connecting the sections. They are:

- steps
- attacking soldiers, running people, and people wounded or dead
- mother with baby in carriage
- student — spectator
- woman with pince nez whose violent death concludes sequence

The cinema languages Eisenstein invoked were interpersonal (Chapter 10), parallel (Chapter 12), and collision (Chapter 12) (see Figures 11.1 and 11.2).

Case Study: Hitchcock's *The Birds*

Hitchcock is one of the best practitioners of constructive cinema language. In *The Birds* a sequence begins with the mother arriving at her neighbor's farm. The sequence is bracketed with (1) long shots of the truck driving down the road, coming and going from the farm, and (2) a repeated shot pattern that makes excellent use of Vorkapich cinema language (discussed later in this chapter).

Hitchcock's Vorkapich builds suspense because he sets up the pattern of the mother's arrival, entry into the farmer's house, and finally her discovery of the dead man. She leaves the house in the same way she had come, except Hitchcock constructed the shots for her departure in such a way as to add to the nightmare and to the suspense. When she enters the house, she walks down the hallway to the room. The angle and lighting of

Figure 11.1 *Constructive Cinema Language.* Potemkin's *baby carriage as it rolls down the steps at the conclusion of the Odessa steps sequence.* (Courtesy of Janus Films.)

the hallway were designed to seem like a "dream" of running down a long hallway with great depth. We expect her rapid departure, but the hallway shot had been designed to add to the horror of the experience, and she runs down that hallway past us, reminding us of horror dreams.

Logically, invoking Vorkapich, we should have expected a shot of the living room, since when the mother first entered the house we saw the living room. But Hitchcock knew that her running out of the living room was not going to heighten the suspense, so he elected to jump that. Her running out would have been logical but boring.

Interestingly enough, the purpose of the living room was to build suspense. When she entered the house, going directly into the living room, she went for the hallway, but as she arrived at the doorway, she sees a series of broken cups held by hooks on the hutch. The smashed cups remind us of the previous evening when the mother and her family had been attacked by the birds and her favorite cups had been smashed.

Figure 11.2 POTEMKIN, *Construction Cinema Language. This mother carries her dead child up the step to the soldier during the Odessa steps sequence.* (Courtesy of Janus Films.)

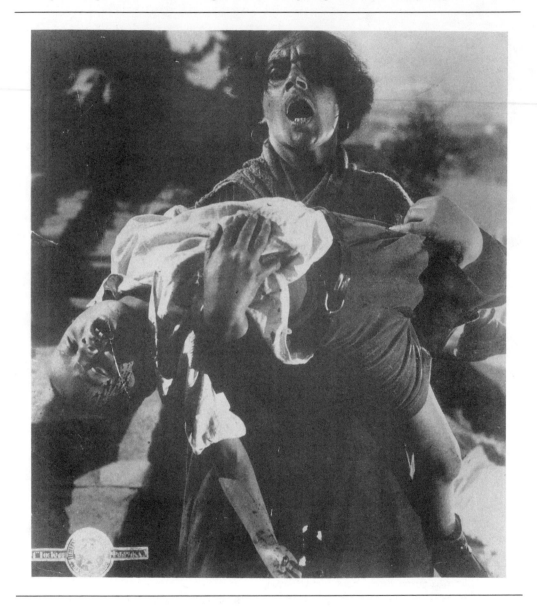

This sequence begins with the mother (Jessica Tandy) visiting the farmer next door. The sprawled figure of the farmer is smashed into a close-up by three jump-cut shots to the farmer's face. His eyes have been plucked.

This bizarre death is similar to Eisenstein's three shots that concluded the Odessa steps sequence. Hitchcock in his constructive sequence used those jump-cuts to climax the sequence, as did Eisenstein 40 years earlier.

Like Eisenstein, Hitchcock repeats his camera positions and patterns, though the audience is unaware of it. By design he tricks the audience into believing that it is the same shot when anchorage and/or geography is necessary.

The rule of three seems to prevail when changing the height of the camera. Hitchcock's placement from high to low shots is rarely motivated by point of view—a common error among beginning directors. Beginning directors often follow the point-of-view camera placements lavishly in their honest desire to be correct.

• • • • • • • • • • • • • • • • • • •

FRAGMENTED CINEMA LANGUAGE

Fragmented cinema language has no master shots, nor are there combinations of sequential shots. It may be best to describe it as a collage of shots, usually short in duration, expressing feelings, textures, and ambience, rather than situation or location, though it may be used for that as well. The insight of fragmented cinema language goes beyond the simple statement of a master shot.

Fragmented cinema language captures the essence of the action, the location, or the feelings of the observer. It is the marriage of various shots, combined in a unique constructive design that extrapolates the essence of the scene. Each shot should be like an add-on, giving more information but leading the viewer, who is anxiously waiting for the next shot.

It has a unity of location, yet it does tend to isolate people and things. It appears to be without prejudice or involvement with any on- or off-screen character, unlike the interpersonal cinema language. When correctly matched with the right shots, it instills great emotion or insight, or a three-dimensional feeling for a place, a relationship, or an action.

The pattern is begun by a shot that is repeated to give the anchorage an audience needs. When properly planned, the final viewpoint is three-dimensional. Like I-P and the master scene, it dovetails with other cinema language procedures, but needs to be preplanned and done carefully.

Case Study: *Raiders of the Lost Ark*

Another example of constructive cinema language, using fragmented cinema language, is Steven Spielberg's *Raiders of the Lost Ark* whip and gun sequence. The shots are described here in detail to give the reader a better sense of how to create the organized fragmentation. Spielberg does this so well and so logically that it may go unnoticed by the viewer. This following sequence begins as the main titles complete.

Raiders of the Lost Ark

CONSTRUCTIVE-FRAGMENTED CINEMA LANGUAGES

Shot	Description	Time

———————————— Opening threat ————————————

Shot	Description	Time
1	M.S. of Guide #2. He X's down into a shoulder shot.	03
2	CLOSE-UP Pistol in its holster. He pulls it out of the holster and cocks it, making an audible sound.	03

———————————— Indy Jones hears it ————————————

3	SHOULDER SHOT OF JONES IN SILHOUETTE POV Guide #2. He cocks his head in response to the "click."	02

———————————— Threat followed through ————————————

4	SHOULDER SHOT of Guide #2 as he raises the pistol, pointing it toward: (REPEAT OF SHOT #1)	007

———————————— Action Whip ————————————

5	CLOSE SHOT OF WHIP ON HIP . . . He turns as his hand moves down . . .	007
6	CLOSE-UP OF HAND . . . holding the whip above his head . . . snapping it back, frame left. SOUND OF WHIP CRACKING	007
7	CLOSE-UP HAND . . . Cracking the whip toward frame right. In the B.G. in a thigh shot is Guide #1 watching in amazement.	007
8	2—SHOT, B.G., WAIST OF Guide, F.G. Jones in silhouette, appearing to snap the whip. Actually you don't see the whip but YOU HEAR ITS RESOUNDING CRACK!	001

———————————— Reaction to Whip ————————————

9   CLOSE-UP GUIDE #2. His eyes are bulging with   01
     surprise and fear as he raises his hand . . .

10   MEDIUM SHOT OF ROCK AT THE EDGE OF   01
     STREAM . . . PISTOL falls onto the rock and rolls
     into the stream.

11   CLOSE-UP OF GUIDE #2 (REPEAT OF SHOT #9).   01

     He holds his hand, then runs off frame left . . .

─────────── JONES IS A MAN TO RECKON WITH ───────────

12   MEDIUM SHOT OF INDY JONES . . . Still sil-   05
     houette . . . now he steps forward into the sun-
     light. We see his face for first time (REVEAL-
     MENT. He watches:

──────────────────── Villain runs off ────────────────────

13   WAIST SHOT OF GUIDE #2. Holding his hand.   03
     He is running back in the direction he came
     from frame left. He stops for a moment, looking
     back frame right, and then continues running
     off into the jungle. He gets smaller as he runs
     off.

──────────────── Completes whip action ────────────────

14   CLOSE SHOT OF INDY'S HAND COILING THE   03
     WHIP . . . Guide #1 watches increduously.
     (REPEAT OF SHOT #7, SYMMETRY OF COM-
     PLETED ACTION)

─────── He is strong and can take care of himself ───────

15   CLOSE-UP OF INDY. He now moves frame left,   11
     looking frame right. CAMERA PANS WITH HIM
     TO GUIDE #1 who continues to look after Indy.
     His eyes are filled with a mix of respect and
     fear. He moves off frame left following Indy.

16   2-LONG SHOT. INDY leading the GUIDE as they   14
     climb up the hill when Indy disappears into the
     cave.

     Running time of the entire sequence is 1 minute, 17
seconds, with a total of 16 shots.

───────────

Figure 11.3   Psycho. *The shower slasher, who in truth never lands a cut, demonstrates the magic of fragmented cinema language invoked by Hitchcock.* (Copyright © by Universal Pictures, a Division of Universal City Studios, Inc. Courtesy of MCA Publishing Rights, a Division of MCA Inc. Courtesy Leland Fauste Esquire)

Further Examples

Hitchcock's famous *Psycho* shower sequence is an excellent example of fragmented cinema language (see Figure 11.3). See *Hitchcock,* by François Truffaut, where this sequence is storyboarded. In Brian De Palma's *Dressed to Kill* the art gallery sequence is a mixture of movement cinematic language, master scene, and interpersonal and subjective cinema language which is truly remarkable.

The impression that fragmented cinema language is used only in highly emotional situations is simply not true. It was used quite effectively by Norman Jewison in his Academy Award – winning film *In the Heat of the Night* on the occasion when Sidney Poiter searched a car for clues to a murder. Sam Peckinpah's opening sequence in *The Wild Bunch* stands as one of the more complicated examples of fragmented cinema language ever put on film. It borders on excess, but it is worth examining.

Chapter **12**

OTHER CINEMA LANGUAGES

The remaining cinematic languages are often used for specific circum-stances. Each language has a purpose and creates a specific mood. Parallel cinema language, for instance, is used to create a sense of dual action, which builds a feeling of suspense in the audience. Collision cinema language provides action adventure movies with conflict and discord. With subjective cinema language, the camera becomes a character in the scene, pulling the audience self-consciously into the scene as well.

. . . .

SYMBOLIC CINEMA LANGUAGE

Symbolic cinema language is a series of disconnected images conveying an "idea" through the use of a symbol that relates to the central theme and/or story. Its main characteristic is found in its disregard for matching shots or action or time or space. This draws attention to the symbols, which may be abstract or realistic.

Mixed Symbols

In Hitchcock's *Spellbound,* when Ingrid Bergman and Gregory Peck kiss for the first time many doors open up. Slowly, each door is swung open. Hitch-

147

cock uses the opening doors to indicate how she opens her heart to this man.

Animate Symbols

In *To Catch a Thief* Hitchcock uses the black cat to represent the cat burglar, Cary Grant. The audience understood the "cat burglar" was stealing again when they saw a black cat running across the rooftops. Continuing with his joke, Hitchcock cut in a shot of a black cat luxuriating on the couch in Cary Grant's French chateau. When the police arrive to interrogate Grant, the cat runs off, foreshadowing Cary Grant's hasty departure. This clear statement of guilt in the viewer's eyes is in fact a deliberate red herring planted by Hitchcock to keep the viewer engaged.

Inanimate Symbols

Again, in *To Catch a Thief* in the first love scene between Grace Kelly and Cary Grant, fireworks are seen through the window of their hotel room. As they kiss, Hitchcock cuts in the fireworks as the music swells. It may sound corny now, but Hitchcock was one of the first to use the fireworks symbol.

In *Potemkin* Eisenstein uses three separate marble statues of lions, though unrelated, and in different locations, but he does so by cutting them together, making it appear that the lion has awakened, his head lifted up, listening, and then finally on his feet, alert, ready for action. Eisenstein wrote later that the lion was to represent the people awakening to the evils of the czarist government.

Advantage   The advantage of symbolic cinema language is that it can turn an abstract idea into a visual image that has a strong emotional impact, capturing the essence of the idea, making the image superior to the "real thing." The result is an outstanding, indelible image.

Disadvantage   The disadvantage is the symbol may be too esoteric. The selection of the symbol and its execution need careful thought.

Vogue

If you choose a symbol that is popular today, then be aware of the pitfalls. The question that should be asked is, Will it be understood in the future? There is nothing worse than selecting a symbol that is outdated or, worse, misunderstood.

Symbolic cinema language transcends the commonplace. It is a tool that distills reality to make a statement or to lead to insight into the human condition, and it is an excellent tool for the filmmaker.

• • • • • • • • • • • • • • • • • •

PARALLEL CINEMA LANGUAGE

When you see the heroine tied to the railroad tracks as the train is hurtling toward her, while at the same time the hero is rushing to save her, you are seeing an example of parallel cinema language. By *parallel cinema language* we mean cutting back and forth between two different action sequences, making them appear as if they were happening simultaneously and/or in tandem. This language compares the relationship between the two and increases tension. Though each sequence is independent of the other, they eventually converge to heighten the climax.

Rescue, search, and pursuit sequences often use parallel cinema language. When switching from one sequence to the other, time can be expanded, compressed, or even moved into the past or the future. The audience will accept these aberrations of time, though it will not in some of the other cinema languages.

Repetitive Sequences

The primary sequence is established at the beginning of the parallel cinema language configuration. It is identified by the way it takes up more screen time.

The secondary sequence starts with a dramatic close shot (signature shot) that sharply brings it to the attention of the viewer. In crosscutting, the signature shot signals to the audience that they are into the secondary sequence. The cycle has to occur at least three times to be effective.

Sync Sound and Time

Unlike master scene cinema language, which requires that the language be in "real" time, parallel does not have a real time requirement. Time manipulations can occur only when cutting to and from the primary, or to and from the secondary sequence. You may even enter earlier the primary or secondary, or return as if it were the same time, or you can enter later. The audience will accept time manipulations.

But when you are in the primary or secondary sequence, then you are unable to manipulate time. The events must appear to be happening in real time within the sequence.

This language accepts sync sound as well as nonsync sound. It permits compression and expansion of real time within the same language; hence "wild" sound is acceptable when changing over to the next sequence.

Unlike master scene, where a violation of sync sound would destroy the film's credibility, in parallel language there is greater latitude.

Matching

Parallel cinema language requires transitional planning so that crossing over to the other sequence will be understood. The rule is to design one sequence as the primary sequence and the other as the secondary one. This may be dictated by the screenplay.

By using a visual device common to both sequences, effective crosscutting is done. For instance, by matching an element common to both the incoming shot and the outgoing shot, the transition is smoothly done or, in the primary sequence, a close shot of a round train wheel is matched (dissolved) to a close shot of a round coin in the hand of a character in the secondary sequence.

Crosscutting

The primary sequence must end with a wide shot that comfortably cuts into the signature shot of the secondary sequence.

Composition and Opticals

Composition and opticals are worked out to support the primary and secondary sequences. This ties in with the chosen signature shot and the matching device. In addition, opticals like dissolves or wipes are used to soften the change from one sequence to another.

Primary Sequence

The primary sequence is the main story line; it takes more screen time than does the secondary.

Secondary Sequence

The secondary sequence bursts on the screen in an abbreviated fashion. It should be quickly identified by its "signature shot." A signature shot functions to identify quickly the secondary sequence so the filmmaker can move the story rapidly forward. That "coin in hand" mentioned earlier can also become a signature shot if it is repeated when cutting back from the primary to the secondary sequence again, in the way that Hitchcock used the cigarette lighter in *Strangers on a Train*.

Case Study: *Strangers on a Train*

Hitchcock uses parallel cinema language to advance the story and move quickly to the climax of the film. The story has Guy (Farley Granger), a professional tennis player, wanting to divorce his estranged wife. He is approached on a train by a stranger, Robert Walker, who wishes to kill his father. He proposes an exchange of murders. Walker assumes Granger's agreement and kills his wife. Granger is horrified and refuses to kill Walker's father. To get revenge and to protect himself from prosecution, Walker decides to plant Granger's cigarette lighter at the scene of his wife's murder. He chooses to do so at the time Granger, watched by the police, has to play a tennis match. Granger has to finish the match and catch Walker before he can plant the incriminating evidence.

Primary and Secondary Sequences   The crosscutting between the tennis match and Walker making his way to the crime site, elevates the tension of the film, and brings it to a climactic conclusion. The tennis match takes more screen time, as Walker goes to the crime site. For a period of time, the tennis match is the primary sequence.

Switch   As the film continues, the crime site/amusement park sequence gains in screen time. Hence, the secondary becomes the primary sequence, while Granger's hurrying to catch Walker becomes the new secondary sequence.

Parallel cinema language is used by the director. But whether it is dictated by the script or chosen by the director does not matter. When using parallel cinema language, obeying the rules is compulsory.

• • • • • • • • • • • • • • • • • • •
COLLISION CINEMA LANGUAGE

Collision cinema language was suggested by Eisenstein. It was inspired by dramatic theory. The premise is that the more elements in conflict, the better the drama, hence, the better the movie.

Compositional Conflict

The use of conflicting compositional elements abounds in movies. In *Citizen Kane* Orson Welles used compositional conflict throughout the entire film. It is notable in the signature shot of the whispered "Rosebud." Welles used size and volume in the close-up of the huge lips. Welles also used other compositional devices. For instance, darkness obscured the enigmatic Citizen Kane, while the light, representing the new element, hope, was another compositional factor. (In Chapter 9, compositional elements were examined in detail.)

In action pictures, collision cinema language is mandatory. Oblique lines, which are the most dynamic, are generally used throughout this genre. When used in conjunction with other lines, they heighten the tensions.

Opposite Emotions

A scene beginning as a "love scene" and ending as a "hate scene" is an example of the use of opposite emotions. For instance, when the hero, with love in his heart and a bouquet of flowers in his hand, enters to discover his lover in bed with another man, a melodramatic change from love to hate takes place. This scene started with a man in love and ends with a man full of hate.

Movement

Movement can be used to create and heighten conflict. In Chapters 13 and 14 we will examine movement in detail. Shadows moving quickly across a vertical plane is an example of creating conflict with movement. This device was used in *Potemkin*'s Odessa steps sequence.

Picture and Sound

The sound track can be placed in conflict with the picture. Robert Altman constantly pits his visual images against the sound track. He deliberately neutralizes the picture, giving dominance to the sound track. The film *The Long Goodbye* is an example of this.

Music Conflicts   When the music is contrapuntal to the picture, the effect is arresting. Music's "opposite emotions" theory is designed by composers to add another dimension to the emotional impact of a film. Stanley Kubrick used classical music as a counterpoint to the visual content most of the time—see his *Dr. Strangelove*. Jerry Goldsmith's score to Franklin Schaffner's *Planet of the Apes* added a frighening dimension to the film.

Sound Effects   Jacques Tati in *Hulot's Holiday* used sound effects to turn a mundane, sterile world into a zany and bizarre yet funny one. In the peaceful world of films, sharp sounds startle us, from the horror film genre, as in *Halloween,* to the action films, like *Batman.*

Dialogue   Dialogue may be in conflict with the picture, another device used in collision. In Hitchcock's *The Birds,* the hero pleads for help from the local sheriff, while his mother picks up the remaining pieces of her cherished teacups, shattered by the attacking birds. The dialogue is mundane; at the same time the action suggests the poignant emotional state of the mother.

Dialogue indicating the character's feelings may be put in conflict with compositional elements of the picture. In Joseph Mankiewicz's Academy Award—winning film *All about Eve,* Bette Davis, as the attractive, glamorous Broadway stage star, remarks in her cool jocular manner, "This is going to be a bumpy night." The sharp, rapier dialogue is in conflict with the sophisticated, sleek look of the movie.

Rhythmic Cutting

Cutting a sequence by the beat of music or a sound effect is another choice. King Vidor's *Give Us Our Daily Bread* was one of the first pictures to use this technique. Vidor cut to the rhythm of a sledgehammer. There are two kinds of rhythmic cutting.

Metric   In this case, the cutting is dictated by the film footage counter. Shots are cut according to a predetermined rhythm. This was used in *Beetlejuice,* in which the dinner party scene had the characters moving in rhythm to Harry Belafonte's calypso music. Many other examples can be found in animated films and in commercials, especially in the soft drink area and abound in music videos.

Tonal   Tonal cutting is dictated by the shades of sound. In John Avildsen and Sylvester Stallone's *Rocky,* when Rocky is hit in slow motion, the blows are shattering. The emotional response is commensurate with the volume and duration of the manipulated sound.

• • • • • • • • • • • • • • • • • • •
VORKAPICH CINEMA LANGUAGE

Breaking an activity down into a series of shots encourages involvement in the activity; this is called Vorkapich cinema language. It is named for Slavko Vorkapich, a famous Hollywood cinematographer who promoted special effects through creative use of the camera.

Bike riding, when broken down into a series of separate actions, has a cause and effect correlation. That is one of the rules of Vorkapich cinema language: it must follow logically. One shot may show hands holding on to the handlebars; another, the feet pushing the pedals down; followed by the flywheel turning the rear wheel; followed by the bike rolling down the path. By cutting these shots together in a logical, rhythmic sequence, the audience will experience bicycle riding.

When applying Vorkapich, the activity can be made into a poem of movement or into a nightmare of suspense. For instance, in an early British film, made during the Second World War, called *Sabotage,* Hitchcock has a young boy on a bicycle deliver a package. The youngster does not know that the package contains a bomb and he dawdles, as ten-year-old boys are wont to do. But he takes too long; the bomb goes off, and the boy is killed. It was sabotage!

Director Ridley Scott used Vorkapich to build suspense in *Alien.* The cyclical shots of the crew searching for the alien in the twisted, wet, dark, cavernous corridors were nerve racking. Lee Katzkin used Vorkapich at the beginning of his racing picture *LeMans.* He took the audience through the start of the grueling 24-hour race. It is Vorkapich expertly used. In *The Getaway* Sam Peckinpah's nonlinear cutting documents Steve McQueen's life as a prisoner in a Texas jail. He violates real time, yet Peckinpah captures the humiliating experience of life in prison. In the *Rocky* movies, Vorkapich cinema language is used to set up the climactic fight. It has become a trademark for this type of film. The pattern is the same. After a few sequences of Rocky's training, the payoff is Rocky demonstrating that he is getting stronger, that his training is working. For the first time, there is hope that he may do well in the championship fight.

Vorkapich cinema language is constructed to repeat, in cycles, series of shots, in a particular order, capturing the event in such a way that the viewer participates in the activity. There are no time constraints and no rational order, except the logic of the action. The discipline itself does not require a master shot, though an establishing shot is usually used to bracket the activity.

• • • • • • • • • • • • • • • • • • •

SUBJECTIVE CINEMA LANGUAGE

Subjective cinema language means using the camera as a character in the story. It is used in two ways: (1) when shots see things or hear things from character's viewpoint, or (2) when the onscreen character talks to the camera as if it were a character in the story. The purpose is to involve the audience. The camera plays either the offscreen character or the onscreen character.

Offscreen Character

The onscreen character talks to the camera, making direct eye contact, addressing the audience as if it were the offscreen character, which is not the case in interpersonal cinema language. The audience is forced into a personal confrontation with the onscreen character. Though the audience is forced into role-playing, its reactions are "programmed" by the onscreen character. The character on the screen reacts to supposed reactions of the offscreen character.

Though subjective cinema language is not used as often as some of the others in features and television, *China Syndrome* and, more recently, *Shirley Valentine* are notable exceptions.

In *China Syndrome* Jane Fonda played a television reporter. She effected one character on the air, and quite a different character when she was "herself." Subjective cinema language showed us, the audience, the difference.

In Lewis Gilbert's comedy *Shirley Valentine,* Shirley addresses the audience directly. We share her confidences and her interpretation of her experiences. This gives us insight into her soul and adds a great deal of charm and amusement to the film. It makes Shirley sympathetic, resulting in a satisfying picture. Gilbert used subjective cinema language quite correctly.

The Camera as an Onscreen Character

A rather common device found in murder mystery stories is another use of subjective cinema language. It is used to represent a viewpoint without revealing the identity of that person.

In the early 50s, Robert Montgomery's *Lady in the Lake* was shot exclusively in subjective cinema language. On- and offscreen subjective cinema language were used. The camera "played" Philip Marlowe, the hard-bitten, sarcastic detective. He was rarely seen onscreen, except in mirror shots. The onscreen characters looked directly into the lens and addressed the camera as if they were talking to Marlowe. Marlowe's voice then responded. The onscreen character reacts directly into the camera as if it was Marlowe.

To simulate Marlowe's walk, the camera was tracked and the audience hears footsteps (an example of subjective movement cinema language). To simulate Marlowe's viewpoint, the camera would pan as if it was Marlowe's eyes. Other movements of the camera interpreted Marlowe's eye or head movements.

Disadvantages

The major disadvantage of subjective is that if forces confrontation between the audience and the onscreen character. This confrontation can be harsh and can turn the audience off. In addition, the feeling of confrontation, plus a "forced" reaction by the onscreen character, may compound the audience's negative reaction.

The major difficulty Robert Montgomery had with using subjective cinema language almost exclusively was that he had only one viewpoint, and this limited the film. The other problem Montgomery ran into was transitions. Getting from one time, place, or location to another presented another problem, because he tried to keep everything in "moment to moment" time.

But that fascinating element of direct eye contact is compelling. In the right circumstance, it can effectively overwhelm an audience. With the advent of interactive video, and the coming three-dimensional contact holograms, this language may find a power never known before.

• • • • • • • • • • • • • • • • • • •

TRANSITION CINEMA LANGUAGE

Transition cinema language moves the audience from a scene, a time, or a place, or it capsulates an event or an emotional state in an abbreviated manner.

Transition cinema language, unlike other cinema languages, is an answer to the challenge of "moving" the audience from one scene to the next.

The Grammar of Transition

At the beginning of filmmaking, certain traditions were established so that the audience could recognize changes of time, place, and location. Just cutting to black was simply too harsh. Over the years, transition cinema language developed symbols to indicate shifts in time, place, or location.

Fade-out or Fade-in. *Fade out* means to reduce the intensity of the picture until the screen is black. Conversely, *fade in* means that the screen starts out black, and then the picture gradually appears, filling the screen.

Traditionally, silent films used fades as if they were dissolves. They did this for economic reasons: the lab charge for fade-outs and fade-ins was the cheapest. However, recent technological breakthroughs have led to a variety of transitional devices at reasonable prices.

Dissolve. A dissolve is the fading out of one one picture, while another picture is fading in: the new picture replaces the other. During the dissolve both pictures are on the screen for a short period of time. That moment is called a superimposition.

A dissolve represents a change of time, place, or location. It is similar to a theatrical scene. The test is, if there is no black between the rotating shots, then it is a dissolve.

Sometimes a dissolve is used to soften a cut that is considered an abrupt change of picture. The "soft cut" lends itself to mood pieces. It softens the shift to another shot usually without changing location or place, but there may be a modest shift of time. Audiences are familiar with this tradition and accept it.

Wipe. A wipe is creatively similar to a dissolve. It also uses replacement of one picture by another without any black. The difference is that a "line" or some other device removes one picture to reveal the second.

There are many types of wipes, such as the "iris," the "window," the "door," and the "spiral"; the names describe the way in which they operate in removing the picture. Most labs have a chart displaying the many kinds of wipes available. In television, the electronic switchers in the control room usually have templates diagramming the various wipes. The major rule is that a wipe has the same creative function as a dissolve.

Illustrative. Illustrative transition cinema language uses real objects to indicate the passage of time. The leaves of a tree changing color, from green to red to dark brown, indicating the change of season is an example. Through use of time-lapse photography, we see the sun move across the sky. Nature is the source of many symbols.

Telescopic. Telescopic transition cinema language is a series of events tied together to express a change of time, place, or relationship. In *Citizen Kane* Kane and his wife are seated at their table, eating their wedding breakfast. They are joyously in love. A swish-pan (a transitional device in the category of a wipe) is then used, indicating a change of time, to reveal them at the breakfast table over the next dozen years or so. We watch their relationship deteriorate until they are no longer speaking to one another, eating their breakfast in deathly silence.

• • • • • • • • • • • • • • • • •

CINE VERITÉ CINEMA LANGUAGE

Cine verité cinema language simulates a newsreel style of coverage. The event appears as if it were happening as you view it, unrehearsed, moment to moment, without manipulation of time, space, or place. The subjects show that they are aware of the camera or they act as if they are caught off-guard by it. Apparent violation of this rule destroys this cinema language. It should not be mistaken for subjective cinema language.

History

In the 1960s, when the Maisel brothers put together packages of light, portable cameras and sound kits to do "guerrilla" filming to capture reality, cine verité was born.

People like Frederic Wiseman filmed actual events. A famous documentary of a family was accomplished by a three-man crew who practically lived with the family. They recorded the family moment by moment; even seeing the camera or microphone was acceptable. On occasion, the family members would address the crew people by name and make comments to them, which added to the "honesty." The theory was that if the crew became part of the family—that is, like furniture—then the family would act normally. This cinema language mandates the following features.

Camera Placement

Camera placement is ordinary. There are no unusual angles, and bad framing is acceptable since it should look like "candid camera." The camera's rocky movement, as if it were hand-held, draws attention to the clumsy operation and convinces the audience that the film is unstaged and spontaneous.

Sync Dialogue

Only dialogue is spoken, and it must be in sync. "Good" sound makes it suspect. If the sound is poorly modulated, then, the belief is, it seems to be happening as being viewed and is unaltered. Sync dialogue adds credibility and a feeling of spontaneity.

Ad-lib Style

The actors and all the participants do their dialogue in an improvisational manner, as if there were no written script. This means an informal, off-the-cuff style.

Narrative Style

The narration or voiceover should be addressed directly to the audience. There should be no literary allusions or dramatizing of the action. Narration should be simple, clear, concise, without frills, and spoken in an ad-lib style.

Editing Style

Editing style is straightforward, sometimes deliberately poorly cut. This style of cutting may in some cases, add to the "reality."

Cine verité seems to provide a "reality" to the viewer. This cinema language requires careful planning and a calculated compromise of technical standards if it is to convince the viewer.

With the new videocameras now in the hands of many laypeople, a new era of cine verité is blossoming. The recent success of the low-budget, non-establishment feature *Sex, lies, and videotape* opens avenues of cine verité not thought possible before.

. . . .

COMBINATIONS OF LANGUAGES

It should be apparent by now that cinema languages are not used in isolation from each other. Most cinema languages work well together. In some instances, they are so inextricably intertwined that it seems almost impossible to separate them. They work by weaving a complex fabric of film experiences. For example, in *Cotton Club* Coppola used constructive, collision, metric, interpersonal, symbolic, and transition cinema languages to conclude his film.

Cinema languages are able to reach viewers on many levels of perception. The images become part of the audience's unconscious, often distilling the story into indelible pictures that may stay with people for the rest of their lives. This ability of cinema languages elevates film to an art form.

Chapter 13

MOVEMENT

The introduction of movies marked the first time an art medium captured movement. This was fascinating because it gave the viewer the ability to see movement as it appeared in life. Film careened crazily, jerked us around, moved us through time and space, and demonstrated to us the strong connection with the movement of life. Film uniquely captured and froze movement so we could experience it from its inception, going from point to point, and finally to its completion. We watched in awe the ballet of life. We recorded it and played it over and over again, watching it unfold in the same space and time as when it was originally conceived.

This chapter will examine movement and how composition, picturization, and cinema languages use and react to movement. We are examining it not merely as camera movement or screen movement, but as a powerful tool. We will also consider the implications in a medium that incorporates the word *movement* into the description of what we call moving pictures.

From this viewpoint, we are interested in understanding movement and all its ramifications. We study the obligatory movement dictated by the script, movement and its use in the various cinema languages, including, but not limited to, the rules of composition and picturization. We investigate movement and how differently it operates within the actor's language, and finally, how it achieves its own identity in the production language.

Movement has greater emphasis than a static shot, as you know. We are interested in understanding how to manipulate it, how it is perceived by the viewer, and how we use it within the context of the story we are telling. But let us first define movement before we are overwhelmed by the scope of this chapter.

• • • • • • • • • • • • • • • • • • • •

DEFINITION

Movement takes time and occupies space while it connects a series of points and/or events toward a more or less definite end. Movement cinema language is composed of moments of definite picturization, supported by composition, and dictated by the specific discipline of the chosen cinema languages. When correctly used, movement creates meaningful pictures as it flows from moment to moment.

We know from Chapter 7 that composition has mood value and picturization tells the story. Movement abides by the composition and picturization rules discussed in Chapter 7. There are some exceptions and variations, which will be examined in this chapter.

• • • • • • • • • • • • • • • • • • • •

THE PURPOSE OF MOVEMENT

Movement gives images their intrinsic life. We betray that trust if we see it as only a mechanical tool. Life never stops, is never at rest, is forever moving. Though governed by the rules of composition and picturization and by the cinema languages, movement has some characteristics that are peculiar only to it.

Before we begin to catalogue and launch into a deep examination of movement, it is important to understand how camera movement as a kinetic tool can move us in a unique manner, somewhat akin to the way music moves us. It plays to those sensibilities that have to do with appreciation of three-dimensional perception. All pictures are two-dimensional. The still picture can show only one surface of the object in its motionless world. In moving pictures we capture the form as it moves through time and space. These moves of the camera and/or the subject combine the art of dancing, sculpture, and music. No painting or sculpture has this unique ability. Interestingly, cubism reflects the artist's desire to show an object in three dimensions, within the limitations of a painting.

Kinetic camera movement can open a new door of perception, as moving pictures lead us to the joy of understanding and loving the world around us. This chapter intends to begin this process.

There are four categories: plot movement, cinema languages; character movement, and how the actor applies the techniques; and finally, putting it all together in the production language.

Plot Movement

Plot movement is in the screenplay. The entrances and exits of characters, serving meals, fighting, dancing, hiding objects, observing an action to further the plot—these are all examples of plot movement. The plot obligates the director to follow certain movements; otherwise, the story does not make sense. The director chooses to fulfill that obligation by using cinema language as well.

Background Movement

In addition to plot movement, there is another kind of movement in the screenplay, which is indicated by the description of the background activity. This is implemented by the director.

For instance, say the hero is walking down a city street. The crowd on a New York City street, however, moves quite differently from a crowd on a street in Calcutta. Background is seldom spelled out in a screenplay but falls into the province of the director.

Arbitrary Movement

Another kind of movement is superimposed on a type of script that is mainly dialogue. Movement is then used to reinforce the wit or the underlying movement of the emotions within the dialogue of the script. Films coming from stage plays, like those of Noël Coward with their snappy dialogue, or original films like *All about Eve* are examples of films in which movement has to be invented and is arbitrary.

In farce and comedy, geometric movements like parallel and counter movements are often introduced to enhance situations. The danger in this style of movement is that the audience recognizes the movement as unrelated to any of the elements of the play. For this reason, the director should be careful to make the arbitrary movement pertinent to the line, situation, or character.

● ● ● ● ● ● ● ● ● ● ● ● ● ● ● ● ● ● ● ●

COMPOSITION RULES OF MOVEMENT

Movement also has a picturizing value. Movements can contribute to mood expressions. When discussing the mood effect of line, mass, and form in composition, we previously considered only the static viewpoint. A film, however, is usually in motion, and the mood achieved must be visualized dynamically by seeing those lines, masses, and forms in motion. In all cases the mood achieved exists in composition, but in actual execution it becomes a composition in which movement is included.

In order to sense the composition rules of movement in films, one must think of it as a ballet. The characters move through the space and time, like Marcel Duchamp's painting *Nude Descending a Staircase*. The movie characters weave in and out of playing out their lives but always in movement.

Another way of looking at movement is to imagine that there is a string attached to the subject. One can then watch the subjects weave in and out and around objects in the film, appreciating their choreographic movement.

Form Expressed in Movement

As we know from Chapter 7, form is classified as either form or space. Like the ying and the yang, one cannot exist without the other. Patterns of form exist in movement.

The different arrangements of form in composition can also be thought of as existing in action. Movement in a film may be irregular or regular in execution. It may extend through all planes, spread all over areas, or it may be restricted to one or two areas. Form in movement may be symmetrical, asymmetrical, shallow, deep, compact, or diffused.

Symmetrical Movement   Symmetrical movement, like the shot, implies formality, grace, or rigidity. Films that need symmetry to capture the time period, like *The Three Musketeers, The Count of Monte Cristo*, or, even more recently, *Dangerous Liaisons*. In Stephen Frears's *Dangerous* the film was mostly designed with symmetrical movement. But as the plot thickened and grew serious, the love affairs came home to the characters, as did the consequences of their actions. Symmetrical movement was abandoned for asymmetrical movement. Stephen Frears succeeded in making the audience feel the appreciation and reality of that final end.

Asymmetrical Movement   Asymmetrical movement implies flexibility, casualness, and lack of order. A group leaving a movie theater is a good example of asymmetrical movement.

Frears brought home the feeling of impending doom and final dissolution by changing from symmetry to asymmetry. The audience sensed the change but was at loss to explain it.

Movement in Depth   Movement in depth expresses warmth, richness, mellowness, sincerity, and realism. In his more recent films John Huston used shots in depth, staging moves from the far background to the foreground. This was noticeable in his *Man Who Would Be King*.

In the *Raiders of the Lost Ark* scene set in Marian's bar in Nepal, Spielberg used movement in depth. By having Marian cross at a right angle to the camera from the foreground to the background, and from background to the foreground, he created an oblique movement pattern that signified Marian's anger and frustration. Examine the screenplay (in the Appendix) and the film and note how the action (beat) of Marian and Indiana was expressed in movement. The closing shot of the scene has Indiana walking through the door into a close-up as Marian's taunting line is laid over his face, capturing the expression of disbelief, suppressed anger and frustration. With a final shift of his eyes mirroring his frustration, he departs. An exclamation of Marian's revenge follows.

Shallow Movement   Shallow movement expresses quaintness, artificiality, shallowness, excitement, effectiveness, and an alert quality. This form is especially appropriate for musicals like *My Fair Lady, Hello Dolly,* and *Funny Girl,* which went in and out of musical comedy reality. *Guys and Dolls,* which needed a feeling of "Damon Runyon's Broadway," used few shots in depth. In contrast, Robert Wise's production of *West Side Story* used depth for realism and to accommodate the choreography of Robbins. Huston's *Maltese Falcon* is another example of the use of shallow movement, capturing the strange world of Sam Spade, which worked quite well.

Compact Movement   Compact movement expresses warmth, force, horror, and power. Good examples of compact movement are found in Walter Hill's *The Warriors.* The film, about a gang from Coney Island (the heroes) passing through other territories to return to their own turf, turns out to be a filmic ballet of movement. This is surprising, since Hill is deeply interested in "action" pictures, and his choice of choreography is fascinating. He had different gangs assigned a movement. Those movements and backgrounds posed the threat to the hero group. The strength of the gang was characterized by its composition. The tighter the composition, the more compact the group, the greater the determination and power of the group.

   Compact movement staging is frequently found in confrontation scenes between police and the bad guys. This kind of shoot-out staging is used over and over again. The movement has the police surround the others, but the format is the same. In *The Warriors,* the "compact" group was trapped because the other gang surrounded them. This pattern was used in the film; the tightness of each group was the measure of its strength and determination.

Diffuse Movement   Diffuse movement expresses indifference, coldness, turmoil, defiance, and individualism. The lone cowboy riding out into the night conjures up associations with individualism or defiance, but his diffuse movement expresses any of the above qualities when set into the plot. These shots are not clichés but are in fact visual shorthand, communicating to an audience that loves recognizing symbols.

Mass in Movement

Mass in movement has to do with the weight of the mass in a picture. The effect of mass in composition depends on the number of people used, and on the handling of the group in relation to the space intervals between the members of the group, as well as the body positions they assume.

   In *The Warriors* the gang (the heroes) had to move through sections of New York City controlled by other gangs to get home to their own turf. When the warriors were confronted by another gang, their mass and movement indicated their strength. This was quickly determined by the space they occupied, as well as by the movement within their space.

Movement Stability

Movement needs to be tied down, following the natural law of gravity. Violations are used for special effects, as in the *Star Wars* when, in the final dogfight to destroy the Emperor's mammoth spaceship, the aircraft were violating gravity in an acceptable way.

Balance in Movement

Movement has balance, and it works simply within the form selected. Movement that is balanced has symmetry. Symmetrical movement is best represented by classical ballet, while interpretative dancing is more often asymmetrical.

Today, action films use movement with asymmetrical balance, challenging the audience's sense of balance. Examples are found in programs like "Star Trek: The Next Generation," and in films like *Raiders of the Lost Ark, Die Hard 2,* and *Lethal Weapon* and *Lethal Weapon II,* to name but a few.

Strength of Movement

Movement may be classified as either strong or weak, or dynamic or static. The value of movement, whether it is good or bad, is based solely upon the intent of the director. Value judgment is based on the purpose needed to express the needs of the moment. These choices are translated by using composition and picturization for support.

A strong move is toward the camera; this is one of the strongest moves possible. It may be executed by the subject moving from the background to the foreground, or by having the camera move toward an object. The weakest move is the opposite—that is, by having the subject walk away from the camera.

A camera view from a high angle makes a man appear to be weak. The story content of the shot indicates that he is indecisive. He makes a decision and then rises to his feet, as the camera arcs down to floor level. The resulting picture has this man move from a weak position to an enormously powerful one. This shot was used in Eisenstein's *Ivan the Terrible.* Czar Ivan was indeed terrible. The shot just described showed how he grew into such a monster. The emotional value of the shot is seeing this man go from being weak and uncertain to being a powerful, ruthless killer of the people.

A number of elements moderate movement from strong to weak and from weak to strong. This has to do with contrast. Say a strong move is made, such as frontal cross down to the foreground, with the character then delivering his line. This is a powerful, strong move, but it can be instantly changed by a weak action. Continuing with this example, say the character crosses to center, then pulls out a chair and sits down. Sitting is a weak move because of the drop in height. In this instance, the strong move is compromised by ending in a weak move. If it were reversed—that is, if the move went from weak to strong—then it would be a strong move. The rule is that a weak move is made strong if it is preceded by a weaker move, and a strong move is made weak if it is followed by a weak move. Simply stated, the move that ends the action decides whether it is strong or weak.

Dynamic and Static Motion

A move can be dynamic or static. The word *dynamic* is used to express the amount of attention the movement commands. A dynamic move creates the feeling that it is aggressively moving. For instance, using a wide-angle lens to cover the action makes it appear dynamic, since the peculiarity of the lens exaggerates the movement.

   The term *static movement* seems contradictory. How can a move be static when by definition movement must be moving and static means non-movement? Static movement feels like frozen movement. We can create static movement. For instance, we know the subject is moving but does not appear to be moving. Slow motion has a person or object moving but slowly or not at all. The effect is static movement. This effect is frequently accomplished by using a telephoto lens. A common shot is to show an athlete running down a field. Then a close shot cuts in so that the runner does not seem to be moving; instead the close shot accentuates the concentrated effort of that human being marshaling all his strength. This is an example of static movement in action.

Line

Line movement rules are the same as for line in the shot. That is, horizontal, perpendicular, diagonal, curved, straight, or circular lines generate the same feeling and/or mood in line movement. Movement line is treated in a straight, curved, or broken manner to obtain the various mood effects and match line in the shot. Movement is achieved by the subject's movement or by the camera's movement, or through a combination of both. In the Appendix, the *Raiders of the Lost Ark* bar scene in Nepal appears; movement is detailed, as is the use of the movement line.

Amount of Movement

Films of constant excitement, characters requiring no detailed characterizations, no dialogue innuendoes, no thought or sharp contrasts in mood, like melodramas, rowdy farces, or suspenseful stories, usually demand constant movement. The amount of movement adds to the intensity of a scene. In "Hill Street Blues" the constant movement added to the tension and vitality of the series. Less movement makes the scene feel less cluttered, less zany, more anchored, and in some cases less interesting.

Length of Movement

Should movement be short or long? The length of the movement refers to how long the move takes to accomplish its action, from the beginning to the end.

If the move is short and quick, it adds tension and heightens suspense, excitement, sharpness, irritability, impulsiveness, and gaiety. Long, lengthy moves are associated with composure, deliberation, futility, languor, lack of emotional strain, aloneness, entrapment, the romantic, the feminine. Long movement has a legato, or smooth, quality.

Short movement has a staccato, or sharp, quality. The longer the movement, the weaker it becomes.

Intensity

The intensity of the movement depends upon the emotional content and/or state of the character in the scene. Heightened emotion is conveyed by greater intensity. Lax movements are unconvincing but are excellent in contrast to the zany universe of comedy or farce. The intensity of the move has the reaction of causing excitement, intense, hot action.

Rhythm

All movement, whether it is executed by the camera or by the subject or by a combination of both, has rhythm. The rhythm of the move affects how it is perceived. The rules of rhythm prevail with movement as well. For instance, slow, luxuriating motion is associated with romantic movement. Consider the loving couple walking into the bright orange sunset. Their slow, languid rhythm indicates their emotional involvement. Obviously the additional support of line, mass, and form may be needed. Tempo and pace are the other variables. See Billy Wilder's hilarious 1950s film *One, Two, Three*, with James Cagney, to see pacing and rhythm wonderfully done.

Direction

Whether the movement is right to left or left to right has a psychological impact in the countries that read from left to right. In East Asia, where people read in a vertical manner, this theory would not have significance. The theory is that movement traveling across the screen in the same way we read — that is, left to right — is more acceptable. Consequently, according to this theory, if the movement goes right to left, the feeling is that it is more difficult. So if the director wanted to impress upon a Western audience the difficulty of the action, then she would stage it from right to left.

• • • • • • • • • • • • • • • • • • •

MOVEMENT IN PICTURIZATION

Picturization movement translates the psychological, intellectual, or emotional concept of a scene into physical movement. Like static shot picturization, movement picturization has meaning and tells the story but does so by translating it into movement and movement patterns.

Analysis with Central Theme

As character relationships shift and change in the scene, so does movement picturization. Movement communicates the subtext of the scene and leads the viewer to pleasurable insight into the action of the scene. But all this ties directly to the central theme. Again, consider the movement pattern of the *Raiders of the Lost Ark* Nepal bar scene (see Appendix). Examine its floorplan and note its camera similarity to *Big Country* master scene cinema language. The movement is relevant and meaningful to the interior of the characters.

Marian makes deep crosses in the frame of *Raiders of the Lost Ark* which go from background to the foreground, then foreground to background, with Indy acting more like an anchor, as she picks up the glasses from the table. In an explosion of final frustration, she tumbles the glasses from her tray into the sink, illustrating her internal rage. That is a practical demonstration of movement in picturization.

Point of View

Movement, like the static shot, has a point of view. Point of view obviously asks, whose point of view is represented in this scene?

In the scene between Marian and Indiana, whose viewpoint did Spielberg have represented? Intuitively, you know whose viewpoint you are seeing or hearing or feeling when you read the script or watch the film. The screenwriter most often implies it. Ultimately, the decision is up to the director. It is not uncommon for the director to take another viewpoint.

Raiders of the Lost Ark is almost entirely from Indiana's viewpoint. We follow his journey, his raid, to get the lost Ark. The hero's viewpoint is usual for action films, but there are exceptions, like *Halloween,* which had more than one storyline, or *Lethal Weapon,* which had two heroes.

Labeling the Scene

In movement picturization there are several basic movement patterns. The patterns remain the same, though the specific subject changes. The movement patterns are:

1. The *breaking pattern* is a series of small, repetitive moves coming from a center. The movement is a thrusting out and then returning to the center, then thrusting out in a different direction. The move itself is short and direct. It is like a series of short, jabbing moves. If we drew a diagram with arrows representing the direction of the move, then the picture would contain a series of arrows in a circle pointing out toward the outer edges of the frame. This type of movement is found in scenes that have subjects like seeking or looking for some lost item, breaking up furniture in an angry manner, chasing after an animal, and so on.

The intensity of movement should be in keeping with the content of the scene. This breaking pattern may be aggressive or introspective. The manner of playing the move depends on the content of the scene. If anger is the underlying emotion then it can be directed at things, persons, objects, or the subject himself. The movement pattern, though, is consistently the same.

If it is comedic in manner, the movement may not need to have serious commitment, or it can be slightly exaggerated, which may make it feel comedic. Again, note that the pattern remains the same.

Movement pattern is not necessarily restricted to one shot but may be incorporated into the selected cinema language. An example would be a lynch mob coming to hang a prisoner. The sheriff appears in front of the crowd, rifle in hand, telling them to disperse. The dispersing crowd is an example of the breaking-up pattern. This sequence would be done with several shots.

2. *Opposition movement* is where the two forces are in direct confrontation. The pattern looks like two arrows, each pointing at the other, confronting the other.

This opposition movement is used all the time. It may be used in one shot, or it can be structured within a cinema language. Two forces moving toward each other may be translated by using parallel cinema language. One of the forces is the primary and the other is the secondary, as was discussed earlier.

High Noon is an excellent example of the use of parallel movement cinema language. In the final shoot out at the climax of the film, the sequence is an excellent use of opposition movement.

In Peckinpah's *Wild Bunch* opposition movement is used throughout the entire film. John Ford's classic film *Cheyenne Autumn* includes many examples of the opposition pattern. A static example has already been cited in *Big Country*. Peck and Ives face off from master camera position B.

3. *Intervention movement* has two or more forces separated by a third party. That is picturization. This movement pattern is frequently used in scenes of mediation. The two forces are separated, moving toward a showdown. The third force steps between them and acts like a mediator.

4. *Change of mind movement pattern* is somewhat similar to a breaking pattern, with this major difference: the breaking pattern is thrusting out, then retreating back. In the change of mind pattern, the diagram has the movement going out, then the character realizes that he didn't want to go out, and he turns back on himself. The result is that the character is unable to make up his mind. As soon as he is sure, he changes his mind again.

5. *Enmeshing and trapping* is a movement pattern similar to placing the victim in the center of an open area. Another party may be able to walk to and around the victim. This pattern of movement is found in courtroom scenes in which the attorney walks up and around the person seated in the witness chair.

6. *Pounding pattern movement* is found in police stations when practicing cross-examinations. The staging pattern is to have the victim in the center, and the "pounders" encircle the victim and begin their verbal and/or physical pounding. This movement pattern operates as long as it implies some kind of threat by the "pounders."

7. *Discovery movement pattern* occurs when a character is surprised, then repelled by the sudden discovery, and then returns to claim the surprise.

8. *Fight movement patterns* are quite obvious and call for direct confrontation with the other subject.

9. Using many *s* curving moves and gestures, or soft moves in a circular fashion is what is meant by *love pattern*.

10. In the *chase pattern* one character is running away from the other. All kinds of chases are used, again depending on the script. Here too the diagonal line pattern may be employed.

● ●

EMPHASIS

Movement is one of the more powerful tools of emphasis and immediately commands attention. The obligation of the director is to give emphasis and to select the method. There are only three ways to gain emphasis, apart from postproduction special effects.

Subject's Movement

The subject's movement gains emphasis by its very nature. But the pattern of movement is determined by the props. The placement of doors and furniture creates a pattern of movement.

The rules guiding furniture placement come from the theater. Yale University professor Alexander Dean wrote a book, *Fundamentals of Play Directing*, which is an excellent source for theater staging, and is very thorough on blocking.

Most situation comedies, such as "The Cosby Show," "Married with Children," "What's Happenin'," and "The Jeffersons," just to name a few, have living room sets that are carefully designed for a flow of movement. Most of these sets include a sofa, an adjoining chair or two, and sometimes a piece of furniture that connects to an adjacent group. That available area makes a transition to another French scene easy. The use of doors and zany staging patterns can be seen in the play *Room Service*. It is a wonderful example of the use of the doors and how doors can manipulate the pattern of the play.

The sofa placement in relation to the exterior door and staircase, and/or the kitchen door, determines the overall pattern of movement for the entire piece. If the kitchen door is placed on camera right, and the staircase is the middle of the set, this forces the actors to enter and exit in a definite pattern. Hence the director has to determine the flow of the traffic. On occasion an art director/production set designer will do furniture placement on the set, which can lead to problems. Obviously, the flow of movement determines the camera placement and shots, and these must remain under the control of the director.

Say an actor enters through the exterior door, on camera left, then moves frame left to right. Once a sofa is encountered, she has to cross above or below the sofa. If the path is clear, then the actor moves in a sweeping, or direct, movement pattern.

Suppose the line of this movement is not in keeping with the spirit of the piece. Rather, a feeling of informality is wanted. Remembering that a broken line creates that feeling, the director places a table and a chair near the door, forcing the actor to negotiate in and around the table and chair. This is an example of how an actor is forced to move in a broken movement design.

Creating a pattern of movement on locations may be accomplished by staging around things like a tree, a fence, a road, and so on. For instance, say the movement requires a long, languid straight line across the screen to give the feeling of peace and solitude. Then the actor needs to walk down the road, right to left, or left to right, depending on the strength of the move; this pattern is determined by the selection of the road.

These rules are particularly helpful when moving large numbers of people, like armies marshaling to fight. When shooting on location the only other major determining factor is where the "big key light" is going to be and at what hour you need to be there to shoot. The big key light is the sun, of course. Its placement is not controllable, and allowance must be made for its use in the shot. Reflectors and artificial light are the other alternatives if you must have a certain shot at a certain hour.

Camera

Camera placement and selection of the lens constitute the second way for the director to control emphasis. Obviously, one approach is the single shot and additional emphasis is gained with the close-up of the subject. If a subject is to have emphasis in a shot with more than one person, then placing the subject in the foreground immediately gains emphasis. But once the subject moves, that gains him emphasis. In the theater the joke about gaining emphasis centered on the waving of a long handkerchief while the leading man was doing his lines. Movement commands attention.

Focus is another way. In "Hill Street Blues" the use of a telephoto lens as the subject moved quickly, but in focus, through the halls and corridors of the police station gave the subject emphasis. In this case, two camera elements gave the emphasis: the focus and the telephoto lens.

Soaps and sitcoms use two to four cameras. The pattern is the same as that of the master scene cinema language. The discipline of shooting a continuous pattern multicamera show is dramatically different in production procedure, but the cinema languages rules of directing apply equally as well.

Combination of Both

Examples of the combination of subject and camera working together can be found in many films. One of the more dramatic uses is seen in a couple of turntable shots in Brian DePalma's *Body Double* and in Milos Forman's *Hair*. These rather startling examples of subject and camera combination movement shots are created by placing the subject on a turntable with the camera tied to the platform at a fixed distance, assuring focus, while the backgrounds whirled by. In Orson Welles's *Touch of Evil* the opening crane shot is a ballet of camera crane and subject movement. Welles used movement master scene cinema language brilliantly here.

This was the first shot of the picture in the production shooting schedule. The studio bosses were about to close down the film. Welles, without going through studio channels, pulled together a crew and made the shoot happen. When the studio bosses viewed the dailies, they permitted him to continue, especially because of the support of Charlton Heston, who was a hot studio property at the time.

• •

MOVEMENT RULES FOR SUBJECTS

The philosophy of creative partnering between the actor and the director is a win-win situation for the film. Most actors prefer to take the director's lead and support. Frequently actors come up with excellent suggestions that supersede the director's preplanning. Most actors who have achieved success are accomplished artists (despite the publicity agent's propaganda that this star was discovered overnight) and should be respected. The years of training and emotional deprivation are rarely revealed since press agents know that audiences prefer to believe in the Cinderella Hollywood myth.

There are some exceptions when working in a stressful limited time frame like daytime drama. Placement of two to three cameras and shooting in a continuous pattern, requires blocking the actors prior to rehearsal. The show is to be shot and edited instantly on the same day. The actors under these circumstances appreciate all the help they can get. Remembering lines and blocking are the first priority for the actors. For the director it is getting the best quality but on a tight schedule. This situation is reminiscent of summer stock days when the requirement was a play a week, and knowing lines, blocking, and being on time for entrances and exits were the actors' concerns. Many actors, writers, and directors have honed their skills as a result of their daytime drama experience. Many stars have come out of soaps and sitcoms.

Today's daytime and sitcoms are the closest form to the excitement and vitality of live theater. In television the director has more control than in the theater. His ability to control the actor's performance and the other elements have to do with controlling the editing.

The principal factor in directing actors' movements is the motivation of the characters. Whether an actor feels he can move on a certain line is determined by the beat of the scene. We will examine this in Parts 5 and 6.

Generally some stage actors tend to move too much in film and television. In the theater, the actor's movement is necessary to get better picturizations. But in film this is accomplished through camera placement and cutting.

Body Movement

Stepping up, straightening up, placing weight on the foot nearest to the camera, rising, and walking forward are all considered strong body moves. In contrast, weak subject movement is stepping backward, slouching, placing the weight on the back foot or leaning backward away from camera, turning around, and walking away from the camera. Not only is body movement classified as strong or weak, but so is the line of movement.

A simple rule to follow is that if a strong movement is made and then followed by a weak movement, then the audience reads it as a weak move. Conversely, if a weak move is followed by a strong one, then the audience reads it like a strong move.

Dialogue

An actor has three choices in delivering dialogue: it can occur before, during, or after the movement. Each way of delivering these lines assumes a static camera for the following rules to prevail.

There are three ways for an actor to move and deliver a line. To say the line then move, to move with the line, or move, then deliver the line. Delivering the line prior to the movement gives emphasis to the movement. Saying the line as the actor moves throws focus on the move. The third way, the line gains emphasis because the movement points to it.

• • • • • • • • • • • • • • • • • • • •

THE GRAMMAR OF CAMERA MOVEMENT

The moving camera shot affords us opportunities to see the universe in ways we have never seen it before. All the camera moves need to be smooth and must not draw attention to the move itself. There are exceptions, however, where the use of a sharp move gives a special effect.

Tracking

Tracking is an old term going back to the days when the camera and dolly equipment were heavy and cumbersome. The least little bump caused the picture to jump. To make the picture appear smooth when the camera had to be moved, a track was laid down on the floor over the bump. The camera was mounted on a dolly with wheels that would run on the tracks. Many camera moves were made this way and in some instances still are. But it was and still is tedious, time consuming, and costly. Today, this approach is less of a problem because of lighter and more portable equipment. A track is used in cases where the floor is bumpy or the ground is rough.

Today *tracking* has come to imply another meaning. The camera and the subject are moving in sync, together. The subject is kept in the frame as she is moving . . . somewhere. It appears that the background moves, but the subject remains in focus and the same size. Four or more people may be involved in moving the camera. Hence the requirement from the actors is consistent, regular movement, but slower than normal. It will appear normal when screened. This type of move is sometimes called dollying.

Dolly

To dolly in or dolly out means the camera moves toward or away from the subject, but not parallel to the subject as with tracking. It is possible that a camera can be dollying and tracking in the same move. That is, the move may have the camera track with a character, then dolly in to a part of the scene for a close-up.

Crane

A camera placed on a large crane, similar to those used in the construction business, as well as to other, smaller cranes used in studios, is what we mean by a crane shot. These cranes are able to elevate and lower the camera. Yet all the crane shots, defying gravity and moving magically, as in Welles's *Touch of Evil,* are accepted by the audience. Somehow the audience attributes unlimited power to the camera. No matter what it does, as long as the content makes sense, the viewers accept the pictures.

Crane shots are wonderful. With ingenuity and the most recent technological breakthroughs they can give us a tool to do things that past masters could only dream of.

Arc

To arc a camera means to move it laterally in some up or down position. The term *arc* is used to describe certain crane moves or combinations of dolly and track shots.

Tilt

Tipping the camera up or down without moving the tripod is what we mean by *tilt*.

Pan

To pan the camera we move the head of the camera in a lateral fashion, right or left. The term comes from the word *panorama*—that is, to see the world in a sweep.

Combinations

Many of the moves described here are made together. For instance, it is not uncommon for the camera to dolly and tilt, or pan and track. To avoid confusion and to promote good communication, directors and camera operators need to agree on these definitions of terms.

• •

PERSPECTIVE MOVEMENT RULES OF THE CAMERA

Some peculiarities are intrinsic to the camera and lens and their relationship to the subject. Since the camera has monocular vision, an object moving along the center line of its angle of view indicates that its perspective is in reverse proportion to the retrogression from the lens. Everything comes out of depth, moves toward the center of the frame, and departs at the same rate of speed. The question is how we can use these characteristics of the camera.

Hitchcock used them effectively in *Vertigo*. When Jimmy Stewart looked down the staircase, this triggered a vertigo attack. Hitchcock believed that if the audience could experience vertigo, then they would relate even more to the hero, played by Jimmy Stewart. Hitchcock arrived at a practical game plan. He had a miniature scale model of the staircase built which matched the appearance of the staircase seen in the earlier shot. He had the camera dolly into the model and simultaneously zoom the lens back. Obviously this created a confused visual signal. Hitchcock hoped that this would make the viewer feel queasiness somewhat similar to the experience of vertigo.

Movement on the perspective main line may be made to appear static or dynamic. (Later we will examine the methodology for achieving static and dynamic shots.) In a perspective shot, the camera holds the subject in the frame, keeping it the same size. The subject does not appear to be moving; rather, only the background moves. This has a strong kinetic feel to the viewer and gives emphasis to the subject. The background feeds into the mood of the scene.

This technique can be further exploited. In *Charade*, starring Cary Grant and Audrey Hepburn, the director, Stanley Donen, used it to enhance his climax. In the climax Cary Grant is chasing Walter Matthau (the villain in this case) down a street. In the background are the pillars of a state building. As the camera tracks with Grant, the pillars pop into the shot and race across the frame; as one disappears, another pops in. The moving pillars act like kinetic hits upon the psyche of the viewer and increase the tension of the scene. This shot reinforces the theme of the film. A charade, of course, involves acting out something to give information. In this film, everyone was "acting out" another character. Audrey Hepburn and Cary Grant seemed to be the two who were not. At the end of the film we discover that even Cary Grant was doing a charade, pretending he was someone else.

One of the more interesting uses made of this perspective movement can be seen in Akira Kurosawa's classic film *Rashomon*. As Toshiro Mifune rushed through the forest, the trees flicked by one after another, crazily leaping across the picture. They created an instant barrier, splitting the beams of light. In his constant use of these "flashing trees" Kurosawa captured the feeling of this medieval forest, filled with lyric magic and eerie mysticism. Kurosawa asked the eternal universal question, What is truth? He is one of the few Asian filmmakers whose films are successful in the West.

Emphasis

Perspective strength can be used to advantage. Placing an object far from the camera and then whipping it into a close-up is a powerful way of gaining emphasis.

Static Movement

Static movement seems to be a contradictory term. It means movement that does not seem to move, though in fact movement is going on. It is a non-aggressive movement. It is an excellent tool for supporting specific emotional needs and yet also for creating a feeling of frustrated movement.

There are three static movement formats. Each has a different formula and a different creative function.

Earlier, we discussed briefly the tracking shot. Essentially the moving subjects are held in a static format while the background moves. The power of this procedure is in its secondary emphasis and in its contrast to the primary.

The background may be something as simple as crowds of people. But the pressure of "hurrying crowds" on the foreground characters may appear to be minimal or dynamic, depending upon the choice of the director. This has more to do with the way the director, with the DP's support, decides to register the emotional content of the shot. Contrasting a frenetic background with a calm foreground of characters is one choice, and it makes one type of comment. The background can also be used to show pending threat. This means that at some point the secondary emphasis will shift to become the primary. This may be done for shock effect, but the method is the same.

For example, say a couple of friends are walking down a lonely, deserted road in the country. They are talking. We dolly the camera back, holding them in a medium two-shot. The focus is foreground so the deep background is soft but discernable, barely. As the friends are chatting away, a shape appears in that background. We cannot make it out, but it moves rapidly toward the "heroes" in the foreground. Threat has created empathy for them. The shape moves quickly on the road. At this point we shift the focus imperceptibly, increasing the depth of field. This makes the shape real that is heading for the heroes.

We are now watching this fast-moving object, and our concern increases; we grow more tense. In effect the process of shifting focus from the secondary to the primary has occurred. The viewer is curious to know what the threatening object is.

Consider a picture in which the foreground and the background are both static; then the moving subject seems to be in a state of frozen stasis. A telephoto lens has the ability to create that feeling of static movement. The composition choices depend on the emotions dictated by the content of the story.

Dynamic Movement

Dynamic movement creates the feeling of opposition. In the previous section's scenario, the contrasting moving shots, like the object moving down the road, were dynamic shots.

• • • • • • • • • • • • • • • • • • •

THE SUBJECT AND CAMERA OPTICS

Creatively using lenses in movement is an important skill. Most static shots require a telephoto lens. The narrow depth of field makes it work. The wide-angle lens accentuates movement. Action placed in depth and moved forward appears to move twice as fast and is dynamic when a wide-angle lens is used, as we have cited previously.

The combination of both static and dynamic movement with the proper lens support enhances the overall effect. Frequently a knowledgeable cameraman is helpful and may suggest combinations of lenses and dolly gear which produce results far beyond the director's expectations.

In this chapter we examined the variations of the rule of movement, how it operates with people (subjects) and with the camera, and finally the overall kinetic and aesthetic principles. We have up to this point avoided discussing the specific details of how movement weaves into the various cinema languages themselves. That is the purpose of the next chapter.

Chapter 14

MOVEMENT
CINEMA LANGUAGE

Movement cinema language is different from any of the other cinema languages because its principles operate within the other cinema languages. Each movement cinema language has rules similar to its non-movement counterpart but with exceptions. These exceptions are the focus of this discussion.

First, all the rules stated in Chapters 9, 10, 11, and 12 are in force with the movement cinema language counterpart. The difference is in the limitations that movement places on the specific cinema language. Movement occupies space and takes time, just like all the other cinema languages, except movement can be lengthened or shortened, compressed or expanded. The manner of its execution has an impact on the viewer.

Since movement cinema language is designed to cut into the film as single unit, it invokes constructive cinema language discipline. Specific detailed planning is necessary. The requirement is that the move must end at a definite point before the nonmovement cut is initiated. This is constructive cinema language.

• • • • • • • • • • • • • • • • • •

RULES

There are rules for cutting movement into the selected cinema language which the director needs to know in order to plan for it. To avoid jarring the viewer and drawing attention to the move, the movement must come to a full stop before a cut is made to the next nonmovement shot. In addition, the move must begin and end at a definite point and be seen in the shot.

The exception is when the cut is to another moving shot. Generally, the connective shot is a form of matching movement or shape. Matching screen direction is another example of a connective device that modifies the cut.

The realm of editing movement gets to be quite interesting. Being able to move the images around, unlike nonmovement shots, opens up vistas never imagined previously. There is a freedom that is not available in static cutting. This concept is not restricted to moving shots but applies as well to what appear to be nonmovement shots—these are in fact a form of movement shots.

Every director knows that camera movement and subject movement constitute a useful creative tool when operating within the disciplines of the various cinema languages. But the tool some directors may not be aware of is this remarkable ability to jiggle the image so the figure moves, jumps, or snaps into various positions. From a traditional viewpoint this was once considered a "mistake" and classified as a "jump cut," meaning that the image jumps without matching the exact position in the previous frame. Like many discoveries it came out of the desire to avoid a mistake. This mistake may have originated in a shot with a damaged frame or two which somehow was mistakenly cut into a sequence with a missing frame or two. When the layperson saw the result, he was startled and fascinated by these little shifts.

Master filmmakers now use it constantly. Examine Hitchcock's *Psycho* shower sequence, for example. At the beginning of the sequence, before the entrance of the killer, Janet Leigh in the shower was jumped around in the frame to startle the viewer. Hitchcock used this technique throughout the shower sequence and concluded the scene with it. These shots appeared to be static, nonmovement shots. Yet they turned into moving shots without the audience's knowing it. Most viewers believe the shots are continuous and are not aware of the cutting.

In most action sequences, there are opportunities to shift the image, making the sequence more exciting. There are camera position procedures that gracefully accomplish and implement this "jump cut" philosophy.

Multiple cameras are often used to shoot an event that is not repeatable, like the burning of a building or a car race. Cutting back and forth between the two cameras is common coverage in action events involving racing cars or airplanes. These camera position choices are made simply to cover the action of the event, creating, in a sense, a master shot of each phase of the event. That is not what we are talking about!

To make it appear as if the images jump, lock two cameras together into the same position, with a minor difference in the size of the subject but not such a major difference that it appears to be another shot. If camera A has a car in a full-length shot, while camera B has it in another full-length shot, they are not exactly the same shot, though their angle of view and the subject size of the shot is almost identical. When the two shots are cut together it makes the cars or subjects seem to jump around in the frame. The excitement of the action is greatly enhanced, and it is rare for the viewer to be aware that these are two different shots being cut together.

Rules are lessons to learn from. Another case in point is the rule concerning crossing the "axis" to avoid reversing the direction of the subject. Avoiding crossing the axis is a rule supported mainly by editors or inexperienced directors. Crossing the axis is simply another tool for moving the image around. Matching direction when cutting from one camera to another is common sense. The confusion occurs when the theory is couched in mysterious terms that sound so ominous.

Crossing the axis means the subjects in the frame appear to reverse their position. The camera is placed on the opposite side of the subject, making the subject looking frame right in fact looking frame left.

Giving the other side, or a three-dimensional feel, is the wonderful part of filmmaking. As a matter of fact, constructive and fragmented cinema language often use it. Master scene and interpersonal cinema languages practitioners are fearful that the cut is jarring and that it violates the space and time of these cinema languages. The audience, however, accepts direct cuts without the neutral cut when some of the other cutting techniques are used. Often, cutting on action into a reverse position is acceptable. For instance, the entrance into a room which reverses the direction of the movement is acceptable. Another trick to remember is to place the subject in the same third of the frame on the reverse cut.

Going from a detail to a long shot, or the reverse (starting with a wide establishing shot, then going into some detail), revealing a shocking piece of unexpected information, was one of Hitchcock's favorite uses of movement cinema language. To slip in and discover some intimate detail that denies the appearance of what it seems or that throws a new and startling light on that event is one of the more popular devices. You may recall that this is one of the rules of cinema language but in this case the rule concerns the relationship to movement.

Hitchcock has the camera move off the center axis and into a lateral direction, which keeps the viewer fascinated. Spielberg does the same in *Raiders of the Lost Ark* bar scene (see Figure 14.1).

Movement cinema language is more than just a category; it has its own aesthetic principles. Movement is a powerful tool within the cinema

Figure 14.1   Raiders of the Lost Ark *bar scene.*

MOVEMENT PATTERN FLOORPLAN

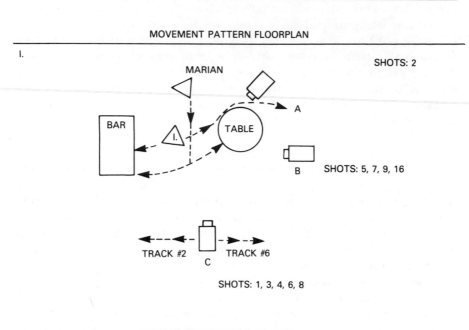

(MARIAN X HITS INDY X TO BAR)

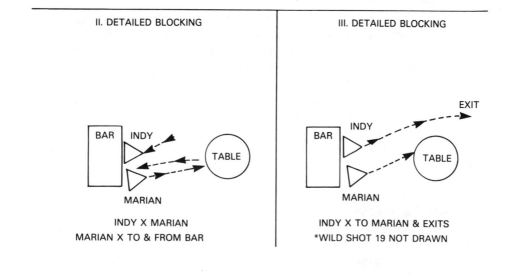

II. DETAILED BLOCKING

INDY X MARIAN
MARIAN X TO & FROM BAR

III. DETAILED BLOCKING

INDY X TO MARIAN & EXITS
*WILD SHOT 19 NOT DRAWN

language. Like all artistic tools it must be explored and used. Scorcese did it in *Taxi Driver, GoodFellas,* and *Raging Bull;* more recently, directors like John McTiernan (*Die Hard*) and Richard Donner (*Lethal Weapon*), to name a few, are using movement in different and exciting ways.

As you read this chapter on movement, be aware that you have just begun its exploration. There is more here than meets the eye, because it moves.

• • • • • • • • • • • • • • • • • •

MOVEMENT MASTER SCENE

In *Twelve Angry Men,* Sidney Lumet, the director, invoked movement master scene. The camera glides around the closed room, eavesdropping on the panel of jurors who are there to determine the life or death of the defendant. In this moving shot Lumet elected not to use any close-ups. The film is a study of the interpersonal relationships of the twelve men on the jury. The dynamics among these men and how they arrive at their decision is the theme.

Director Lumet uses movement master scene cinema language expertly. A shot running about 6 minutes begins the film.

This sequence begins with a bird's eye view of the holding room for the jurors to determine their verdict. They file into the room. It is a hot, humid evening in New York City. This is the master scene cinema language obligatory establishing shot setting the geography of the players. Then the camera arcs down and follows each person as he expresses his opinion about their situation, about the trial, and about the other people and their situations.

In this one running movement master shot, we are introduced to the members of the jury. The camera glides with each of them as they pair off from the group and we eavesdrop. When we gain insight into each pair, we move to meet another pair. Lumet motivates the camera by character movement and has done it so artfully that the viewer is never conscious of the camera moves. We gain an intimate view of each person as the reality of the jurors' is brought home to the viewer.

Though this is classified as movement master scene, it does not follow the master scene rules exactly. The payoff in each vignette comes in the way of dialogue, with pictorial composition support, but with no payoff close-ups.

Orson Welles's *Touch of Evil* is a tour de force movement master scene sequence.

This sequence is intricate and what makes it even more remarkable is that it was executed more than 30 years ago. Both *Touch of Evil* and *Twelve Angry Men* use the crane quite artfully but in dramatically different ways.

In *Touch of Evil* the sequence starts with a close-up of a bomb. The camera moves back to reveal a figure standing in an alley with a bomb in his hand. A couple, laughing, is coming down the alley toward us. The figure darts off. The camera tracks with him to a parked convertible. He places the bomb in the trunk. We hear a burst of laughter as the figure darts off but not before slamming the lid closed on the trunk.

The couple gets into the convertible and drives off. The music starts. Though it is dated, it has a jazz, romantic, syncopated beat, with a clear "tick-tock" in the music. (Perhaps this borders on excess, but it worked with the picture using collision cinema language.)

We crane back over rooftops to discover and hold the convertible in the frame as it moves down a darkened city street and stops at a traffic light. As the car moves toward us, we arc down to street level; as the car passes off frame, we pick up on this couple crossing into the frame we hear their dialogue.

They are recently married. We continue to track them walking down a busy street past other structures to a barrier that turns out to be the checkpoint for entrance to the United States from Mexico.

In the background comes the convertible as our couple walks up to the immigration officer. He recognizes Charlton Heston as a Mexican national policeman who recently broke up a drug ring. His comment indicates that Heston may be in for a lot of trouble because of the power of the drug traffickers.

The important thing to note is that the rules for the master scene cinema language are the same in movement master scene, except for some of the obvious restrictions. Time in this discipline happens moment to moment. The first shot is an establishing shot that sets up the place and people. The moving camera does not draw attention to itself, nor are there obtuse angles or jumps in the continuity.

Interestingly enough, the need for repetitive shots or cycles of shots is still there. The repetition is more kinetic than a repeated shot pattern. That is, the camera moves are repeated either by execution or by similar moves.

In *Twelve Angry Men* the camera moves are clearly repeated. The camera pans with one subject into a two-shot, then the same pattern is repeated over and over again. On a couple of occasions Lumet varied the moves by having a person carry the camera over to a new two-character scene, while the subject who brought the camera over wanders off. Obviously, the camera moves are motivated by the movement of the subject. This follows the invisible camera cut rule of master scene cinema language.

It is jarring to watch a camera move without a motivation within this cinema language. This mistake is apparent to the layman viewer. There are times when the director elects to fool the viewer into believing that she is using master scene cinema language but actually using another.

In master scene, invisible cutting and movement are mandated because the concept of moment to moment reality must not be violated; the scene must look as if it were happening right there at that moment without any artificial means of control. When the camera becomes intrusive into the consciousness of the viewer, it violates the viewer's treasured make-believe. The viewer, without understanding why, may get angry at the film. So caution is necessary when the director decides to violate the integrity of the cinema language.

In another instance, Lumet had a character re-enter and carry the camera over as he picked up another scene with another participant. But the move was deliberately repeated, and expected, and accepted by the audience. Again, these patterns make the audience feel safe because they know exactly where they are and who the characters are. Another rule of the master scene cinema language is similarly followed in movement master scene cinema language.

In *Touch of Evil* Welles's movement pattern is repeated and the audience is tantalized more by the unexpected. That is Welles's style. When the viewer thinks the pattern is going to change, this builds tension, and so Welles repeats the move and the viewer is happily relieved.

Welles uses this technique over and over again. It gained for him a strength, familiarity, and popularity that made his style unique. The variations of his moves are made more exciting because of the breadth and depth, and the visceral moves violating gravity made the events exciting and different.

The use of movement in movement master scene is quite exciting because it marries with other cinema languages — with collision cinema language, for instance, in *Touch of Evil*. The music track was essentially a form of collision cinema language, which gave the scene a pulse and a counterpoint to the content, until finally the car explodes.

• • • • • • • • • • • • • • • • • • •

MAKING DIALOGUE VISUAL

Now is the time to review and note how Steven Spielberg made the dialogue visual in the Marian's bar scene. Spielberg used stage business and precise crosses to carry the camera into the close shots for emphasis, yet he held the scene in a two-shot because he wished us to view Marian and Indy's relationship continuously. Obviously, the close-ups were put in for emphasis.

The point of view is Indy's. You sense that from the moving two-shots. Spielberg used different movement to make the dialogue visual and have correct picturization.

Using the form of a shooting script, we have diagrammed the character's movement and the camera position as well. See Figure 14.1.

Raiders of the Lost Ark

MOVEMENT PATTERN

Shot   Description

BEAT _____ <1>

1   MEDIUM SHOT OF MARIAN . . . POV INDY ("C"
       Camera)

       AS MARIAN PUTS HER COLD SHOT GLASSES TO HER
       HEAD, A SHADOW LOOMS OVER HER.

                    INDY (OFFSCREEN)
               Hello, Marian.

                    MARIAN
               Indiana Jones. (X's TO HIM)
               I always knew someday you'd
               come walkin' through my door.

2   OVER HER SHOULDER . . . TO INDY ("A" Camera)

                    MARIAN
               I never doubted that. Something
               made it inevitable. (X's TO
               STRIKING DISTANCE) So what
               are you doing here in Nepal?

3   OVER HIS SHOULDER . . . TO MARIAN ("C" Camera)

                    INDY
               I need one of the pieces your
               father collected.

       SHE HITS HIM WITH A SOLID RIGHT TO THE JAW.

                    MARIAN
               I learned to hate you in the last
               ten years.

MARIAN X's FRAME LEFT AND EXITS. CAMERA
HOLDS INDY IN A SINGLE SHOT.

BEAT _____ <2>

> INDY
> I never meant to hurt you.

> MARIAN (OFF-SCREEN)
> I was a child. I was in love.

4   TWO MEDIUM SHOT OF MARIAN AND INDY . . .
FAVORING HER ("C" Camera)

> MARIAN (CONT'D)
> It was wrong. You knew it.

INDY X's TO BAR. CAMERA TRACKS WITH HIM.

> INDY
> You knew what you were doing.

MARIAN FOLLOWS HIM, SHOT GOES INTO OVER
INDY'S SHOULDER TO MARIAN.

> MARIAN
> Now I do!

MOHAN IS SEEN ENTERING THROUGH THE EX-
TERIOR DOOR IN THE BACKGROUND. SHE GESTURES
AT MOHAN.

> MARIAN
> This is my place! Get out!
> (speaks in Nepalese)

MOHAN RESPONDS IN NEPALESE AND EXITS
THROUGH THE DOOR.

> INDY
> I did what I did.

BEAT _____ <3>

> INDY (CONT'D)
> You don't have to be happy
> about it but maybe we can help
> each other out now.

5   TWO LONG SHOT . . . ("B" Camera)

MARIAN CROSSES TO TABLE . . . IN THE
FOREGROUND

INDY X's TO HER

> INDY
> I need one of the pieces your
> father collected. A bronze piece
> about this size with a hole in it,
> off-center, with a crystal. You
> know the one I mean?

HE MAKES A CIRCLE WITH HIS FINGERS. SHE PICKS
UP THE GLASSES.

6   TWO MEDIUM LONG SHOT ("C" Camera)

SHE PICKS UP TRAY WITH GLASSES AND X's
TOWARD THE BAR

> MARIAN
> Yeah, I know it.

CAMERA TRACKS WITH HER TO BAR . . . ENDING IN
A CHEST SHOT OF HER

BEAT _____ <4>

> INDY
> Where's Abner?

MARIAN DOESN'T ANSWER. INDY X's TO ABOVE HER
AT THE BAR ENDING IN A TIGHT TWO SHOT.

                    INDY
          Where's Abner?

                    MARIAN
          Abner's dead.

INDY'S ATTITUDE CHANGES INSTANTLY. THIS IS
SAD NEWS.

                    INDY
          Marian, I'm sorry.

BEAT _____ <5>

                    MARIAN
          Do you know what you did to me,
          to my life?

7   TWO LONG SHOT ("B" Camera)

                    INDY
          I can only say I'm sorry so many
          times.

MARIAN DUMPS THE GLASSES ONTO THE BAR WITH
A LOUD CRASH.

                    MARIAN
          (X's TABLE IN F.G.)
          Well, say it again, anyway.

                    INDY
          (X's OFF FRAME RIGHT) Sorry.

BEAT _____ <6>

                    MARIAN
          (AT TABLE PICKING UP
          GLASSES)
          Yeah, everybody's sorry. Abner
          was sorry for dragging me all

over the earth looking for his little pieces of junk. I'm sorry to
still be stuck in this dive. (X's
BACK TO BAR)

8   M.S. SHOT OF INDY AT BAR . . . MARIAN X's INTO
      BACKGROUND ("C" Camera)

                    MARIAN
            Everybody's sorry for some-
            thing.

9   TWO LONG SHOT AT BAR

                    INDY
            It's a worthless bronze medal-
            lion, Marian. Are you going to
            give it to me?

                    MARIAN
            (X's BACK TO TABLE) Maybe. I
            don't know where it is.

INDY TURNS TO HER.

                    INDY
            Well, maybe you could find it.
            Three thousand bucks.

HE HOLDS THE MONEY IN HIS FIST.

                    MARIAN
            (X's BACK TO BAR) Well, that'll
            get me back.

10   M.S. OF INDY AT BAR

MARIAN X's TO BAR ABOVE INDY

                    MARIAN
            But, not in style.

                         INDY
              I can get you another two when
              we get to the states.

11   OVER HIS SHOULDER . . . TO CLOSE UP OF MARIAN

                         INDY
              It's important, Marian.

12   CLOSE UP OF INDY . . . POV MARIAN

                         INDY
              Trust me.

13   OVER HIS SHOULDER TO CLOSE UP OF HER

BEAT _____ <7>

              MARIAN WENT TO HIT INDY AGAIN BUT INDY
              CAUGHT HER HAND IN MID-FLIGHT, AND THRUST
              THE MONEY INTO HER HAND.

14   CLOSE UP OF INDY

                         INDY
              You know the piece I mean.

15   TWO CLOSE SHOT AT BAR . . . FAVORING HER

                         INDY
              You know where it is.

                        MARIAN
              (LAUGHING) Come back tomor-
              row.

16   CLOSE UP OF INDY

                         INDY
              Why?

17   OVER SHOULDER TO HIM

MARIAN
Because I said so, that's why.

18   TWO LONG SHOT ("B" Camera)

MARIAN X's TO THE TABLE IN F.G.

19   MEDIUM OF INDY AT BAR

INDY X's TOWARD:

20   MEDIUM TWO SHOT OF MARIAN & INDY

INDY X's ABOVE HER . . . EXITS FRAME RIGHT

MARIAN
Ha!

21   CLOSE SHOT OF EXTERIOR DOOR INDY OPENS

THE DOOR AND COMES INTO CLOSE-UP

MARIAN
See you tomorrow, Indiana Jones

INDY DOES NOT LOOK HAPPY. HE CLOSES THE DOOR.

_____ END OF SCENE _____

Courtesy Lucasfilms Ltd.

• • • • • • • • • • • • • • • • • •

MOVEMENT INTERPERSONAL

As we know interpersonal cinema language is based on isolating shots of the participants. In the moving shot, the director has several choices for achieving the isolation: the camera can move to each subject, or the subject can move to the stationary camera, or a combination of both. The combination often involves a trick, such as using a mirror or "racking" the focus.

The camera moving to each of the participants is quite obvious and does not require additional instructions. The camera pans, tilts, arcs, dollies, or tracks, isolating each subject. This implies that the subjects are moving while the camera is isolating the subjects.

Having the subject move into single shots is quite common. This approach has the character cross to another offscreen character, and as they turn, the camera discovers the second person. The first is then off-camera. This is similar to a counter-cross form used in the theater.

The combination of camera and subject movement is used most frequently in I-P. When two characters are walking toward the camera down a street, the manner of creating I-P is by having the camera track with each character in a single shot. The track and the dolly depend on the beat of the scene and the choice of the director.

Again, the same rules apply to movement I-P as to the nonmovement I-P. The unity of time and place and viewer replacement in the relationship is necessary to make it work.

• • • • • • • • • • • • • • • • • • • •

CONSTRUCTIVE MOVEMENT

Movement must be in constructive cinema language because of the obligation of cutting in and out of the other nonmovement sequences; this makes it necessary to plan it. In addition, movement in film has to cut in as a unit.

Detailed planning of sequences in sections, linking them with repeating shots, and the dynamics come through because it is constructive movement cinema language. Whether it matches or violates time and space depends on which other cinema language is being used.

• • • • • • • • • • • • • • • • • • • •

FRAGMENTED MOVEMENT

To use movement in its most poetic, dramatic form is to invoke fragmented cinema language. The opportunities abound today because of fast films, portability, and the visual propensity of many people, since they were weaned on the moving image through television. Their level of sophistication and acceptance is remarkable.

The portable camera, with all its special lenses, such as the snorkel, and the antigravity camera tripod give us the extraordinary opportunity to examine things in motion in great detail. The ability to capture an action in this manner is dramatic and fascinating.

Content has little to do with the director's choice in using one of the specific movement cinema languages but still should be considered as part of the orchestration plan for the film.

An example of fragmented movement cinema language is found in Scorsese's *Taxi Driver*. In an unbroken move the camera examines the universe of steel and wheels and chrome in a 360-degree circling movement around the taxi as Robert DeNiro drives down through New York. We understand the fragmented world the protagonist lives in.

In this case, the director was writing his film with a cinema language. A series of fragmented shots could have accomplished the same creative goal, but the move added depth and reality superior to a shot.

SYMBOLIC MOVEMENT

Movement lends itself to symbolic movement cinema language quite comfortably. Nature abounds with moving symbols, such as the sun and the stars. Again, the same rules carry through in this cinema language.

PARALLEL MOVEMENT

Many of the old silent movies used parallel cinema language as their staple in the old melodramas, especially in chase sequences. Today we may use parallel with more subtlety, but it essentially is the same.

This cinema language is frequently invoked in action sequences. The same rules when cutting action sequences in parallel prevail as in non-movement parallel.

The same rules for manipulating time in and between sequences, and the rules that govern switching from the primary to the secondary, remain in force for parallel movement cinema language as well.

COLLISION MOVEMENT

Introducing movement to collision cinema is quite natural since the principle of conflict is inherent in this cinema language. The use of dynamic and static movement lends itself to this cinema language.

The rules for using metric and tonal cutting in collision movement cinema language are the same, except of course it is in motion.

VORKAPICH MOVEMENT

Vorkapich is used in movement but infrequently. Since the repetitive actions must be done in cycles, this presents a challenge in using movement (though when it is used the results are quite dramatic).

SUBJECTIVE MOVEMENT

Like Vorkapich movement, subjective movement cinema language is limited. Rapport between the viewer and the action on the screen is needed.

Many subjective shots incorporate movement. This simulates the movement of the offscreen character. The same rules apply to subjective movement as to subjective cinema language.

• • • • • • • • • • • • • • • • • • •
TRANSITION MOVEMENT

Examples of the use of transition movement include the telescopic transition device described earlier in the *Citizen Kane* sequence. You may recall the scene in which Kane and his new bride had their first breakfast together. The sequence stayed with them over the next dozen years, and we saw the falling apart of their relationship. The swish pan (or whip pan, as some call it) is a good example of how movement can be used to invoke transition movement cinema language.

• • • • • • • • • • • • • • • • • • •
CINE VERITÉ MOVEMENT

The "shaky" style type of movement required in this cinema language has been discussed. It simulates an extemporaneous style of filming that needs to be maintained in this cinema language. The same rules of the cine verité apply to movement. Always bear in mind that movement in this language must be motivated.

• • • • • • • • • • • • • • • • • • •
MIXTURE OF MOVEMENT

The mixture is frequently found in action pictures where movement and action are the prime need. The mixing of these movement cinema languages presents some startling and wonderful challenges, especially with the new technology.

It is clear that there are many opportunities and challenges in invoking movement cinema languages in different combinations, opening avenues for exploring filmic movement in ways not dreamed of before.

PART **5**

THE ACTOR'S LANGUAGE

Chapter **15**

UNDERSTANDING THE ACTOR

Actors bring the flesh, blood, and sinew to their characters. Depending on their talent, their contribution can be enormous.

The director understands that the actor's training is unlike the training of any other artist. First, the instrument is the actor himself. Second, the artist-actor has been trained in a unique way. His training concerns personal feelings since his discipline requires that he deliver an emotion on cue. To make it more difficult, the actor must deliver the "right" emotion as scripted. This can be very difficult, since life does not prepare us to come up with feelings on cue. Nevertheless we expect and demand that the professional actor do just that.

• • • • • • • • • • • • • • • • • • •

THE GRAMMAR OF THE ACTOR

If the actor, for reasons unbeknownst to us, does not perform on cue, then we are annoyed or even angry. Sometimes this annoyance will show up in the crew's attitude. The crew members may grow impatient if the actor does not deliver on cue; they do their job, why should they expect less from an actor? Adding to this is the common belief that there are hundreds of actors anxiously waiting in the wings.

The bottom line is that an actor brings emotion and life to the material. This unique marriage between the heart and the mind of the actor is difficult, and unless the director understands and appreciates the process she will not be able to assist the actor. It is an excellent idea for the director to do some acting as well.

Rapport

Knowing the actor's training and background helps the director to communicate with the actor. Rapport brings trust, and with trust, the actor has no limit. The actor and the director should form a partnership and be collaborators in the creative process.

Case Study: *John "Pappy" Ford*

John Ford built rapport using the principles of Yevgeny Vakhtangov. Ford set up a permanent location camp in Monument Valley in Utah. It was there that most of the famous Westerns were shot (as a result, many viewers of Westerns have mistaken Monument Valley as representing the West). Most of the Ford troupe of actors came to stay at this location and to live for months at a time. Some liked it so much and felt so at home that they stayed beyond their required time. Though never directed to do so by Ford himself, each person somehow played his or her role offcamera as well as on. Ford had set up the location in a manner that encouraged this playing of roles on an everday basis. For instance, if a movie included a family, the actors portraying the onscreen family were housed together as if indeed they were living together.

Every day after the day's shooting, the company assembled to have dinner, and then for storytelling or group singing. When casting his movie, Ford cast the actor not only for his role in the movie but for his ability to integrate with the company during the off-hours. In fact, he cast the actors who were as close to the character as possible. Almost all his actors were used over and over again. They frequently became associated with the classic Western types that they and Ford invented. That was total rapport.

The actors lived together and performed their roles in a day to day manner. When they performed in front of the camera, they did what they had been doing every day since their arrival. It was so natural for them. They were at their best when they worked in a Ford film.

Some actors' work was so superior to any of their other past work that Ford was thought to be a genius to get such fine performances out of them. But the technique Ford used was unknown to him; he was following his own instincts. It was a technique practiced in Russia by a young fiery student of Stanislavsky, Yevgeny Vakhtangov. He practiced the concept of having his theater company live together and live their roles on a daily basis. The difference was they consciously worked at it. Ford was much subtler. But the bottom line was that it worked, and they both had a good deal of success.

It was also said that Ford never explained the action or talked about objectives or beats, but rather kept his direction simple. He would tell an actor to get off his horse and walk through those doors into the saloon. It was deceptively simple. He did not give the actor any baggage or inner meaning, but simply requested he do it.

In other words, he knew that people do not act, they do things, simply. In the most dramatic situation, people just do things they do every day and they do it simply. Dwelling on the meaning of the script or on the message to the audience is just not "actable," let alone directable. Human beings just do what they do every day. What makes us extraordinary is we do these simple things in extraordinary circumstances. Ford knew that and approached his films and actors that way. In truth he used Vorkapich, but with style.

John Wayne was a Ford Protégé. Wayne was never as good as he was in the films he made for Ford. It was Ford who helped develop his "star persona." He discouraged Wayne from going to acting school, but rather encouraged him to be himself, to be his own man, and never to permit his fears, or fears of his limitations, to appear on the set. He gave him the gift of love and total protection.

• • • • • • • • • • • • • • • • • •

ACTING LANGUAGE

Like all professions, acting has its own langauge.

History

The Group Theater was formed out of a WPA project during the Depression era. It included such people as Lee Strasberg, Cheryl Crawford, Harold Clurman, Robert Lewis, Martin Ritt, Luther Adler, and Stella Adler, just to name a few. Members of this group became the leaderes who set the style of acting that has gained world attention and now is considered the American acting school. It has so strongly affected the world of theater and film that many leading films and stage productions have set the standard. The American actor has become the standard that many systems emulate. Ironically the system was born in the Soviet Union. The soul-searching artistic director of the Moscow Art Theater, Igor Stanislavsky, was the founder of the American system we refer to as the "method."

Today most of the actor's language is based on the method. This is short-hand for the Stanislavsky method of acting. This technique was used by almost all the great actors of past generations like Luther Adler, John Garfield, Lee J. Cobb, and recently Marlon Brando. Today's practitioners of the method include Al Pacino, Paul Newman, Robert Redford, and Dustin Hoffman. The method has left an indelible mark upon the American actor, as well as on the worldwide acting community. This discipline is built upon a series of training procedures that have to do with internal techniques.

The Method's Prime Directive

The prime directive of the method is to train the actor to access his emotions. This is quite a task.

Suppose you question yourself and ask where your emotions are. Our emotions and memories are stored in the unconscious in minute detail. Some believe we even remember our birth. This is the part of the brain that carries all our history, all the wonderful happy and unhappy feelings we have ever experienced. It does not forget anything. We think we can't remember, but if we lived through it, it is stored in the unconscious. Hypnosis proves it every time.

To command consciously the unconscious is difficult. To command the unconscious to bring forth an emotion at the precise moment required is truly impossible. Try it: command yourself to feel anger, love, or jealousy.

The prime directive of the method is to give the person tools ("methods") to tap into the unconscious. The romantic image from the master scene cinema language supports the actor. If the actor has "natural" talent—which means the ability to access an empathic personality—that actor may become a star. Such actors include Marilyn Monroe, Cary Grant, Judy Holiday, Dustin Hoffman, Al Pacino, Paul Newman, and John Wayne. Wayne is the most obvious example because he did not take acting lessons. Wayne simply did it.

Many Methods

In truth, the method has many methods. It gives the actors tools for tapping into their unconscious and getting the emotions that are needed. Some unusual procedures have to be used in order to encourage the unconscious to participate in this process. But first let's deal with some of the method terms.

Different Terms, Different Schools

Method acting schools have common concepts, though each splinter group has its own terminology. Terms like *superobjective, spine, action, motivation,* and *through line* simply mean, what does the character want. As in life, we have an objective, we want something, or a person, or we wish to achieve something—that is our purpose, and how we try to achieve it is what the script is about. This is true for a play or a screenplay.

When the terms *superobjective, spine,* or *action* are used, they simply refer to the objective the character has throughout the entire screenplay. In *Raiders of the Lost Ark* Indiana Jones's superobjective, or the spine of his character, was to find lost treasures and bring them to the public. His was a dedication bordering on obsession. From the actor's language, Indiana Jones's superobjective was to find artifacts. The term *spine* means the same thing.

This objective concept is common to all the various method schools, whether Strasberg's or the Neighborhood Playhouse, or the individual schools: they all subscribe to the same concept. They are based on the method.

One of the first questions the director asks the actor is, Are you a method actor? If so, what school of acting did you attend? How can I best serve you when it comes to your personal way of working? Then the director should keep quiet and allow the actor to talk. Many actors will, but some may not be able to verbalize it. Listen patiently to those actors especially. The story goes that Richard Burton learned to listen when he got into film acting. Listening is healing.

Finally the principle actors should be reminded that the technicians are here to serve them, that no matter what happens, the creative artist makes the difference in the film. This statement is important because too many have the impression that the technician is king. Generally, most actors are intimidated by the technicians. It is the director's job to make the actor feel safe. No matter how experienced the actor is, or how much bravado he projects, when he appears on the set, the simple fact is that he is scared.

Don't be fooled by actors; just understand that they are scared. And it is okay to be scared. Turn the experience into fun. Set aside "judgment" and become the child at the movies. Never lose that sense of wonder and innocence. In this way, you, the director, become the audience.

The actor who has achieved stardom requires special handling. Most actors test the director in their own way. It has to do with a feeling of trust. Actors know how vulnerable they are.

If the director does not violate the actor's trust, then the bonding process happens. This is what we mean when we speak of rapport. Rapport between the director and the actors is necessary for performances and films to be made which are extraordinary. Every director has a group of actors he works with only because it is so efficient. The shorthand between the actor and director sometimes borders on telepathy.

● ● ● ● ● ● ● ● ● ● ● ● ● ● ● ● ● ● ● ●

FILM ACTING

Film acting is not the same as stage acting. Surprisingly, many excellent theater people teach acting as if it were only for the stage. Of course many procedures and techniques do travel well to the dramatically different world of film and television acting. But there are differences as well. The purpose of stage acting is to rehearse over and over so the play can be performed dozens of times, with the hope that it may run for years.

This is the exact opposite of film acting. It is rare that the actor will get the opportunity to rehearse more than twice. Normally, if the actors are rehearsing a play, there is no instant performance requirement. Not so in film. Rehearsal is brief, the time to repeat more than two or three times is rare, and the need to perform is immediate.

In addition, there is a different creative position for performing than for the stage. In films the need for the actor to be himself or herself is essential. Hence there are additional procedures and techniques for film acting which need to be developed to help the actor with the challenge of developing film acting skills.

• • • • • • • • • • • • • • • • • • •

PROFESSIONAL FILM ACTING

Requirements

The professional film actor has learned some rules that make his experience on the set easier and gain the respect of the crew and cast members. Directors recognize this skill.

Hitting the Mark

Unlike stage acting, film acting requires precision. Since a lens has a narrow view, the actor has to be at his designated position. To make it more of a challenge, rarely does the actor have the luxury of hours of rehearsal as in the theater. The film actor's discipline requires trust, facility, and spontaneity.

Camera and Sound Characteristics

It is helpful for the actor to know the size of the shot he is in. Obviously, in a close-up the actor cannot make broad gestures. It is wise for the director to tell the actor of those restrictions. Actors need to learn to act with their eyes, their fingers, their mouths, and so on.

The actor needs to be sensitive to the limitations of the microphone. It is difficult for the sound people to handle great variations in sound level. If you shout one minute and then talk softly, this causes extreme difficulties for the sound mixer and will be a problem in mixing the picture. Generally, talking on the same level is acceptable and preferred by the director as well.

Opening Up

The technique of opening up is known by stage actors as well. "Opening up" means showing both eyes to the camera. Inevitably, when casting, actors turn away from the camera. Is it shyness or ignorance? No matter what the explanation, the director, and the good actor, should be aware of this tendency and should take care to avoid it.

Inner Life

The film actor needs to have a powerful inner life for her character. It is the reaction, the goings on within the soul, that make the film actor fascinating. Spencer Tracy was brilliant. His inner life, his twists and reactions, obligated the editor to cut to him so that viewers could see what he was doing. It made him the star.

Camera Intimacy

Camera intimacy is hard to acquire. Some think that the actor has it, or he doesn't. Some think it can be learned. In an environment that feels safe, actors can blossom into wonderful characters.

Marilyn Monroe had this characteristic, as did Jean Harlow and Clark Gable. Richard Gere has it, Paul Newman has it, and so does Barbara Streisand. It is a vulnerability, an empathy, an identification, that goes beyond the scene or the film, but that actor is watched with complete fascination by the audience. It has been discussed earlier under empathy. That is a subject, however, much beyond the scope of this book.

Chapter 16

THE DIRECTOR PREPARES
FOR THE ACTOR

How does the director prepare for the actor? The method automatically prepares her to direct the actor. A few modifications, notes, and the checklist are all she should need.

The first reading of the script is the most important one; this is detailed in Part 6, Chapter 19.

The second reading, like the first, is read out loud. That is, the entire screenplay is read out loud, and everything is read in a loud voice so it makes sense to the reader. This reading is to be done with gusto and without reserve. The director, with pencil in hand, makes notes as the script is read. The notes should include anything that does not make sense, or loopholes in the script, character questions — anything that is interfering with enjoyment of the script.

In addition, the notes should also include the "fun" you are having with the script. Perhaps the script has wonderful moments of triumph, great sadness, or great joy; or there are moments in the script that almost make it but not quite.

This is unfortunate, but it is a common failing of scripts. They work hard to get you into the story, but then there is a modest conclusion. Spielberg and Lucas understand the importance of the distance from high to low, and the release necessary to make a film wonderful. Look at the experiential graph back in Figure 4.1 and match up the screenplay with the graph. Is there a clear definite climax and is it high enough in emotional strength? Does the resolution extend the feelings of resolution and does the audience get their payoff? Do you need to extend that moment to allow the final conclusion to be enjoyed by the audience? Obviously you are making notes on your own reactions.

FINDING THE BEAT

The beat is a group of lines linked together by a common objective, a subject, or an action. Once that character's objective or action changes, then it signals a new beat.

Director's beats and the screenwriter's dialogue linkage coincide, as mentioned earlier. It is important to know that because actors' beats and directors' do not have to coincide. As a matter of fact, that usually adds more inner life to the character. The next question is how you match the actor's beats to yours. The answer, you don't.

First, the director is seeking out the beat changes and wishes to draw those lines in. Do it lightly because as you read ahead you may discover that your choice could be improved by moving the beat, or the actor may choose to delay the change. It does not matter, as long as the change does occur. As long as the changes do not violate the central theme, you should encourage the actors to make choices that are different because they add excitement and personalizations to the film.

When working with the actors, do not get "intellectual," filling the actors with creative theory, or have "head" discussions about the "beat" or its placement. This is not a contest to see who is right. There is no right or wrong here. Remember, keep the actor out of his head. His discipline responds best to feelings. As long as it makes sense and does not violate the objective, encourage the actor in his creative freedom. Often, actors will come up with powerful ideas and interpretations that the director might never have dreamed of.

When the director is reading the script at home and comes to dialogue, he acts it by reading it out loud. This helps him to understand what the character wants and why the character does certain actions. It is important that the director do this reading feeling totally free and comfortable. Few directors, even those who have been professional actors, try to shortchange this process, for it leads to difficulties.

This is the time to mark off the beats. Remember, the beats you mark off are the screenplay's beats, not the character's beats. The acid test of your best notes is when you return to that portion of the script and by rereading your notes you know what is going on internally with the characters, as well as what the action of the script is.

In addition, doing this reading is extremely helpful when you are preparing the film with the heads of the department. They inevitably come up with wonderful suggestions. All your creative choices are right there in case you lose sight of what is going on in the script. On one occasion an Academy-nominated art director made a suggestion on the treatment of the walls of a set for a science fiction pilot. It was accepted. After the film was shot, however, it became clear that the choice did not serve the pilot. Quite the contrary: it went against the whole mysterious, eerie feeling considered desirable.

In addition, these notes are extremely helpful when working with the actors on the set during the shoot. Since the film is shot out of sequence, there is often confusion as to what the scene is about and what has just happened.

NAMING THE CHARACTER'S MOTIVATION

Naming the character's beats and writing them down in your script is essential. That keeps you on track, and eventually forces you to arrive at the central theme. Even if you think you know the central theme, check yourself out and follow the process. This is the way to make certain that you have chosen the correct central theme. This also determines whose viewpoint you wish to represent.

Generally a scene has only one point of view. Perhaps a more precise way to express this is to say that every scene has a major point of view. In order for the action of the scene to proceed, it is necessary for the reaction to be included. An obvious example is when Marian hits Indiana at the beginning of the barroom scene. His reaction of shock and surprise was needed. Though it is his scene, showing his reaction was necessary. Again, look at the analysis.

CHARACTER ANALYSIS

Like the thorough actor, the director must do an analysis of the character. It is obvious in certain film genres (the deductive) that character analysis does not require as much depth as in the inductive film. But do not make the error that some special effects or "action" directors make by not having a sharp, clear character in mind. It may require working with the actor if that character is not clearly delineated in the screenplay. Between the actor and the director, that character should be made clear and locked in. The time for thorough discussion is before shooting, or at least not during shooting, though it is legitimate for a director and an actor who are working through a scene to engage in major discussion. If the matter is not reasonably settled then, it is better to take a break and retire to a private discussion. Egos and probing and proving who is right are not the issue here; creative partnering is.

History

Write the history of the character like a biography. If you are uncertain of the character's history, then imagine that history, but make sure it is logical and explains her behavior in the film. This helps the actor to get reality into her character, and this kind of homework will put you in a good light with the actor, giving the film credibility.

Spine, or Superobjective

One of the ways to check your character analysis is to see if you have the spine of the character. If you have gotten the spine, you will have an excellent handle on the character. Remember, simple is best. The more complicated you feel the character is, the more confused you may be. Most good screenplays are simple and clearly written, while their characters are sharply etched.

Relationship

Understanding the character's relationships to other characters in the screenplay and to himself is essential when writing the history of the character study.

Atmosphere

Always keep in mind when writing the character's analysis the time and place of the scene. For instance, in *Raiders,* Marian's bar was apparently her place, and that had an effect on the scene between Indy and Marian. It affects the "adjustment" Indiana had to make when he arrived. Remember too that it was evening when Indy arrived.

Note in the final shot of that sequence that Marian holds up the medallion while in the background the building is burning; she announces triumphantly that she is his partner — her real objective in the scene. The burning down of Marian's bar makes her statement a fact.

• • • • • • • • • • • • • • • • • • • •

CHARTING ENTRANCES AND EXITS

Most films are shot out of continuity. This tends to confuse the actors. Though they have a call sheet and scenes are duly noted, it does not indicate the preceding action or where the character was or is emotionally.

Anticipating this problem, the director works up a chart or makes notes in her script to answer the anticipated questions of the actor: "Where am I now?" "What just happened to me?" "What time of day is it?" "Why am I doing this?" "What do I want here?"

These questions are not uncommon, and some of the better actors trust their intuitive skills and ability to play a scene moment to moment by avoiding a rehearsed kind of preparation.

Some actors are shy about asking those questions on the set in front of the crew. In this case, talk to the actor prior to his appearance on the set. The other type of actor is thoroughly prepared for each day's shooting and does not require that kind of support.

IMMEDIACY, THE KEY TO FILM ACTING

The need for immediacy in film, unlike stage acting, is paramount. In a film, the actor must know exactly where he is when he enters a room and where exactly he just came from. In the checklist, these questions are asked: "Where did character just come from?" "What did you just do this very moment as you entered?" "What is the character doing at this very moment?" And finally, to help the actor to get rolling in the scene, "What does the character want right now?"

The questions are personalized. It is a good idea to talk to the actor as if he were the character. This helps the actor to continue to identify with his character. As the actor gets into the scene, then the director might ask the following question: "What's the very next thing you (the character) want?"

The questions are to be asked by the actor of himself, or by the director in rehearsal. It is best to do this kind of preliminary work with the actor in privacy—that is, not on the set in front of the entire crew.

If the scene is not working on the set, then, depending upon your relationship with the actor, you may break the crew for a few minutes, or pull the actor to one side, or talk to him quietly and privately in the dressing room or in the director's office. Sometimes, using the crew as an audience helps the actor to get that immediacy, especially in the case of comedy. The moment-to-moment playing is essential in film acting.

Chapter 17

THE ACTOR'S LANGUAGE

In the preceeding chapters we have studied the director's techniques for helping the actor. In this chapter we will deal with some of the techniques practiced in the acting schools.

But first it should be pointed out that these techniques are for stage acting. Most of them were designed to play in that environment, those techniques that lend themselves to film acting have been selected here. Some of the disciplines learned by stage actors do not travel well to film. The reason is that stage acting is predicated on a rehearsal pattern that is spread over weeks and sometimes months. It is rare in film acting that the actor gets that kind of rehearsal period.

The history of film acting goes against the traditions of stage acting. In stage acting the actor is encouraged to be other than or more than himself. In film acting, being oneself is paramount. Those who do that well (like John Wayne) will develop the acting skills necessary for film.

STANISLAVSKY'S METHOD

The prime directive of the method school is to give the actors tools to access their emotions, which are found in the unconscious mind. The unconscious cannot be ordered.

Try it on yourself. Tell yourself to be angry or sad, or glad, or in love. We are human beings, we are not machines. We are not designed to emote on cue. We feel and we react.

To prepare to access our unconscious, we have to be relaxed. The unconscious (or subconscious) will not respond to fear, anxiety, or pressure. This again presents a serious set of challenges because the film production business is a very tense and intense activity, more so, in certain ways than the theater. In film you don't get more than a couple of chances to perform. Once a scene has been filmed, only rarely will an actor have the chance to do the scene again. In the theater, there is always another night to perform. Primarily, then, the actor needs to be in a safe space where his unconscious can feed him.

Relaxation Exercises

Rule number one to help the actor is to get him to relax. Don't just pay lip service to this rule, but rather encourage the actor to use a process. In many cases, trained actors know this and are prepared with their own relaxation exercises. But just in case their approach is not working, you should know some quick fixes. The purpose of these exercises is to get the body relaxed, and, even more important, to get the spirit to participate as well. The purpose, however, is not to induce sleep.

The Standard   Get the actor into a quiet room, comfortably seated in a chair, with his feet planted firmly on the ground, his arms resting on the armrests. Then suggest in a quiet, peaceful voice that he make himself comfortable, while telling him to relax each part of his body, starting with head, then ears, then eyes, then the nose, the mouth, and so on. You lead the actor to focus on each part of the body and to relax that part. Then, when this process is complete, the actor is in a receptive state, ready to begin to access his unconscious.

Heart's Home   This is one of the fastest and more successful procedures. The actor has to be in a comfortable chair, a quiet place, and with no immediate pressure. Ask the actor to think of a place that is her most favorite place in the whole world, the place where she feels the safest and most comfortable, a place filled with love and peace and inner tranquility. It doesn't have to exist or be real; it can be imaginary. It can be anywhere as long as the actor is extremely happy to be there. It can be a lakeside house, or at the ocean, or on top of a mountain—in other words, any place as long as the actor loves being there. That place is what is called the home of the heart or precisely Heart's Home. Tell her to go there and enjoy the place, to see herself walking up the path or driving up the road, but traveling there. Know there is joyous anticipation in your heart because it is peaceful happiness to be at that place . . . And so on . . .

You may also tell her it is okay to bring a loved one, or a pet, but it must be one that gives you only joy and full acceptance.

A word of caution. On one occasion when some actors were engaging in this exercise, at the Television Academy, some of them became upset and agitated. Later it was discovered that they brought someone who had died to their heart's home. They were happy to see the deceased, but were still grieving. Obviously, that issue should be avoided because it defeats the purpose of the exercise.

Here are some key phrases to use when helping the actor: "Be there," "Know you are accepted just as you are," "You are perfect just as you are," "You are wonderful just as you are." Then follow this train of thought. If the actor has a strong spiritual side, encourage that by telling him, "God loves you," "You are loved unconditionally by God," and "God is looking out for you," "Turn it all over to God and trust it will work out." "Be filled with the white light" and "Know you are unique. There is no one like you on earth." This last part of the exercise has had a great deal of success, more than anyone thought possible, and it is used in film acting classes.

Remember to take the actor back; don't merely leave her at "heart's home." Take her back to the studio dressing room, or wherever you are, and then talk to her about the day's work in a relaxed manner. Make it sound easy. It usually is. Give her a feeling of security. This first meeting is usually concluded by the director's saying something like this: "If there is anything that is not working for you, please talk to me. No matter how busy I may appear, there is nothing more important than the work we do when we shoot your scene." All of this is true. This is a fast way to get the actor to relax and gain their support and confidence.

There are many other relaxing exercises to be found in books on meditation which you may wish to try. These two have worked the best for me.

• • • • • • • • • • • • • • • • • • •

METHOD PROCEDURES

Subtext

Paraphrasing the dialogue means asking the actor to put dialogue lines of the script into his own words. Let's say a character has a line, "I am leaving this house because I don't want to be with you."

This line's subtext may mean something dramatically different from the words. For instance, if the character wants his lover to stop him from leaving, his threatened departure is a ploy. With that understanding, the actor may elect to say the line as if he were wanting to continue a relationship such as, "Though I am pretending to leave I want you to ask me to stay."

As a tool to help the actor, if the actor is not giving the interpretation that makes sense to the scene, you could ask the actor to consider the subtext of the line. This quickly brings the attention of the director and the actor to the basis of an incorrect interpretation. This process should be followed away from the eyes of the crew.

In fact when the director is breaking down the screenplay into beats, he is figuring out the subtext. That is what each character means when he or she has some dialogue.

Sense Memory

Sense memory is one of the most powerful tools that method (via Lee Strasberg) has given us to help the actor relive an experience. The trained sense memory actor does not merely re-enact the experience, but rather goes through the experience again.

It takes practice and time, but anyone can use this technique and have success. We have had some of it with our acting students. The degree of success has to do with regular daily practice and trusting the process.

Sense Memory Process   To practice this process, first tell the actor to concentrate on his lead sense (taste, smell, sight, touch, or hearing) and then recall an incident by using that lead sense.

Let's say the incident the actor is trying to recall took place at the ocean. The first thing recalled is the smell of the ocean. Then that odor triggers off the whole scene. The scene is then recalled through the actor's other senses, such as taste, touch, sight, or sound, but not as a series of events.

As the sense memory becomes stronger, it takes the actor right back into the event. He won't merely remember the event but will experience it. The stronger the sense recall, the stronger the feeling for the actor. When sensory recall is used, the actor's brain cannot tell the difference between reality and fantasy. Knowing this technique helps the trained actor to achieve a feeling of reality. This technique is most powerful, and some of the more successul actors in the business use it.

How does the director practice this technique on the set? Some method actors are trained in sense memory and suggesting it may help them. But they need training. If the actor has had sense training and has stored these sense memories, then the director may ask him to bring those memories into play.

Discussing the method of sense memory recall in detail is beyond the scope of this book. Just be aware that there is a method that the actor must know. Please see the bibliography for more information on sense memory, specifically Ned Manderino's book.

Affective Memory

Affective memory is also called emotional memory by some acting schools. Reliving an event that triggers off emotion is how it works. This method is used by beginning and experienced actors. It has been successful. The reservation is that the emotional recall for the actor may be too strong or uncontrollable, or the value of the emotion is incorrect.

The director has to be careful with this method when guiding the actor. If the actor is inexperienced, caution is the word. Simply asking the actor if he has had an experience that may be similar to the requirement of the role is one way to initiate this exploration.

A way to encourage the actor to explore that emotion is by asking him to tell you about the incident. Then ask specific questions, like what time of day, what exactly is happening, how was he feeling about it, and so on. The more detailed attention to feelings is the route to explore with the actor.

Improvisation

Improvisation is defined as a scene with a premise. There is no specific structure, like a script or dialogue. The only thing there is the premise.

Improvisation's sole purpose is to bring "realism" to a scene. (Viola Spolin's *Theatre Games for Rehearsal* is an excellent sourcebook.) This may be done by suggesting a similar situation to the actors.

Let's say a scene takes place in the 1880s. The actors find the language, the customs, and the behavior of the 1880s remote and consequently their performance is stiff. We invent an improvisation with a similar situation that takes place in contemporary times. The actors act it out without any concern for lines or staging. Generally this helps the actor to identify with the emotional needs of the scene and gets rid of the stiff performance. Again, this should be done in the privacy of the rehearsal hall or an office.

Moment-to-Moment Playing Improvisation helps the actors get spontaneity in their work. To play a scene moment to moment means that the actors play the scene as if it had never been rehearsed and is happening "moment to moment" as in real life. This is another good reason to use improvisational technique when the work seems stale. Improvisation gives the work and the scene a freshness, a vitality.

Three Improvisation Procedures Paraphrase the dialogue and/or situation we just cited. The 1880s incident is one example.

Opposite Action of the Scene Giving a premise that is in direct opposition to the circumstances of the scene allows the actors to release their inhibitions, and consequently they find new values. For instance, the obligation of the scene requires a deep sadness. The scene does not seem to get the actors. By having the premise to change from a comedy approach may release the actor to be able to play it.

External Technique

There are two groups that use this external technique: trained actors and untrained actors.

Trained Actors The trained actor works with externals to get the desired effect. Sir Laurence Olivier was an example. When talking to the trained actor, you need to describe the character and the situation, but in objective terms. You need to be precise about the resulting behavior you are seeking for the character. This group of performers learns from doing.

Be cautious with nightclub performers turned actors because they have difficulty in working with other performers. Recognize that what they do is the one-person job of entertaining groups of people by simply standing up and talking to them. This is an impressive feat.

Untrained Actors   Many of the techniques in the method section will work with the untrained actor. The general rule is to keep it simple, just as John Ford did. Cast the nonprofessional actor who seems to be the closest to the character you are seeking. That makes your job easier.

Do not underestimate the nonprofessional; with support he performs extraordinarily well. See some of the earlier work of Milos Forman and observe nonprofessionals carrying large parts of his pictures.

The trap to avoid is demonstrating. Do not show the nonprofessional how to do a scene or how to say a line. When a director gives instructions in that manner, he is inviting mindless imitation, and that is death to spontaneity and credibility. Trust your nonprofessional.

PART **6**

THE PRODUCTION
LANGUAGE

Chapter 18

PREPARING THE CHECKLIST FORM

Every time a film is started, it feels as if we are reinventing the wheel. But not now: this method will guide us through the chaos of production and allow the creative process free rein.

Let's start by filling out the checklist, applying the literary, visual, and actor's languages—see Figure 18.1.

PREPARATION

The Central Theme

In Chapter 3 the process of finding the central theme was discussed. We have read the screenplay or seen the film *Raiders of the Lost Ark*, or perhaps we have done both. The Appendix contains Marian Ravenswood's bar scene from *Raiders*. Please review the analysis in Chapter 3 and the movement in Chapter 14. This scene will serve as the example for filling out the checklist.

Clearly, we empathize with Indiana Jones. His empathic viewpoint is established in the prologue. We also recognize that the prologue foreshadows the film's outcome, which adds to the tension.

Figure 18.1   *The checklist form.*

PREPARATION

Title of Film:
1. Central Theme
2. Beat Breakdown of Scene:
    Character "A" objective:
    Character "B" objective:
3. Scene's Central Theme
4. Experiential Graph Placement:
5. Empathy POV Scene—Whose?
6. Scene no.:
7. Scene Label:
8. Cinema Language (s):
9. Picturization:
10. Compositional Support:
11. Storyboard:

IMPLEMENTATION

FLOORPLAN: Camera Placement (Light Quality): Staging Pattern:

ACTING PROCEDURE(S):
1. Been:
2. Just come:
3. Needs now!:

IMPORTANT NOTES:

We need to pay attention to the title: *Raiders*. Certainly, Indy is a raider, as are Belloq and the Nazis. The film is about these raiders. In addition, the picture is about finding the lost Ark. The star of the picture, contrary to popular opinion, is the Ark not Indiana Jones.

But all this theorizing may seem so esoteric. This is an action adventure film that follows classic structure and has a strong, empathic hero.

Then why does a director have to go through all this "theorizing" to direct an action picture? What difference does it make whether the picture is about the "raiders" as long as we know who the hero is and find the action exciting?

And what difference does it make if I understand that Indy is not the star of the film, the Ark is? Most people are going to be rooting for Indy, for he is clearly the hero of the film.

Beat Breakdown

"Theorizing" gives the director the tools to find the objectives (actions) in the beats and to arrive at the correct central theme. Once this has been done, then the film's universe, and all the many decisions made by the director, will support the theme, and, most importantly, the integrity of the film will not be compromised.

The central theme of *Raiders of the Lost Ark* is that the Ark, a relic from the past, is best left in God's hands. Violate the integrity of the Ark and this power will destroy the violators. When the evil Belloq and the Nazis opened the Ark, how did Indiana Jones know to instruct Marian to close her eyes? If they had seen those "spirits," they would have been destroyed as well.

In the prologue, Indiana Jones stole the golden head and avoided trap after trap, including that gigantic ball. But only when he gave that golden statue to Belloq did he finally escape unharmed. This correctly foreshadowed the balance of the film.

A Scene in Relation to the Central Theme

How does the scene in Marian's bar relate to the central theme? Indy's objective was to get the medallion, while Marian's superobjective was to get Indiana. Both of their goals (superobjectives) are met, and their partnership is forged in the fire of the shootout with the Nazis and the burning down of her bar. This locks her into the search for the Ark—the central theme—but her superobjective remains the same, to get Indiana Jones. (See Figure 18.2.)

Experiential Graph

The placement of the scene on the experiential graph (see Figure 4.1) is important. The director directs a scene differently if it occurs in Act III as opposed to Act I. The differences have to do with the degree of the tension in the scene and the relationships of the characters. Obviously a scene in

Figure 18.2   Raiders of the Lost Ark. *This takes place in Marian's bar in Nepal as Indy asks about the medallion. She taunts him.* (Courtesy Lucasfilms Ltd.)

Act I would not have the same intensity if it were in Act III, where the final confrontation between the hero and villain calls for special handling.

Empathy POV Scene

Art by definition requires a "viewpoint"; therefore every scene must have a viewpoint. But when we use the word *scene* we mean two different things. The "literary language screenplay scene" is one meaning, while the second means the shot, which is found in the visual language.

What is the process for determining viewpoint? This is the question every director asks himself consciously or unconsciously. When we speak of a viewpoint, the implied question is, who do we want the audience to empathize with? That is, from whose viewpoint are we to show the event? Again it goes back to whose viewpoint best serves the central theme. Is it the point of view of the writer, or does the director make a choice? Or can it be both ways?

Most scenes have one major viewpoint. Rarely does a scene have more than one, though on occasion it does happen. The power of selecting the empathetic viewpoint falls into the hands of the director.

Interpersonal cinema language states that the onscreen character is perceived as if he were seen from the POV of the offscreen character. The viewer's POV is changed as cut from single shot to single shot. Yet when we examine *Vertigo* we realize that we are seeing Jimmy Stewart from Bel Geddes's POV. (There is only one exception, when Hitchcock cuts in a close-up of Bel Geddes and gives us the insight that she is still in love with Stewart.) We see Jimmy Stewart from her viewpoint, though, through the use of the I-P, we also participate in their personal relationship.

To return to the *Raiders* scene, is the scene from Indiana Jones's viewpoint or from Marian's? Or is it both?

As we examine the scene as Spielberg shot it, it appears to be in movement master scene cinema language. We see Marian from Indiana's viewpoint, but that does not preclude a close shot of Indiana as he was reacting to Marian.

Was this strictly Spielberg's choice, or was it in the screenplay? If the screenplay does not have a POV, then it is necessary for the director to adopt one. Without a POV, the scene becomes flat and reportorial. Sometimes the implied viewpoint of the screenplay is not the one the director selects. The important thing to know is that there must be a viewpoint. There is only one viewpoint in every scene. There may be a "reaction" shot, as in *Raiders of the Lost Ark,* but the primary viewpoint is Indiana's. That was the apparent choice of Spielberg. This is interesting enough, but the primary viewpoint consistently implies less screen time. But the empathy character gives them greater power, and the audience always walks away with the feeling that the "star" got plenty of screen time.

To find the viewpoint of the scene, ask yourself who is seeing this scene. If the scene appears to be objective, that is part of the art of master scene cinema language; even fragmented cinema language has a primary point of view. For instance, in the scene between Kane and his new bride (which was recommended viewing in Chapter 12 to demonstrate the creative use of transition cinema language), we know the scene was structured as a flashback by Kane's best friend, Jedediah, played by Joseph Cotten. When the shot was viewed it appeared to be an objective scene; in fact it was not.

It was movement master scene, and the point of view was the amplification of the central theme. That is, we saw the character Citizen Kane wonderfully responsible and truly idealistic, dedicated to wholesome principles of truth and justice for all, at the beginning of the sequence. Welles's director's point of view coincided with the screenplay's central theme, "Money corrupts the human spirit," and we saw that happen right before our eyes.

Scene Number

A number is assigned to each shot and is marked in the shooting script. It usually is assigned by the production manager or the assistant director. This is more a bookkeeping piece of information.

Scene Label

Is this scene a hate scene, a love scene, or a jealousy scene? The major emotional content of the scene is what prompts the label. This is an excellent way to tune in to the emotional needs of the scene.

Cinema Language

Selection of the cinema language methodology is discussed fully in Part 4. This section of the checklist form (see Figure 18.1) is a matter of following your schedule. This listing is another way of double-checking yourself.

Picturization

Picturization, as you may recall from Chapter 7, is the arrangement of the elements of the picture to tell the story. The test is if the audience sees the picture and understands the content. For instance, say the hero and villain have gathered their forces to do battle. The arrangement of these groups in the shot should be so clear that if someone walked into the movie at that moment he or she would immediately understand that these two forces are in conflict. That is correct picturization.

Compositional Support

Composition supplies the way to express the mood of the scene by using line, form, mass, or color. Using the correct compositional elements, as in the example just given, is important — the use of space to represent the two forces and their comparative strengths, for example. In *Big Country* the picturization was apparent. Burl Ives was on the left side of the frame, on the right side of the frame was Gregory Peck, and in the middle was Jean Simmons, reinforced by Chuck Connors. She was the person Ives and Peck were fighting over.

Storyboard

Storyboarding a film means to select the pictures that you want seen, drawing the picture, as in cartoon strips. This does not require artistic skill, but it is a way for you to remind yourself of the picture you are seeking. With the computer graphics available today, it is possible to storyboard a film on your home computer. In the near future there should be a software package that will include a storyboard graphics capability.

• • • • • • • • • • • • • • • • • • •

IMPLEMENTATION

Floorplan

The floorplan is a visual representation of the things on the floor from a ceiling viewpoint. It includes not only the set and the set pieces, but also the placement of the camera and the blocking of the actors, or simply the staging pattern. This is a simple matter of translating the selected cinema language and the picturization worked out and detailed in the first half of checklist form.

For instance, looking at Figure 10.2 *Big Country* floorplan shows the placement of the camera, as well as the character placement and movement (blocking). This floorplan was deduced by studying the film.

Acting Procedures

Acting procedures are the techniques you may need after doing some research with the participating actors. For instance, after you have met the actor, you realize he works well in a sensory environment. You may prepare some sensory suggestions for the actor. Or say you know that the actor works well in improvisational settings; then you might prepare some "improvs" and plan to film them. This may require some planning with your camera operator.

"Been," "Just Come," "Needs now!"   It is critical that the actor know where his character has *just* been, where he has just come from a moment ago, and what is the immediate thing he needs right now as the scene begins. This very first moment is critical to the actor because it sets the tone of the work. (For more information see Uta Hagan's book, *Respect for Acting*, listed in the Recommended Books.)

This procedure should be ready for every shot and should be kept at your fingertips. This is a powerful tool in helping the actors. The important thing is not to offer it unless it is needed. This is determined by whether the actor is getting immediacy in his work.

Important Notes

This part of the checklist gives us the opportunity to examine the desired results and make notes on things we wish to remember.

Chapter 19

THE DILEMMA'S ANSWER

Lee Strasberg, one of the great American acting teachers, emphasized that the director's first reading of the script is the most important reading of all. The director sees, hears, feels, and reacts to the script as if he were the audience. No other read-through of the script can ever duplicate that first time. This reading guides him through the many challenges of production.

THE FIRST READING

This first reading is the inspiration for all the director's production and creative choices. Some questions the director must ask are: Were the characters real? How did you react to the characters? Did you care for the people? Especially the hero? Did the story lose you? If so, where? Did you like the story? Did you believe the story? Did you get bored at some point? How did you feel right after you left the movie script running through your head? Did the picture stay with you? Precisely, what stayed with you? How long did it stay with you?

Did you relate to the theme, the environment? Are you prepared to spend anywhere from six months to two years with this movie? It could take even more time, depending upon the financing, availability of stars, and so on.

Rules for the First Reading

There are some general rules for that all-important first reading. First, the screenplay should be read in one sitting. This simulates the running time of the film.

Next, and most important, do not come to the material with a "judging" attitude. The guiding principle is to read/view the script as if you had just walked into the movie theater.

Do not make notes the first time. Go with the flow of the script and give yourself permission to react to the material with emotion but without pre-judgment. The obligation of making notes can interfere with reacting to and feeling the material. You will remember everything that was good and bad. Be assured of that.

The director discourages other sources, such as best friends, lovers, or spouses, from commenting on the screenplay prior to this reading. In this way, reactions to the material are pure and uncorrupted.

After you read the script, you may feel inclined to go over it. Do *not* do that until you have made notes. If something is unclear, do not go back over the script to check it out, but instead trust this first reading. The explanation is simple. Assume that if you were confused, then it may be in the script. If you wish to investigate the screenplay, then the next thing is to make notes on everything that was "wonderful for you" and then explain why you thought it was. The "why" should not be theory, but what you felt about it. Then finally, make notes on any parts of the script that confused you.

After having done this, then you may review the script. You may discover that you misunderstood certain sections, or the script was not clear. In your meeting with the author, you will know the questions you need to ask.

Targeted Audience

Every script has a targeted audience. That is in the nature of filmmaking since an immediate financial return is required. Roger Corman is an excellent example of a director who makes pictures for specific groups.

The audience for *Raiders of the Lost Ark,* an action picture, is quite different from the audience that attended *Ordinary People.* It is important that the director know the genre that the script may be addressing. Each genre has traditions and it is important that the director know what they are. Matching up those criteria with the script is another concern.

Empathy and the Central Theme

Probably the most important question the director has to ask himself is, are you rooting for the hero? As you know, without empathy, it is very difficult to make a successful film. Admittedly this problem can be overcome by other factors such as getting a movie star who has an empathic persona or rewriting the script or design of some specific cinema languages, in order to turn the main character into an empathic character.

The next question is, is the film credible? Is the central theme compromised? Does the script have unity and purpose? If all these questions are answered in the affirmative then we are ready to move into phase two.

• • • • • • • • • • • • • • • • • • • •
THE SECOND READING

In Chapter 16, there are rules and instructions for the second reading. There may be a tendency to flash through this reading because of embarrassment or reluctance to act out. That attitude may indicate an internal problem. You need to remember that it is important to do this because as the director you will appreciate your creative partner, the actor. Unfortunately, the "technical" side seems more accessible to the director than helping the actor. We live in a society where we have been trained to deal not with feelings but with machines. Ultimately, the actor is a critical part of the process. Honor the actor and be supportive.

Locking in Reactions
The second reading will lock in your reactions to that first reading by the beat breakdown (review *Raiders of the Lost Ark*). In this reading you should remember that *reading out loud is a must.*

Genre
What films are similar? What are the rules or parameters of this genre? Does this script follow or violate some of the genre rules? For instance, if you are doing a horror film, killings and coarse brutality are expected in this genre. Every genre has some hard-edged parameters, and it is essential that you know these rules.

Structure
The next area is the literary language. As you may recall from Chapters 4 and 5, the questions we ask here are, Does the screenplay conform to the rules? If not, does the violation work? Or is it correctable? Does the structure support the screenplay? What is the story's strength? How can it be best supported? Is there a weakness? Is it correctable? What support does it require, a rewrite? Is the writer available, and is the producer prepared to support a rewrite? As you continue your second reading, there is another element that needs your attention.

Visualizing
As you read the script the second time, "pictures" should be confirmed in your head. We are not saying cinema languages; we are referring to specific pictures, or shots, if you will.

Sketches/Storyboard   Allow your inner movie camera to present you with the pictures, which will be refined later on when you get orchestration. At this point, little sketches in the margin of the script or on the back of the preceding page are helpful. The pictures can be primitive, and they can be kept hidden. But when you look at them you will understand their meaning.

These little pictures are your inspiration, although they may be altered when you get to the third reading. But the concept is there for you to remember. Generally, it works out for the best.

Symbolic Cinema Language   This is the time to look for symbolic visual images that represent the inner life of the characters or the inner meanings of the central theme. These symbols when artfully engaged can make a lifetime impact upon the viewer.

Citizen Kane abounds with symbolic images that are structured through the extensive use of symbolic cinema language. Norman Jewison's film *In the Heat of the Night* has many dramatic symbols. Jewison has an acetylene torch ignited in the background of the picture and at that precise moment Sidney Poitier has just decided to interrogate the most powerful citizen, who is also the most bigoted man, in town. The torch symbolizes the internal burning hatred of both bigots. This adds tension and "heats up" the anticipated scene. This is excellent imagery, because it translates the images.

Translating Images   How to translate the emotional sense of the scene into a visual representation is the next issue to address. In the preceding example, the background action was arranged to symbolize the emotion of a scene. But it does something else as well. At that same time that acetylene torch translated into an emotional image. That is why the audience got it: they understood that bigots burn inside. It is a double whammy. That is excellent filmmaking.

Going back to the beat, understanding the emotional content of that moment is the first step as you remember. Implementation is done through staging, or camera movement, or a combination of both.

In *Raiders of the Lost Ark* in Marian Ravenswood's bar, Spielberg used the movement of his characters to indicate their emotional state. Marian's crossing back to the bar and dumping the glasses into the sink was an example of using business to indicate her emotional state. Spielberg's movement master cinema language was designed to cut from the opposite diagonal. When one expected Spielberg to follow the diagonal movement with the traditional over-the-shoulder reverse, he threw in a shot that crossed that angle and suddenly thrust us off in another direction. He surprised us and fascinated us, but without confusing us. He avoided confusion by consistently placing Indy and Marian in the same area of the frame. But when he had them switch position, he made certain it was seen onscreen. In this way, Spielberg made the "visual" statement that the hero was twisted around by Marian's refusal to give him the medallion. The staging reinforced the emotional state of Indiana. Every time Indiana thought he had the situation under control, it suddenly took off in another direction. Spielberg's shooting the sequence in those unexpected diagonals illustrated the emotional state of the hero because we the audience were forced to go through the same disorienting experience. Spielberg expertly demonstrated that expository scenes with some fancy film footwork can be made fascinating as well.

• • • • • • • • • • • • • • • • • • •

THE THIRD READING

The third reading is to orchestrate the film. Selections are made in the visual language. Refer back to Chapter 9 for the rules that deal with orchestration.

The Climax

By definition the climax is the highest point of excitement in the film. If the film is to be properly orchestrated, then the climax should be unique, unlike anything else in the film. There are several ways to accomplish this.

Cinema Languages

Mixing cinema language is one method, and it can yield wonderful results. Consider the climax and the conclusion of *Cotton Club,* as described earlier. Reviewing that film clip, you may note that Coppola used as many as six different cinema languages. Symbolic, collision, parallel, constructive, transition, and fragmented cinema languages were used to heighten the climax of the film and bring the film to a heart-rending conclusion. People often ask whether the ending was scripted, or whether the decision was made by the director. It happened that Coppola was both writer and director in this case, so the question might appear to be academic. But in truth it is not. To paraphrase the famous remark by President Truman, the buck stops here, because the director selects the various cinema languages and decides how to use them.

Warren Beatty created some wonderful climactic sequences using transition cinema language in a fairy tale cartoon film, *Dick Tracy.* His unusual way of creating climaxes came out of a long tradition in filmmaking, but because it is rarely used in contemporary films it appeared new and fresh.

Location

Location is another method of heightening the climax. Finding a location that has never been seen before in the film is the rule. Hitchcock did it consistently in most of this films, though he added another element. If he shot a picture in a well-known locale, then he selected a historic landmark associated with the locale. In *North by Northwest,* for instance, the famous Mount Rushmore was used in the concluding climax sequence. In *Raiders of the Lost Ark* note how the climax occurred in a location never seen before in the film.

Costume and Special Props

Adding a costume or a "magical" hand prop is another popular way of heightening the climax. This device is popular in action pictures. Consider the use of the saber in George Lucas's *Star Wars,* or the "special" karate stance in *The Karate Kid.*

In *Raiders of the Lost Ark* note that the Ark itself became the special prop, and finally the mystery of opening it had everyone waiting for the outcome. Using the deus ex machina was a classic device. As you recall, dues ex machina refers to the machine that would lower one of the gods from Mount Olympus to solve all the mortal problems. It was a respected device in the ancient Greek theater of Aeschylus and Sophocles. The *Raiders* device worked basically the same way. The variation was that those gods were forces unleashed that simply solved Indiana's problems by melting the bad guys. The special effects people had a ball and so did the audience. The application of an ancient technique was well done.

A Camera Signature Shot

Claude Lelouch's *A Man and a Woman* used a camera circular shot that had not been done quite in the way he executed it. Lelouch had worked out an antigravity camera mount that made the camera rotate in a 360-degree move around the image. With a wonderful piece of music and this unique signature shot, Lelouch changed the texture of the film. It became one of the more successful foreign pictures in the United States.

Chapter **20**

CONCLUSION

After learning about the art of directing, it is time to look at the real world of production. The question asked of the director by the producer or the production manager is whether the picture can be shot at their published budget. This is an important question. The budget determines the basic crew, the number of shooting days, the setups that have to be shot during a given day, the number of pages that must be shot to stay on schedule, and finally whether the picture can be shot on location or at a distant location or in the studio.

The budget is not the real problem; rather, it is the Hollywood system. The director is often brought in after the budget has been made up. If it is a studio picture, the creative people are rarely involved in the budgeting process. Nicholas Roeg, the internationally known director of such films as *Don't Look Now, Walkabout,* and *The Man Who Fell to Earth,* drily wondered out loud how a budget can be made without including the vision of the director.

In our method, making a budget is easier because the director's visual languages are figured in. Examine the checklist, which clearly outlines the shots. This would resolve the conflict between the production manager's budget and the director's vision.

Simply applying this method in preparing the screenplay for production will put the professional and the beginning director ahead of the needs of shooting a film. If you follow the procedure, without omitting any steps, you will achieve success.

APPENDIX

Raiders of the Lost Ark is an action picture; hence, the dialogue is minimal and the beats are short and precise. The scene takes place in Nepal in Marian Ravenswood's bar. Indiana Jones arrives, seeking a medallion that is the key to finding the Ark.

Raiders of the Lost Ark

BEAT _____ <1>

As Marion puts her cold shot glasses to her head, a shadow looms over her .

> INDY
> Hello, Marian.

She turns and walks toward him.

> MARIAN
> Indiana Jones. I always knew someday you'd come walkin' through my door. I never doubted that. Something made it inevitable. So what are you doing in Nepal?

> INDY
> I need one of the pieces your father collected.

She hits him with a solid right to the jaw.

> MARIAN
> I learned to hate you in the last ten years.

BEAT _____ <2>

She turns away from him.

INDY
I never meant to hurt you.

MARIAN
I was a child. I was in love. It
was wrong, you knew it.

INDY
You knew what you were doing.

She gestures at the door as Mohan enters.

MARIAN
Now I do! This is my place! Get
out! (Speaks in Nepalese)

MOHAN
(Responds in Nepalese)

INDY
I did what I did.

BEAT   _____   <3>

INDY
You don't have to be happy
about it, but maybe we can help
each other out now. I need one of
the pieces your father collected.
A bronze piece about this size
with a hole in it, off-center, with
a crystal. You know the one I
mean?

He makes a circle with his fingers, watching Marian as she
picks up the glasses on the bar.

MARIAN
Yeah, I know it.

BEAT   _____   <4>

                                    INDY
                            Where's Abner?

Marian doesn't answer.

                                    INDY
                            Where's Abner?

                                  MARIAN
                            Abner's dead.

Indy's attitude changes instantly. This is sad news.

                                    INDY
                            Marian, I'm sorry.

BEAT   _____   <5>

                                  MARIAN
                            Do you know what you did to me,
                            to my life?

                                    INDY
                            I can only say I'm sorry so many
                            times.

Marian behind the bar dumps the glasses she's been
carrying.

                                  MARIAN
                            Well, say it again, anyway.

                                    INDY
                            Sorry.

BEAT   _____   <6>

                                  MARIAN
                            Yeah, everybody's sorry. Abner
                            was sorry for dragging me all
                            over the earth looking for his lit-

tle pieces of junk. I'm sorry to
still be stuck in this dive. Everybody's sorry for something.

                    INDY
It's a worthless bronze medallion. Marian are you going to
give it to me?

                    MARIAN
Maybe. I don't know where it is.

                    INDY
Well, maybe you could find it.
Three thousand bucks.

He holds the money in his fist.

                    MARIAN
Well, that'll get me back, but not
in style.

                    INDY
I can get you another two when
we get to the states. It's important, Marian. Trust me.

Marian looks at him in disbelief as he puts the money in
her hand.

(PRODUCTION NOTE: In the film, Marian actually went to
hit Indy again, but Indy caught her hand in midflight and
thrust the money into it.)

BEAT _____   <7>

                    INDY
You know the piece I mean. You
know where it it.

                    MARIAN
(laughing) Come back tomorrow.

                    INDY
        Why?

                    MARIAN
        Because I said so, that's why.

Indy turns and goes to the door.

                    MARIAN
        Ha! See you tomorrow, Indiana
        Jones.

RECOMMENDED FILMS

1. *Big Country,* William Wyler, 1958, 168 minutes
2. *The Birds,* Alfred Hitchcock, 1963, 120 minutes
3. *Blow-Up,* Michelanglo Antonioni, 1966, 111 minutes
4. *Butch Cassidy & the Sundance Kid,* George Roy Hill, 1966, 112 minutes
5. *Citizen Kane,* Orson Welles, 1941, 119 minutes
6. *Cotton Club,* Francis Ford Coppola, 1984, 127 minutes
7. *Doctor Zhivago,* David Lean, 1965, 197 minutes
8. *Dressed to Kill,* Brian De Palma, 1980, 105 minutes
9. *Exorcist,* William Friedkin, 1973, 122 minutes
10. *French Connection,* William Freidkin, 1971, 118 minutes
11. *Gone with the Wind,* Victor Fleming, 1939, 219 minutes
12. *Hamlet,* Laurence Olivier, 1948, 153 minutes
13. *In the Heat of the Night,* Norman Jewison, 1967, 110 minutes
14. *High Noon,* Freddie Zinnemann, 1952, 85 minutes
15. *Lady in the Lake,* Robert Montgomery, 1946, 103 minutes
16. *Potemkin,* Sergei Eisenstein, 1925, 67 minutes
17. *Psycho,* Alfred Hitchcock, 1960, 109 minutes
18. *The Quiet Man,* John Ford, 1952, 129 minutes
19. *Raiders of the Lost Ark,* Steven Spielberg, 1981, 115 minutes
20. *Romeo & Juliet,* Franco Zeffirelli, 1968, 152 minutes
21. *Strangers on a Train,* Alfred Hitchcock, 1951, 101 minutes
22. *Vertigo,* Alfred Hitchcock, 1958, 128 minutes
23. *The Wild Bunch,* Sam Peckinpah, 1969, 135 minutes
24. *The Wizard of Oz,* Victor Fleming, 1939, 102 minutes

RECOMMENDED BOOKS

1. Alton, John. (1949). *Painting with Light.* New York: MacMillan Company

2. Arijon, Daniel. (1976). *Grammar of the Film Language.* Boston: Focal Press

3. Nilsen, Vladmir. (1985). *The Cinema As a Graphic Art.* New York: Garland

4. Truffaut, Francois. *Hitchcock.* New York: Simon and Schuster

5. MacCann, Richard Dyer (Ed.). (1966). *Film: A Montage of Theories.* New York: E.P. Dutton

6. Sharff, Stefan. (1982). *The Elements of Cinema.* New York: Columbia University Press

7. Leyda, Jay, and Vonow, Zina. (1982). *Eisenstein at Work.* New York: Pantheon Books

8. Halsman, Philippe. (1961). *On the Creation of Photographic Ideas.* New York: Ziff-Davis

9. Bouleau, Charles. (1980). *The Painter's Secret Geometry.* New York: Hacker

10. Black, Campbell. (1981). *Raiders of the Lost Ark.* New York: Ballantine

11. Morris, Eric, and Hotchkis, Joan. (1979). *No Acting Please.* New York: Putnam

12. Hagan, Uta. (1973). *Respect for Acting.* New York: MacMillan

13. Clurman, Harold. (1974). *On Directing.* New York: MacMillan

14. Easty, Edward Dwight. (19xx). *On Method Acting.* Orlando, Fl,: House of Collectibles

15. Dean, Alexander, and Carra, Lawrence. (1980). *Fundamental of Play Directing.* New York: Holt, Rinehart, & Winston

16. Spolin, Viola. (1985). *Theatre Games for Rehearsal.* Evanston, Ill.: Northwestern University Press

17. Manderino, Ned. (1977). *The Transpersonal Actor.* Los Angeles: Manderino Books

INDEX